WITHDRAWN
WRIGHT STATE UNIVERSITY LIBRARIES

NATIONAL STANDARDS

FOR

UNITED STATES HISTORY

EXPLORING
THE AMERICAN
EXPERIENCE

Grades 5–12

Expanded Edition

Including Examples of Student Achievement

National Center for History in the Schools

University of California, Los Angeles

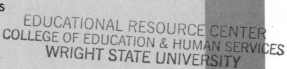

EDUCATIONAL RESOURCE CENTER
COLLEGE OF EDUCATION & HUMAN SERVICES
WRIGHT STATE UNIVERSITY

D1070323

The development of the United States History Standards was administered by the National Center for History in the Schools at the University of California, Los Angeles under the guidance of the National Council for History Standards. The standards were developed with funding from the National Endowment for the Humanities and the U.S. Department of Education. This publication does not necessarily represent positions or policies of the United States government, and no official endorsement should be inferred. With the exception of photographs and other visual materials, this publication may be freely reproduced and distributed for educational and research purposes.

Project Co-directors:	Charlotte Crabtree Gary B. Nash
Project Assistant Director:	Linda Symcox
Book and cover design:	Robin Weisz
Production planning:	Chris Coniglio
Production:	UCLA Publication Design Services
Document control:	Marta Hill
Photo Research:	John Pyne, Gloria Sesso and David Vigilante
Copyright procurement:	Leticia Zermeno

Ordering Information

National Standards for United States History: Exploring the American Experience
ISBN 09633218-1-1

Write to:

National Center for History in the Schools
University of California, Los Angeles
10880 Wilshire Blvd., Suite 761
Los Angeles, CA 90024-4108
FAX: (310) 825-4723

PREFACE

Publication of the *National Standards for United States History* could not be more timely. These standards address one of the major goals for education reform contained in the landmark legislation, **Goals 2000: Educate America Act**, signed into law by President Bill Clinton in March 1994. This statute affirms that by the year 2000, "All students will leave grades 4, 8, and 12 having demonstrated competency over challenging subject matter" in the core academic subjects of the school curriculum, history among them. Heralding passage of this legislation by the Congress, Secretary of Education Richard W. Riley announced, "Final passage of the Goals 2000 legislation moves us one step closer to the day when we can assure every parent in America that their children . . . are receiving an education that is up to world class standards." It is a goal broadly supported by the American people, their state governors, their legislators in the United States Congress, and two successive presidential administrations.

Support for the development of internationally competitive national standards of excellence for the nation's schools was first voiced in the National Education Goals adopted by the nation's fifty governors in their 1989 meeting in Charlottesville, Virginia. The third of the six education goals adopted in that meeting identified history as one of five school subjects for which challenging new national achievement standards should be established.

In October 1992 President Clinton reaffirmed his commitment to achieving these goals, including the "establishment of world class standards [specifically to include history] and development of a meaningful national examination system. . . to determine whether our students are meeting the standards. . . , to increase expectations, and to give schools incentives and structures to improve student performance." That same year, the importance of national standards in history was again affirmed in *Raising Standards for American Education,* the report to Congress of the National Council on Education Standards and Testing, appointed by the Congress to advise on these matters under the co-chairmanship of Governors Roy Romer (D-Colorado) and Carroll A. Campbell (R-South Carolina).

It was in this robust climate of education reform that the National History Standards Project was born. Funded in the spring of 1992 by the National Endowment for the Humanities and the Office of Educational Research and Improvement of the United States Department of Education, this project sought to develop broad national consensus for what constitutes excellence in the teaching and learning of history in the nation's schools. Developed through a broad-based national consensus-building process, this task has involved working toward agreement both on the larger purposes of history in the school curriculum and on the more specific history understandings and thinking processes all students should have equal opportunity to acquire over twelve years of precollegiate education.

In undertaking this process, it was widely agreed that the History Standards, as finally drafted, would in fact mark a critical milestone but not the final destination in what must be an ongoing, dynamic process of improvement and revision over the years to come. History is an extraordinarily dynamic field today, and standards drafted for the schools must be open to continuing development to keep pace with new refinements and revisions in this field.

This present publication, *National Standards for United States History: Exploring the American Experience,* marks the first milestone in the development of standards of excellence for the nation's schools. It is the result of over two years of intensive work by hundreds of gifted classroom teachers of history; of supervisors, state social studies specialists, and chief state school officers responsible for history in the schools; of dozens of talented and active academic historians in the nation; and of representatives of a broad array of professional and scholarly organizations, civic and public interest groups, parents and individual citizens with a stake in the teaching of history in the schools.

The National Council for History Standards, the policy-setting body responsible for providing policy direction and oversight of the project, consisted of thirty members, including the present or immediate past presidents of such large-membership organizations directly responsible for the content and teaching of history as the Council of Chief State School Officers, the Association for Supervision and Curriculum Development, the Council of State Social Studies Specialists, the National Council for the Social Studies, the Organization of American Historians, the National Council for History Education, and the Organization of History Teachers. In addition, members included the Director and Associate Director of the Social Studies Development Center, supervisory and curriculum development staff of county and city school districts, experienced classroom teachers, and distinguished historians in the fields of United States and world history. To foster correspondence in the development of these standards with the work under development for the 1994 National Assessment of Educational Progress (NAEP) in United States history, several participants in the NAEP Planning and Steering Committees were included in the National Council for History Standards. For similar reasons two members of the congressionally mandated National Council for Education Standards and Testing also served on this Council. Finally, the two directors of the National Center for History in the Schools, responsible for administering this Project, served as co-chairs of the Council.

The National Forum for History Standards was composed of representatives from major education, public interest, parent-teacher, and other organizations concerned with history in the schools. Advisory in its function, the Forum provided important counsel and feedback for this project as well as access to the larger public through the membership of the organizations represented in the Forum.

Nine Organizational Focus Groups of between fifteen and twenty-nine members each, chosen by the leadership of their respective organizations, were contracted with to provide important advisory, review, and consulting services to the project. Organizations providing this special service included the Council of Chief State School Officers, the Association for Supervision and Curriculum Development, the American Historical Association, the World History Association, the National Council for the Social Studies, the Organization of American Historians, the National Council for History Education, the Council of State Social Studies Specialists, and the Organization of History Teachers.

Finally, three Curriculum Task Forces were formed, totaling more than fifty members, with responsibility for developing the standards for students in grades K-4, and for students in grades 5-12 in the fields of United States and world history. Composed of veteran classroom teachers from throughout the United States who had been recommended by the many organizations participating in this project, and of recognized scholars of United States and world history with deep commitments to history education in schools, these groups have worked for many months in grade-alike writing teams and in meetings of the whole to ensure continuity of standards across all levels of schooling, elementary through high school.

The Appendix presents the rosters of all these working groups. Deep appreciation is owed to every one of these participants, all of whom gave unfailingly and selflessly of their time and professional expertise during the more than two years of intensive work that went into the development, recurrent national reviews, revisions, and final editorial refinements of this volume. Special appreciation is due the many school districts and administrators who time and again agreed to the release time that allowed the gifted teachers who served on the Curriculum Task Forces to meet at UCLA for week-long working sessions throughout the school year in order to complete the development of the standards and of the grade-appropriate examples of student achievement of the standards. In particular we express the special appreciation due the team of editorial writers — John Pyne, Gloria Sesso, Kirk Ankeney, and David Vigilante — who over the closing months of the project addressed the final changes requested in the third national review of the United States History Standards and helped bring the project to completion.

As co-directors of this project, we express special appreciation, also, to the many thousands of teachers, curriculum leaders, assessment experts, historians, parents, textbook publishers, and others too numerous to mention who have sought review copies of the Standards and turned out for public hearings and information sessions scheduled at regional and national conferences throughout these two years, and who have provided their independent assessments and recommendations for making these Standards historically sound, workable in classrooms, and responsive to the needs and interests of students in the schools.

Finally, we note with deep appreciation the funding provided by the National Endowment for the Humanities and by the Office of Educational Research and Improvement of the United States Department of Education to conduct this complex and broadly inclusive enterprise.

In this most contentious field of the curriculum, there have been many who have wondered if a national consensus could be forged concerning what all students should have opportunity to learn about the history of their nation and of the peoples of all racial, religious, ethnic, and national backgrounds who have been a part of that story. The responsiveness, enormous good will, and dogged determination of so many to meet this challenge has reinforced our confidence in the inherent strength and capabilities of this nation now to undertake the steps necessary for bringing to all students the benefits of this endeavor. The stakes are high. It is the challenge that must now be undertaken.

Charlotte Crabtree and Gary B. Nash
Co-directors

TABLE OF CONTENTS

CHAPTER 1

Developing Standards in United States History for Students in Grades 5-12

Significance of History for the Educated Citizen

Setting standards for history in the schools requires a clear vision of the place and importance of history in the general education of all students. The widespread and growing support for more and better history in the schools, beginning in the early grades of elementary education, is one of the more encouraging signs of the decade. The reasons are many, but none are more important to a democratic society than this: *knowledge of history is the precondition of political intelligence*. Without history, a society shares no common memory of where it has been, what its core values are, or what decisions of the past account for present circumstances. Without history, we cannot undertake any sensible inquiry into the political, social, or moral issues in society. And without historical knowledge and inquiry, we cannot achieve the informed, discriminating citizenship essential to effective participation in the democratic processes of governance and the fulfillment for all our citizens of the nation's democratic ideals.

Thomas Jefferson long ago prescribed history for all who would take part in self-government because it would enable them to prepare for things yet to come. The philosopher Etienne Gilson noted the special significance of the perspectives history affords. *History*, he remarked, *is the only laboratory we have in which to test the consequences of thought*. History opens to students the great record of human experience, revealing the vast range of accommodations individuals and societies have made to the problems confronting them, and disclosing the consequences that have followed the various choices that have been made. By studying the choices and decisions of the past, students can confront today's problems and choices with a deeper awareness of the alternatives before them and the likely consequences of each.

Current problems, of course, do not duplicate those of the past. Essential to extrapolating knowledgeably from history to the issues of today requires yet a further skill, again dependent upon one's understanding of the past: differentiating between (1) relevant historical antecedents that properly inform analyses of current issues and (2) those antecedents that are clearly irrelevant. Students must be sufficiently grounded in historical understanding in order to bring sound historical analysis to the service of informed decision making.

What is required is mastery of what Nietzsche once termed "critical history" and what Gordon Craig has explained as the "ability, after painful inquiry and sober judgment, to determine what part of history [is] relevant to one's current problems and what [is] not," whether one is assessing a situation, forming an opinion, or taking an active position on the issue. In exploring these matters, students will soon discover that history is filled with the high costs of decisions reached on the basis of false analogies from the past as well as the high costs of actions taken with little or no understanding of the important lessons the past imparts.

These learnings directly contribute to the education of the *public citizen*, but they uniquely contribute to nurturing the *private individual* as well. Historical memory is the key to self-identity, to seeing one's place in the stream of time, and one's connectedness with all of humankind. We are part of an ancient chain, and the long hand of the past is upon us — for good and for ill — just as our hands will rest on our descendants for years to come. Denied knowledge of one's roots and of one's place in the great stream of human history, the individual is deprived of the fullest sense of self and of that sense of shared community on which one's fullest personal development as well as responsible citizenship depends. For these purposes, history and the humanities must occupy an indispensable role in the school curriculum.

Finally, history opens to students opportunities to develop a comprehensive understanding of the world, and of the many cultures and ways of life different from their own. From a balanced and inclusive world history students may gain an appreciation both of the world's many peoples and of their shared humanity and common problems. Students may also acquire the habit of seeing matters through others' eyes and come to realize that they can better understand themselves as they study others, as well as the other way around. Historical understanding based on such comparative studies in world history does not require approval or forgiveness for the tragedies either of one's own society or of others; nor does it negate the importance of critically examining alternative value systems and their effects in supporting or denying the basic human rights and aspirations of all their peoples. Especially important, an understanding of the history of the world's many cultures can contribute to fostering the kind of mutual patience, respect, and civic courage required in our increasingly pluralistic society and our increasingly interdependent world.

If students are to see ahead more clearly, and be ready to act with judgment and with respect for the shared humanity of all who will be touched by the decisions they as citizens make, support, or simply acquiesce in, then schools must attend to this critical field of the curriculum.

Definition of Standards

Standards in history make explicit the goals that all students should have opportunity to acquire, if the purposes just considered are to be achieved. In history, standards are of two types:

1. *Historical thinking skills* that enable students to evaluate evidence, develop comparative and causal analyses, interpret the historical record, and construct sound historical arguments and perspectives on which informed decisions in contemporary life can be based.

2. *Historical understandings* that define what students should *know* about the history of their nation and of the world. These understandings are drawn from the record of human aspirations, strivings, accomplishments, and failures in at least five spheres of human activity: the social, political, scientific/technological, economic, and philosophical/religious/aesthetic. They also provide students the historical perspectives required to analyze contemporary issues and problems confronting citizens today.

Historical thinking and understanding do not, of course, develop independently of one another. Higher levels of historical thinking depend upon and are linked to the attainment of higher levels of historical understanding. For these reasons, the standards presented in Chapter 3 of this volume provide an integration of historical thinking and understanding.

Criteria for the Development of Standards

The development of national standards in United States and world history presents a special challenge in deciding what, of the great storehouse of human history, is the most significant for all students to acquire. Perhaps less contentious but no less important is deciding what historical perspectives and what skills in historical reasoning, values analysis, and policy thinking are essential for all students to achieve.

The following criteria, developed and refined over the course of a broad-based national review and consensus process, were adopted by the National Council for History Standards in order to guide the development of history standards for grades kindergarten through 12.

1. Standards should be intellectually demanding, reflect the best historical scholarship, and promote active questioning and learning rather than passive absorption of facts, dates, and names.

2. Such standards should be equally expected of *all* students and all students should be provided equal access to the curricular opportunities necessary to achieving those standards.

3. Standards should reflect the ability of children from the earliest elementary school years to learn the meanings of history and the methods of historians.

4. Standards should be founded in chronology, an organizing approach that fosters appreciation of pattern and causation in history.

5. Standards should strike a balance between emphasizing broad themes in United States and world history and probing specific historical events, ideas, movements, persons, and documents.

6. All historical study involves selection and ordering of information in light of general ideas and values. Standards for history should reflect the principles of sound historical reasoning — careful evaluation of evidence, construction of causal relationships, balanced interpretation, and comparative analysis. The ability to detect and evaluate distortion and propaganda by omission, suppression, or invention of facts is essential.

7. Standards should include awareness of, appreciation for, and the ability to utilize a variety of sources of evidence from which historical knowledge is achieved, including written documents, oral tradition, popular culture, literature, artifacts, art and music, historical sites, photographs, and films.

8. Standards for United States history should reflect both the nation's diversity exemplified by race, ethnicity, social and economic status, gender, region, politics, and religion and the nation's commonalities. The contributions and struggles of specific groups and individuals should be included.

9. Standards in United States history should contribute to citizenship education through developing understanding of our common civic identity and shared civic values within the polity, through analyzing major policy issues in the nation's history, and through developing mutual respect among its many peoples.

10. History Standards should emphasize the nature of civil society and its relationship to government and citizenship. Standards in United States history should address the historical origins of the nation's democratic political system and the continuing development of its ideals and institutions, its controversies, and the struggle to narrow the gap between its ideals and practices. Standards in world history should include different patterns of political institutions, ranging from varieties of democracy to varieties of authoritarianism, and ideas and aspirations developed by civilizations in all parts of the world.

11. Standards in United States and world history should be separately developed but interrelated in content and similar in format. Standards in United States history should reflect the global context in which the nation unfolded and world history should treat United States history as one of its integral parts.

12. Standards should include appropriate coverage of recent events in United States and world history, including social and political developments and international relations of the post-World War II era.

13. Standards in U.S. history and world history should utilize regional and local history by exploring specific events and movements through case studies and historical research. Local and regional history should enhance the broader patterns of U.S. and world history.

14. Standards in U.S. and world history should integrate fundamental facets of human culture such as religion, science and technology, politics and government, economics, interactions with the environment, intellectual and social life, literature, and the arts.

15. Standards in world history should treat the history and values of diverse civilizations, including those of the West, and should especially address the interactions among them.

Developing Standards in United States History

Periodization

Students should understand that the periods into which the written histories of the United States or the world are divided are simply inventions of historians trying to impose some order on what is inherently a messy past that can be read and conceptualized in a variety of ways. In a nation of such diversity as the United States, no periodizing scheme will work for all groups. American Indian history has benchmarks and eras that sometimes but not always overlap with those of European settlers in the colonial period. Iroquois history would have to be periodized differently from Sioux or Zuni history. African American history would have its own watersheds, such as the shift from white indentured servitude to black slave labor in the South, the abolition of the slave trade, the beginning of emigrationism, and so forth. So also with women's history and with Mexican American history.

Nonetheless, we believe that teachers will appreciate a periodization that attempts to blend political and social history. For this purpose, political events in United States history such as the American Revolution, the Constitution, the Civil War, Progressivism, the New Deal, and the Cold War — all of which have fairly definite beginning and end points — are still useful ways to provide breakpoints in the United States history curriculum. The industrial revolution, the labor movement, environmentalism, shifts in childrearing and family size, and so forth have no such precise beginning and end points and cut across eras defined by revolution, civil war, depression, and the like. In fact, none of the college texts in United States history that have tried in recent years to infuse social history into political and institutional history have been able to get around the general determinancy of wars and political reform movements and the indeterminacy of demographic, cultural, and social transformations.

We have tried to overcome, in part, the difficulties inherent in periodizing history by overlapping eras to demonstrate that there really is no such thing as an era's beginning or ending, and that all such schemes are simply the historian's way of trying to give *some* structure to the course of history. The ten eras selected for periodizing United States history are presented below:

Era 1. Three Worlds Meet (Beginnings to 1620)

Era 2. Colonization and Settlement (1585-1763)

Era 3. Revolution and the New Nation (1754-1820s)

Era 4. Expansion and Reform (1801-1861)

Era 5. Civil War and Reconstruction (1850-1877)

Era 6. The Development of the Industrial United States (1870-1900)

Era 7. The Emergence of Modern America (1890-1930)

Era 8. The Great Depression and World War II (1929-1945)

Era 9. Postwar United States (1945-early 1970s)

Era 10. Contemporary United States (1968-present)

Historical Understanding

History is a broadly integrative field, recounting and analyzing human aspirations and strivings in various spheres of human activity: **social, political, scientific/technological, economic,** and **cultural**. Studying history — inquiring into families, communities, states, nations, and various peoples of the world — at once engages students in the lives, aspirations, struggles, accomplishments, and failures of real people, in all these aspects of their lives.

Through social history, students come to deeper understandings of society: of what it means to be human, of different and changing views of family structures, of men's and women's roles, of childhood and of children's roles, of various groups and classes in society, and of relationships among all these individuals and groups. This sphere considers how economic, religious, cultural, and political changes have affected social life, and it incorporates developments shaping the destiny of millions: the history of slavery; of class conflict; of mass migration and immigration; the human consequences of plague, war, and famine; and the longer life expectancy and rising living standards following upon medical, technological, and economic advances.

Through political history, students come to deeper understandings of the political sphere of activity as it has developed in their local community, their state, their nation, and in various societies of the world. Efforts to construct governments and institutions; the drive to seize and hold power over others; the struggle to achieve and preserve basic human rights, justice, equality, law, and order in societies; and the evolution of regional and world mechanisms to promote international law are all part of the central human drama to be explored and analyzed in the study of history.

Through history of science and technology, students come to deeper understandings of how the scientific quest to understand nature, the world we live in, and humanity itself is as old as recorded history. So, too, is the quest to improve ways of doing everything from producing food, to caring for the ill, to transporting goods, to advancing economic security and the well-being of the group. Understanding how scientific/technological developments have propelled change and how these changes have altered all other spheres of human activity is central to the study of history.

Through economic history, students come to deeper understanding of the economic forces that have been crucial in determining the quality of people's lives, in structuring societies, and in influencing the course of events. Exchange relationships within and between cultures have had major impacts on society and politics, producing changing patterns of regional, hemispheric, and global economic dominance and permitting the emergence in the 20th century of a truly international economy, with far-reaching consequences for all other spheres of activity.

Through cultural history, students learn how ideas, beliefs, and values have profoundly influenced human actions throughout history. Religion, philosophy, art, and popular culture have all been central to the aspirations and achievements of all societies, and have been a mainspring of historical change from earliest times. Students' explorations of this sphere of human activity, through literature, sacred writings and oral traditions, political treatises, drama, art, architecture, music, and dance of a people, deepen their understandings of the human experience.

Analyzing these five spheres of human activity requires considering them in the contexts both of *historical time* and *geographic place*. The historical record is inextricably linked to the geographic setting in which it developed. Population movements and settlements, scientific and economic activities, geopolitical agendas, and the distributions and spread of political, philosophical, religious, and aesthetic ideas are all related in some measure to geographic factors. The opportunities, limitations, and constraints with which any people have addressed the issues and challenges of their time have, to a significant degree, been influenced by the environment in which they lived or to which they have had access, and by the traces on the landscape, malignant or benign, irrevocably left by those who came before.

Because these five spheres of human activity are also interwoven in the real lives of individuals and societies, essential understandings in United States history often cut across these categories. Thus, to comprehend the causes of the American Revolution, students must address the *philosophical ideas* of the Enlightenment, the competing *economic interests* of British mercantilism and colonial self-interest, the *political antecedents* defining the "rights of Englishmen" under English common law, the English Bill of Rights, and the Glorious Revolution, and the varying aspirations of different *social groups* in the colonies, defined by gender, race, economic status, and region.

Similarly, understanding the consequences of the American victory demonstrates how change in any one of these spheres of activity often has impact on some or all of the others. The many consequences of the colonists' military victory included their development of new and lasting *political institutions*, the *social and economic effects* of the American victory on the various groups who entered the war with differing aspirations and who allied themselves with different sides during the conflict, and the long-term *philosophical consequences* of the American Revolution, inspiring what has been called the "Age of Democratic Revolution." Together, these consequences demonstrate the complexity of historical events and the broadly integrative nature of history itself. They also affirm, once again, the unique power of history to deepen students' understanding of the past, and of how we are still affected by it.

Historical Thinking

Beyond defining what students should *know* — that is, the understandings in United States history that all students should acquire — it is essential to consider what students should be able to *do* to demonstrate their understandings and to apply their knowledge in productive ways.

The study of history involves much more than the passive absorption of facts, dates, names, and places. Real historical understanding requires students to think through cause-and-effect relationships, to reach sound historical interpretations, and to conduct historical inquiries and research leading to the knowledge on which informed decisions in contemporary life can be based. These thinking skills are the processes of *active* learning.

Properly taught, history develops capacities for analysis and judgment. It reveals the ambiguity of choice, and it promotes wariness about quick, facile solutions which have so often brought human suffering in their wake. History fosters understanding of paradox and a readiness to distinguish between that which is beyond and that which is within human control, between the inevitable and the contingent. It trains students to detect bias, to weigh evidence, and to evaluate arguments, thus preparing them to make sensible, independent judgments, to sniff out spurious appeals to history by partisan pleaders, to distinguish between anecdote and analysis.

To acquire these capabilities, students must develop competence in the following five types of historical thinking:

Chronological thinking, developing a clear sense of historical time — past, present, and future — in order to identify the temporal sequence in which events occurred, measure calendar time, interpret and create time lines, and explain patterns of historical succession and duration, continuity and change.

Historical comprehension, including the ability to read historical narratives with understanding; to identify the basic elements of the narrative structure (the characters, situation, sequence of events, their causes, and their outcomes); and, to develop historical perspectives — that is, the ability to describe the past through the eyes and experiences of those who were there, as revealed through their literature, art, artifacts, and the like, and to avoid "present-mindedness," judging the past solely in terms of the norms and values of today.

Historical analysis and interpretation, including the ability to compare and contrast different experiences, beliefs, motives, traditions, hopes, and fears of people from various groups and backgrounds, and at various times in the past and present; to analyze how these differing motives, interests, beliefs, hopes and fears influenced people's behaviors; to consider multiple perspectives in the records of human experience and multiple causes in analyses of historical events; to challenge arguments of historical inevitability; and, to compare and evaluate competing historical explanations of the past.

Historical research, including the ability to formulate historical questions from encounters with historical documents, artifacts, photos, visits to historical sites, and eyewitness accounts; to determine the historical time and context in which the artifact, document, or other record was created; to judge its credibility and authority; and to construct a sound historical narrative or argument concerning it.

Historical issues-analysis and decision-making, including the ability to identify problems that confronted people in the past; to analyze the various interests and points of view of people caught up in these situations; to evaluate alternative proposals for dealing with the problem(s); to analyze whether the decisions reached or the actions taken were good ones and why; and, to bring historical perspectives to bear on informed decision-making in the present.

Integrating Standards in Historical Thinking and Understandings

Chapter 2 presents the standards in historical thinking, largely independent of historical content in order to specify the quality of thinking desired for each. None of these skills in historical thinking, however, can be developed or even expressed in a vacuum. Every one of them requires historical content in order to function — a relationship made explicit in Chapter 3, in which the standards integrating historical understanding and historical thinking are presented for all ten eras of United States history for grades 5-12.

Figure 1 illustrates the approach taken to integrate historical thinking and historical understandings in the standards. The example is drawn from Era 3, "Revolution and the New Nation (1754-1820s)." As illustrated, the five skills in historical thinking (the left side of the diagram) and the three historical understandings students should acquire concerning the American Revolution (the right side of the diagram) are integrated in the central area of overlap in the diagram in order to define (immediately below) Standard 1A: What students should be able to do to demonstrate their understanding of the causes of the Revolution.

Pages 10 and 11 provide a further illustration of this same standard, presented this time in the format in which the standards are stated (Chapter 3). The selection is again drawn from Era 3, "Revolution and the New Nation." As illustrated, the standard first presents a statement defining what students should understand: "The causes of the American Revolution, the ideas and interests involved in forging the revolutionary movement, and the reasons for the American victory."

The standard next presents five statements in a shaded box to specify what students should be able to do to demonstrate their understanding of the causes of the American Revolution. Each statement illustrates the integration of historical thinking and understanding by marrying a particular thinking skill (e.g., comparing arguments) to a specific historical understanding (e.g., traditional rights of English people). The particular thinking skill is further emphasized in the bracketed words following the statement (e.g., **Compare multiple perspectives**). The particular thinking skill is not the only one that can be employed but is a particularly apt one. Finally, each component of Standard 1A is coded to indicate in which grades the standard can appropriately be developed.

> **5-12** indicates the standard is appropriate for grades 5-6, as well as for all higher levels, from grades 7-8 through grades 9-12.

> **7-12** indicates the standard is appropriate for grades 7-8 through grades 9-12.

> **9-12** indicates the standard is best reserved for students in their high school years, grades 9-12.

Finally, the shaded box under the subhead "Students Should Be Able to" is supplemented with examples of student achievement of Standard 1A appropriate for grades 5-6, 7-8, and 9-12.

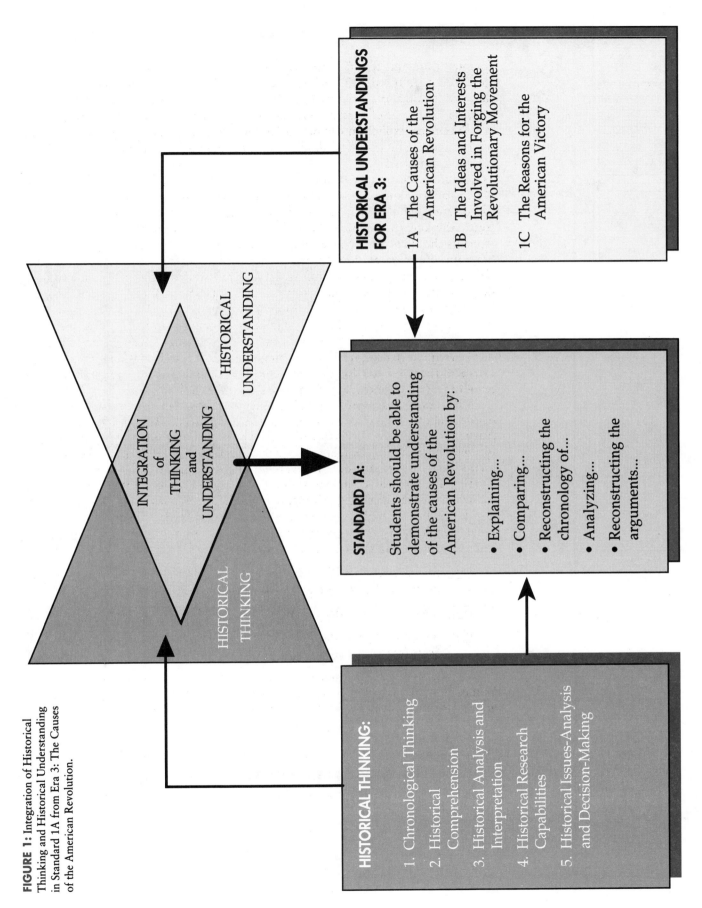

FIGURE 1: Integration of Historical Thinking and Historical Understanding in Standard 1A from Era 3: The Causes of the American Revolution.

NATIONAL STANDARDS FOR UNITED STATES HISTORY: EXPLORING THE AMERICAN EXPERIENCE

STANDARD 1

Students Should Understand: *The causes of the American Revolution, the ideas and interests involved in forging the revolutionary movement, and the reasons for the American victory.*

Students Should Be Able to:

1A **Demonstrate understanding of the causes of the American Revolution by:**

5-12 Explaining the consequences of the Seven Years War and the overhaul of English imperial policy following the Treaty of Paris in 1763, demonstrating the connections between the antecedent and consequent events. [**Marshal evidence of antecedent circumstances**]

5-12 Comparing the arguments advanced by defenders and opponents of the new imperial policy on the traditional rights of English people and the legitimacy of asking the colonies to pay a share of the costs of empire. [**Consider multiple perspectives**]

5-12 Reconstructing the chronology of the critical events leading to the outbreak of armed conflict between the American colonies and England. [**Establish temporal order**]

7-12 Analyzing the connection between political and religious ideas and economic interests in bringing about revolution. [**Consider multiple perspectives**]

9-12 Reconstructing the arguments among Patriots and Loyalists about independence and drawing conclusions about how the decision to declare independence was reached. [**Consider multiple perspectives**]

Grades 5-6

Examples of student achievement of Standard 1A include:

▶ Identify such major consequences of the Seven Years War as the English victory, the removal of the French as a contending power in North America, and the reduced need of the colonists for protection by the mother country.

▶ Select in chronological order and explain the major events leading to the outbreak of conflict at Lexington and Concord.

▶ Create historical arguments or narratives explaining at least one reason why the English Parliament felt it was justified in taxing the colonies to help pay for a war fought in their defense and at least one reason why the colonists, claiming their rights as Englishmen, challenged the legitimacy of the new taxes as "taxation without representation."

Grades 7-8

Examples of student achievement of Standard 1A include:

▶ Assemble the evidence, including the consequences of the Seven Years War, England's new imperial policy and the voices of such resistance leaders as John Adams, Thomas Jefferson, John Dickinson, Thomas Paine, Patrick Henry, and Samuel Adams, and construct a sound historical argument on such questions as:

72

Statement of the historical understandings that students should acquire

Statement identifying the first understanding of Standard 1— The causes of the American Revolution

*Components of Standard 1A, demonstrating integration of historical understanding and **thinking***

Examples of student achievement of Standard 1A

ERA 3: REVOLUTION AND THE NEW NATION (1754-1820s)

Was it reasonable for the English to tax the colonists to help pay for a war fought in their defense? Were the American colonists justified in their resistance to England's new imperial policies?

▶ Explain the divisions in the colonies over these issues by comparing the interests and positions of Loyalists and Patriots from different economic groups such as northern merchants, southern rice and tobacco planters, yeoman farmers, and urban artisans.

▶ Marshal historical evidence including events leading up to "the shot heard 'round the world" and develop a historical argument on such questions as the following: *Was the outbreak of conflict at Lexington and Concord probable? Could any action at that point have prevented war with England?*

Examples of student achievement of Standard 1A

Grades 9-12

Examples of student achievement of Standard 1A include:

▶ Draw upon the arguments advanced by opponents and defenders of England's new imperial policy in order to construct a sound historical argument or narrative on such questions as: *Were the arguments against parliamentary taxation a legitimate and constitutional defense of the historic and traditional rights of Englishmen under common law, or were they merely a defense for tax evasion? Was the British decision to station troops in the colonies at the end of the Seven Years War designed to defend the colonies or did it reflect a conscious decision to keep contentious and expansionist colonists under control?*

▶ Draw upon evidence of the mounting crisis as well as the efforts in Parliament and in the colonies to prevent a rupture with the mother country in order to construct a sound historical narrative or argument on such questions as: *Was the break with England avoidable? Could decisions on either side, other than those which were taken, have changed the circumstances leading to the escalation of the crisis and the outbreak war?*

▶ Drawing upon ideas of religious groups such as Virginia Baptists, mid-Atlantic Presbyterians, and millennialists, assess how religion became a factor in the American Revolution.

Examples of student achievement of Standard 1A

▶ Construct a historical narrative analyzing the factors which explain why a person chose to be a Loyalist or a Patriot. *Why did approximately one-third of the colonists want to remain neutral? Did economic and social differences play a role in how people chose sides? Explain.*

▶ Marshal evidence to explain how a Loyalist and a Patriot would view each of the following: The Tea Act of 1773, the Boston Tea Party, the "Intolerable" Acts, the cause of the skirmish at Lexington Green. *How might a Loyalist have rewritten the natural rights theory of the Declaration of Independence? How might a Loyalist have answered the charges in the Declaration of Independence?*

As demonstrated above, Standard 1A is converted to appropriate achievement expectations for three levels of schooling: grades 5-6, grades 7-8, and grades 9-12. The point here is not to require the study of Era 3 in United States history at all three levels of schooling. Rather, it is to provide teachers with examples of what is appropriate achievement for students in whatever grade (or grades) this era is studied in their local school curriculum.

Questions Concerning These Standards

Q: Do these standards require that Era 3 be taught at all three levels, grades 5-6, 7-8, and 9-12?

A: **No.** The local school curriculum will determine when Era 3 is to be taught, whether at grades 5-6, 7-8, and/or 9-12. Once that curriculum decision is made, teachers can enter these standards to determine which ones are appropriate for their students, and how the standards they select are related to others within a well-articulated curriculum in history, grades 5-12.

Q: Are high school teachers expected to teach all standards identified as appropriate for grades 9-12?

A: **No.** These standards assume that schools will devote three years of study to United States history sometime between grades 5 and 12. Therefore, Era 3 will probably be studied in some depth during at least one earlier school year (e.g., grade 8). In that case, the more numerous standards deemed appropriate for grades 9-12 will, in part, have already been addressed in an earlier grade, and the emphasis can be turned in the high school U.S. history course to those standards judged not to be appropriate for the earlier grades. Again, these are matters of well-designed, articulated curriculum planning, within the jurisdiction of local schools.

Q: Does the thinking skill incorporated in a particular standard limit teachers to that one skill?

A: **No.** Within the shaded box, each standard highlights a particularly important thinking process. However, it is understood that good teaching will incorporate more than a single thinking skill to develop these understandings.

Q: Does the particular thinking skill identified in the standard limit the instructional approaches teachers might adopt to develop these outcomes with students?

A: **No.** To take one example, the second bulleted standard, "Comparing the arguments advanced by defenders and opponents of England's imperial policy," can be developed through any of a number of teaching approaches. For example, students might:

▶ Create a chart listing the competing arguments in two parallel columns.

▶ Assume the roles of defenders and opponents of England's imperial policy and debate the issue whether England was right in developing its policy.

▶ Write "Letters to the Editor" for a July 1775 issue of their classroom newspaper, the *Boston Liberator*, in which the editorial page is devoted to assessing opposing views on England's imperial policy in the context of the mounting crisis.

▶ Create a historical argument in the form of an essay, speech before the English Parliament, or an editorial in which they confront the opposing views on England's imperial policy and justify the position they judge warranted by the data.

In short, these standards are intended to open possibilities, not to limit teachers' options for engaging students in lively activities within what has been called the "thinking curriculum."

Q: **Won't these bulleted standards each require a separate lesson or sequence of lessons, and doesn't the total teaching load therefore far exceed the total number of teaching days available, even over three years of instruction?**

A: **No.** Good teaching, it should be emphasized, will often develop two or more of these bulleted standards in a single lesson or sequence of lessons. The standards appearing as individual statements in the shaded boxes are intended to signify desired *outcomes* of instruction and not to prescribe a particular teaching plan. Teachers will creatively design their own instructional plans, integrating related understandings in a variety of ways to accomplish these ends.

For example, in the teaching approaches just considered, three of these activities — debating England's imperial policy, assessing opposing views on the policy in "Letters to the Editor," and creating a historical argument confronting these opposing views — directly contribute to achieving three of the five bulleted standards: the second, fourth, and fifth. Teachers seeking to make the most of their instructional time will therefore select one of these three activities over the less productive activity of creating a chart listing opposing viewpoints, and in the process snare the proverbial two — or three! — birds with a single stone.

Three Policy Issues

Ensuring Equity for All Students

The purposes of the national standards developed in this document are threefold: (1) to establish high expectations for what all students should know and be able to do; (2) to clarify what constitutes successful achievement; and (3) *most significantly, to promote equity in the learning opportunities and resources to be provided all students in the nation's schools.*

Standards in and of themselves cannot ensure remediation of the pervasive inequalities in the educational opportunities currently available to students. The roots of these problems are deep and widely manifested in gross inequities in school financing, in resource allocations, and in practices of discriminatory "lower tracks" and "dumbed down" curricula that continue to deny large sectors of the nation's children equal educational opportunity.

What the national commitment to high achievement standards for all students *can* do is to serve as an engine of change: (1) defining for all students the goals essential to success in a rapidly changing global economy and in a society undergoing wrenching social, technological, and economic change; and (2) establishing the moral obligation to provide equity in the educational resources required to help all students attain these goals.

As for resources, if students are to achieve the understandings and thinking skills specified in the United States History Standards, they must have equal access to well-prepared history teachers and to engaging, balanced, accurate, and challenging curricular materials. For these reasons the success of Goals 2000 and of the systemic educational reform program it has launched requires the provision of high quality professional development in United States history and in pedagogy for teachers who are not prepared to teach the content or thinking skills presented in this document. Equally important, all students must be provided with the best available textbooks and other curricular materials in U.S. history.

As Robert Hutchins said many years ago: "The best education for the best should be the best education for all." Every child is entitled to and must have equal access to excellence in the goals their teachers strive to help them achieve and in the instructional resources and opportunities required to reach those ends. Nothing less is acceptable in a democratic society; no commitment is more essential to meeting the challenges — economic, social, and ethical — confronting this nation in the years ahead.

Providing Adequate Instructional Time for History

In developing these standards, the National Council for History Standards kept in mind the purposes of Goals 2000, the national education reform program supported by President Clinton, the nation's governors, and the Congress. Developing the internationally competitive levels of student achievement called for in this reform movement clearly cannot be accomplished by limiting the study of the nation's history to one year (or less) over the eight years of middle and high school education. Excellence in history requires the instructional time to pursue an era in some depth and to engage students' active learning through the higher processes of historical thinking.

For these reasons it is important that the schools devote no less than three years of instruction to United States history over the eight years of students' middle and high school education, grades five through twelve. Currently, seventeen states provide three years of United States history, though under a variety of curriculum plans. In formulating national standards for excellence, the Council argued, we should not be setting our sights lower than those of the seventeen states that have already committed three years of instruction to this field.

Accommodating Variability in State and Local Curriculum Plans

Because schools today vary widely as to when and how they offer their courses in United States history, the Council sought a flexible approach to history standards which would accommodate local variability rather than impose a single national curriculum on the nation's schools. Already illustrated on pages 10-11 of this chapter, this approach required converting each standard to appropriate achievement — expectations for students at three levels of schooling: grades 5-6, grades 7-8, and grades 9-12. As mentioned earlier, our purpose is not to suggest that all eras in United States history be taught at all three levels of schooling. Rather, we aim to provide teachers, parents, and students with examples of appropriate achievement on standards for whatever historical eras their local school or school district has determined should be studied at that grade level. Deciding when these ten eras in United States history should be studied, whether in grades 5-6, 7-8, or 9-12, is a *curriculum* decision, and should remain under local or state control.

Thus, under Florida's state course of study, United States history is developed in relation to world history over two successive high school years — grades 10 (to World War I) and 11 (the modern world) — in addition to two successive years of study of state and national history in grades 4 (beginnings to 1880) and 5 (the years since 1880). Teachers of grades 4 and 10 following this plan will draw on the U.S. history standards developed for the earlier eras in U.S. history while teachers of grades 5 and 11 will draw on the standards developed for the later eras. In all cases teachers will focus on the standards designated for their particular grade levels, whether grades 5-6 or 9-12. None will use the standards developed for grades 7 or 8 — two years in Florida's curriculum devoted to studies other than history.

In California, by contrast, where the state framework suggests concentrating upon the study of the early eras of U.S. history in grade 5, the 19th century in grade 8, and the 20th century in grade 11, teachers following this plan will turn to the standards in a different way. Teachers of grade 5 will turn to the standards developed for U.S. history through the Civil War; teachers of grade 8 will *selectively* draw upon these same standards in their initial review but will concentrate upon the standards developed for the 19th-century history of the United States. Teachers of grade 11 will again *selectively* draw upon the standards for the earlier eras in their initial reviews, but will concentrate upon the standards developed for the 20th-century history of the nation. Again, in all cases, teachers will focus within any of these eras upon the standards developed for their particular grade level.

Student mural, Theodore Roosevelt Junior High School, San Diego, CA

Standards in Historical Thinking

The study of history, as noted earlier, involves more than the passive absorption of facts, dates, names, and places. Real historical understanding requires students to engage in historical thinking: to raise questions and to marshal evidence in support of their answers; to go beyond the facts presented in their textbooks and examine the historical record for themselves; to consult documents, journals, diaries, artifacts, historic sites, and other evidence from the past, and to do so imaginatively — taking into account the historical context in which these records were created and comparing the multiple points of view of those on the scene at the time.

Real historical understanding requires that students have opportunity to create historical narratives and arguments of their own. Such narratives and arguments may take many forms — essays, debates, and editorials, for instance. They can be initiated in a variety of ways. None, however, more powerfully initiates historical thinking than those issues, past and present, that challenge students to enter knowledgeably into the historical record and to bring sound historical perspectives to bear in the analysis of a problem.

Historical understanding also requires that students thoughtfully read the historical narratives created by others. Well written historical narratives are interpretative, revealing and explaining connections, change, and consequences. They are also analytical, combining lively storytelling and biography with conceptual analysis drawn from all relevant disciplines. Such narratives promote essential skills in historical thinking.

Reading such narratives thoughtfully requires that students analyze the assumptions — stated and unstated — from which the narrative was constructed and assess the strength of the evidence presented. It requires that students consider the significance of what the author included as well as chose to omit — the absence, for example, of the voices and experiences of other men and women who were also an important part of the history of their time. And, it requires that students examine the interpretative nature of history, comparing, for example, alternative historical narratives written by historians who have given different weight to the political, economic, social, and/or technological causes of events, and who have developed competing interpretations of the significance of those events.

Students engaged in activities of the kinds just considered will draw upon skills in the following five types of historical thinking:

1. Chronological Thinking
2. Historical Comprehension
3. Historical Analysis and Interpretation
4. Historical Research Capabilities
5. Historical Issues-Analysis and Decision-Making

These skills, while presented in five separate categories, are nonetheless interactive and mutually supportive. In conducting historical research or creating a historical argument of their own, for example, students must be able to draw upon skills in all five categories. Beyond the skills of conducting their research, students must, for example, be able to comprehend historical documents and records, analyze their relevance, develop interpretations of the document(s) they select, and demonstrate a sound grasp of the historical chronology and context in which the issue, problem, or events they are addressing developed.

In short, these five sets of skills, developed in the following pages as the five Standards in Historical Thinking, are statements of the outcomes we desire students to achieve. They are not mutually exclusive when put into practice, nor do they prescribe a particular teaching sequence to be followed. Teachers will draw upon all these Thinking Standards, as appropriate, to develop their teaching plans and to guide students through challenging programs of study in history.

Finally, it is important to point out that these five sets of Standards in Historical Thinking are defined in the following pages largely independently of historical content in order to specify the quality of thinking desired for each. It is essential to understand, however, that these skills do not develop, nor can they be practiced, in a vacuum. Every one of these skills requires historical content in order to function — a relationship that is made explicit in Chapter 3, which presents the standards integrating historical understandings and thinking for U.S. history for grades 5-12.

Overview of Standards in Historical Thinking

Standard 1. Chronological Thinking

A. Distinguish between past, present, and future time.
B. Identify in historical narratives the temporal structure of a historical narrative or story.
C. Establish temporal order in constructing historical narratives of their own.
D. Measure and calculate calendar time.
E. Interpret data presented in time lines.
F. Reconstruct patterns of historical succession and duration.
G. Compare alternative models for periodization.

Standard 2. Historical Comprehension

A. Reconstruct the literal meaning of a historical passage.
B. Identify the central question(s) the historical narrative addresses.
C. Read historical narratives imaginatively.
D. Evidence historical perspectives.
E. Draw upon data in historical maps.
F. Utilize visual and mathematical data presented in charts, tables, pie and bar graphs, flow charts, Venn diagrams, and other graphic organizers.
G. Draw upon visual, literary, and musical sources.

Standard 3. Historical Analysis and Interpretation

A. Identify the author or source of the historical document or narrative.
B. Compare and contrast differing sets of ideas, values, personalities, behaviors, and institutions.
C. Differentiate between historical facts and historical interpretations.
D. Consider multiple perspectives.
E. Analyze cause-and-effect relationships and multiple causation, including the importance of the individual, the influence of ideas, and the role of chance.
F. Challenge arguments of historical inevitability.
G. Compare competing historical narratives.
H. Hold interpretations of history as tentative.
I. Evaluate major debates among historians.
J. Hypothesize the influence of the past.

Standard 4. Historical Research Capabilities

A. Formulate historical questions.
B. Obtain historical data.
C. Interrogate historical data.
D. Identify the gaps in the available records, marshal contextual knowledge and perspectives of the time and place, and construct a sound historical interpretation.

Standard 5. Historical Issues-Analysis and Decision-Making

A. Identify issues and problems in the past.
B. Marshal evidence of antecedent circumstances and contemporary factors contributing to problems and alternative courses of action.
C. Identify relevant historical antecedents.
D. Evaluate alternative courses of action.
E. Formulate a position or course of action on an issue.
F. Evaluate the implementation of a decision.

STANDARD 1

Chronological Thinking

Chronological thinking is at the heart of historical reasoning. Without a strong sense of chronology — of when events occurred and in what temporal order — it is impossible for students to examine relationships among those events or to explain historical causality. Chronology provides the mental scaffolding for organizing historical thought.

In developing students' chronological thinking, instructional time should be given to the use of well constructed **historical narratives:** literary narratives including biographies and historical literature, and well written narrative histories that have the quality of "stories well told." Well crafted narratives such as these have the power to grip and hold students' attention. Thus engaged, the reader is able to focus on what the narrator discloses: the temporal structure of events unfolding over time, the actions and intentions of those who were there, the temporal connections between antecedents and their consequences.

In the middle and high school years, students should be able to use their mathematical skills to measure time by years, decades, centuries, and millennia; to calculate time from the fixed points of the calendar system (BC or BCE and AD or CE); and to interpret the data presented in time lines.

Students should be able to analyze *patterns of historical duration,* demonstrated, for example, by the more than two hundred years the United States Constitution and the government it created has endured.

Students should also be able to analyze *patterns of historical succession* illustrated, for example, in the development, over time, of ever larger systems of interaction, beginning with trade among settlements of the Neolithic world; continuing through the growth of the great land empires of Rome, Han China, the Islamic world, and the Mongols; expanding in the early modern era when Europeans crossed the Atlantic and Pacific, and established the first worldwide networks of trade and communication; and culminating with the global systems of trade and communication of the modern world.

Dover Publications

Students Should Be Able to:

A. **Distinguish between past, present, and future time.**

B. **Identify in historical narratives the temporal structure of a historical narrative or story:** its beginning, middle, and end (the latter defined as the outcome of a particular beginning).

C. **Establish temporal order in constructing historical narratives of their own:** working forward from some beginning through its development, to some end or outcome; working *backward* from some issue, problem, or event to explain its origins and its development over time.

D. **Measure and calculate calendar time** by days, weeks, months, years, decades, centuries, and millennia, from fixed points of the calendar system: BC (before Christ) and AD (*Anno Domini,* "in the year of our Lord") in the Gregorian calendar and the contemporary secular designation for these same dates, BCE (before the Common Era) and CE (in the Common Era); and compare with the fixed points of other calendar systems such as the Roman (753 BC, the founding of the city of Rome) and the Muslim (622 AD, the hegira).

E. **Interpret data presented in time lines** and create time lines by designating appropriate equidistant intervals of time and recording events according to the temporal order in which they occurred.

F. **Reconstruct patterns of historical succession and duration** in which historical developments have unfolded, and apply them to **explain historical continuity and change.**

G. **Compare alternative models for periodization** by identifying the organizing principles on which each is based.

Grades 5-6

Examples of student achievement include:

▶ Differentiate autobiographies, biographies, literary narratives, and historical narratives and explain or diagram the temporal structure of events in the story.

▶ Construct multiple tier time lines, entering information on multiple themes developing over the same years: e.g., important social, economic, and political developments in the history of the thirteen English colonies between the years 1600 and 1800; or comparative developments in the English, Spanish, and French colonies in North America between 1500 and 1800.

▶ Group (periodize) events by broadly defined eras in the history of the nation or region they are studying.

▶ Calculate calendar time, determining the onset, duration, and ending dates of historical events or developments.

▶ Interpret data presented in time lines in order to determine when critical developments occurred and what else was occurring at the same time.

Grades 7-8

Examples of student achievement include:

- Measure time by millennia and calculate calendar time BC or BCE, and AD or CE.

- Explain patterns of historical continuity and change in the historical succession of related events unfolding over time.

- Impose temporal structure in developing historical narratives, including biographies, historical arguments, and stories by: working *forward* from some initiating event to follow its development and transformation to some outcome over time; working *backward* from some issue, problem, or event to explain its causes, arising from some beginning and developing through subsequent transformations over time.

Grades 9-12

Examples of student achievement include:

- Reconstruct the temporal order and connections disclosed in historical narratives and biographies and draw upon that information to construct sound interpretations of the text. (For standards in historical interpretation, see Chapter 3, below.)

- Compare at least two alternative systems of recording calendar time, such as those based on a solar year (Egyptian, Indian, Roman, Gregorian, Mayan, Aztec, or Chinese calendars); a lunar year (the Muslim calendar); or a semilunar calendar, adjusting the lunar year to a solar year (the Jewish calendar). Demonstrate understanding of the astronomical system on which the calendar is based, its fixed points for measuring time, and its respective strengths and weaknesses.

- Demonstrate historical continuity and/or change with respect to a particular historical development or theme by reconstructing and analyzing the chronological succession and duration of events associated with it.

- Analyze a model for periodization (such as the one adopted in their history textbook) by identifying the organizing principles on which the particular sequence of historical eras was chosen, and comparing with at least one alternative model and the principles on which it is based.

STANDARD 2

Historical Comprehension

One of the defining features of historical narratives is their believable recounting of human events. Beyond that, historical narratives also have the power to disclose the intentions of the people involved, the difficulties they encountered, and the complex world in which such historical figures actually lived. To read historical stories, biographies, autobiographies, and narratives with comprehension, students must develop the ability to read imaginatively, to take into account what the narrative reveals of the humanity of the individuals involved — their motives and intentions, their hopes, doubts, fears, strengths, and weaknesses. Comprehending historical narratives requires, also, that students develop historical perspectives, the ability to describe the past on its own terms, through the eyes and experiences of those who were there. By studying the literature, diaries, letters, debates, arts, and artifacts of past peoples, students should learn to avoid "present-mindedness" by not judging the past solely in terms of the norms and values of today, but taking into account the historical context in which the events unfolded.

Acquiring these skills begins in the early years of childhood, through the use of superbly written biographies that capture children's imagination and provide them an important foundation for continuing historical study. As students move into middle grades and high school years, historical literature should continue to occupy an important place in the curriculum, capturing historical events with dramatic immediacy, engaging students' interests, and fostering deeper understanding of the times and cultural milieu in which events occurred.

Beyond these important outcomes, students should also develop the skills needed to comprehend "thick narratives" — historical narratives that *explain* as well as recount the course of events and that *analyze* relationships among the various forces that were present at the time and influenced the ways events unfolded. These skills include: (1) identifying the central question the historical narrative seeks to answer; (2) defining the purpose, perspective, or point of view from which the narrative has been constructed; (3) reading the historical explanation or analysis with meaning; and (4) recognizing the rhetorical cues that signal how the author has organized the text.

Comprehending historical narratives will also be facilitated if students are able to draw upon the data presented in historical maps, graphics, and a variety of visual sources such as historical photographs, political cartoons, paintings, and architecture in order to clarify, illustrate, or elaborate upon the information presented in the text.

Students Should Be Able to:

A. **Reconstruct the literal meaning of a historical passage** by identifying who was involved, what happened, where it happened, what events led to these developments, and what consequences or outcomes followed.

B. **Identify the central question(s)** the historical narrative addresses and the purpose, perspective, or point of view from which it has been constructed.

C. **Read historical narratives imaginatively,** taking into account (a) the historical context in which the event unfolded — the values, outlook, options, and contingencies of that time and place; and (b) what the narrative reveals of the humanity of the individuals involved — their probable motives, hopes, fears, strengths, and weaknesses.

D. **Evidence historical perspectives** — the ability (a) to describe the past on its own terms, through the eyes and experiences of those who were there, as revealed through their literature, diaries, letters, debates, arts, artifacts, and the like; and (b) to avoid "present-mindedness," judging the past solely in terms of present-day norms and values.

E. **Draw upon data in historical maps** in order to obtain or clarify information on the geographic setting in which the historical event occurred, its relative and absolute location, the distances and directions involved, the natural and man-made features of the place, and critical relationships in the spatial distributions of those features and the historical event occurring there.

F. **Utilize visual and mathematical data** presented in charts, tables, pie and bar graphs, flow charts, Venn diagrams, and other graphic organizers to clarify, illustrate, or elaborate upon information presented in the historical narrative.

G. **Draw upon visual, literary, and musical sources** including: (a) photographs, paintings, cartoons, and architectural drawings; (b) novels, poetry, and plays; and (c) folk, popular, and classical music to clarify, illustrate, or elaborate upon information presented in the historical narrative.

Grades 5-6

Examples of student achievement include:

▶ Identify the central question(s) the historical narrative attempts to address and the purpose, perspective, or point of view from which it has been constructed.

▶ Demonstrate historical perspectives by taking into account the lives of individuals, their values, and outlooks within the historical context.

▶ Identify specific characteristics of the historical place and time that influenced why events, or actions, developed where and when they did.

▶ Read and interpret the data presented in two-way and three-way tables, classifications, and data retrieval charts.

▶ Read geographic symbols, map scales, and directional indicators in order to obtain and interpret such information from historical maps as: the geographical features of the setting in which events occurred, their absolute and relative locations, and the distances and directions involved.

▶ Read and interpret the visual and mathematical data presented in flow charts, pie graphs, and Venn diagrams.

▶ Read and interpret the visual data presented in historical photographs, paintings, and drawings of the people, places, and historical events under study.

Grades 7-8

Examples of student achievement include:

▶ Read and understand primary sources such as the United States Declaration of Independence, the French Declaration of the Rights of Man and Citizen, and Zapata's "Plan de Ayala." Students should recognize that understanding requires not only what the words say, but where such ideas arose and how they evolved from earlier ideas.

▶ Determine the causes and consequences of events and demonstrate understanding through various techniques such as peer-teaching, Socratic seminars, written analysis, and graphic organizers (flow charts, clustering, Venn diagrams).

▶ Draw upon documentary photographs, political cartoons and broadsides, art, and other visual data presented in historical narratives to clarify, elaborate upon, and understand the historical period. The critical examination of sources, such as caricatures of Louis Philippe or Andrew Jackson, photographs by Mathew Brady and Lewis Hine, paintings by Pablo Picasso and Diego Rivera, and Maoist poster art, assists in understanding historical periods.

▶ Demonstrate the ability to draw warranted conclusions from data presented in political, physical, and demographic maps in appraising the importance of location, region, and movement in history.

▶ Examine historical records to take into account the context of the historical period in which they were written and to avoid "present-mindedness" (i.e., judging the past solely in terms of the norms and values of today).

Grades 9-12

Examples of student achievement include:

▶ Discern the significance of historical accounts and explain the writer's perceptions of movements and trends.

▶ Explain the ways in which historical literature reflects the attitudes, values, and passions of the era. For example, probe the motives of U.S. muckrakers such as Lincoln Steffens, Upton Sinclair, John Spargo, and Ida Tarbell; examine the impact of literary figures of the Harlem Renaissance such as Langston Hughes and Claude McKay; or examine the impact of antiwar novels such as Erich Maria Remarque's *All Quiet on the Western Front*.

▶ Draw upon statistical data presented in charts and graphs in order to elaborate on information presented in historical narratives.

STANDARD 3

Historical Analysis and Interpretation

One of the most common problems in helping students to become thoughtful readers of historical narrative is the compulsion students feel to find the one right answer, the one essential fact, the one authoritative interpretation. "Am I on the right track?" "Is this what you want?" they ask. Or, worse yet, they rush to closure, reporting back as self-evident truths the facts or conclusions presented in the document or text.

These problems are deeply rooted in the conventional ways in which textbooks have presented history: a succession of facts marching straight to a settled outcome. To overcome these problems requires the use of more than a single source: of history books other than textbooks and of a rich variety of historical documents and artifacts that present alternative voices, accounts, and interpretations or perspectives on the past.

Students need to realize that historians may differ on the facts they incorporate in the development of their narratives, and disagree as well on how those facts are to be interpreted. Thus, "history" is usually taken to mean what happened in the past; but *written* history is a dialogue among historians not only about what happened but about why and how it happened, how it affected other happenings, and how much importance it ought to be assigned. The study of history is not only remembering answers. It requires following and evaluating arguments and arriving at usable, even if tentative, conclusions based on the available evidence.

Well written historical narrative has the power to promote students' analysis of historical causality — of how change occurs in society, of how human intentions matter, and how ends are influenced by the means of carrying them out, in what has been called the tangle of process and outcomes. Few challenges can be more fascinating to students than unraveling the often dramatic complications of cause. And nothing is more dangerous than a simple, monocausal explanation of past experiences and present problems.

Finally, well written historical narratives can also alert students to the traps of *lineality and inevitability*. Students must understand the relevance of the past to their own times, but they need also to avoid the trap of lineality, of drawing straight lines between past and present, as though earlier movements were being propelled teleologically toward some rendezvous with destiny in the late 20th century.

A related trap is that of thinking that events have unfolded inevitably — that the way things are is the way they had to be, and thus that humankind lacks free will and the capacity for making choice. Unless students can conceive that history could have turned out differently, they may unconsciously accept the notion that the future is also inevitable or predetermined, and that human agency and individual action count for nothing. No attitude is more likely to feed civic apathy, cynicism, and resignation — precisely what we hope the study of history will fend off. Whether in dealing with the main narrative or with a topic in depth, we must always try, in one historian's words, to "restore to the past the options it once had."

Students Should Be Able to:

A. **Identify the author or source of the historical document or narrative and assess its credibility.**

B. **Compare and contrast differing sets of ideas,** values, personalities, behaviors, and institutions by identifying likenesses and differences.

C. **Differentiate between historical facts and historical interpretations,** but acknowledge also that the two are related: that the facts the historian reports are selected and reflect therefore the historian's judgment of what is most significant about the past.

D. **Consider multiple perspectives** of various peoples in the past by demonstrating their differing motives, beliefs, interests, hopes, and fears.

E. **Analyze cause-and-effect relationships** bearing in mind **multiple causation** including (a) **the importance of the individual** in history; (b) **the influence of ideas,** human interests, and beliefs; and (c) **the role of chance,** the accidental, and the irrational.

F. **Challenge arguments of historical inevitability** by formulating examples of historical contingency, of how different choices could have led to different consequences.

G. **Compare competing historical narratives** by contrasting different historians' choice of questions, and their use of sources reflecting different experiences, perspectives, beliefs, and points of view, and by demonstrating how an emphasis on different causes contributes to different interpretations.

H. **Hold interpretations of history as tentative,** subject to change as new information is uncovered, new voices heard, and new interpretations broached.

I. **Evaluate major debates among historians** concerning alternative interpretations of the past.

J. **Hypothesize the influence of the past,** including both the limitations and the opportunities made possible by past decisions.

Grades 5-6

Examples of student achievement include:

▶ Read historical narratives to identify the author's main points and the purpose or point of view from which the narrative has been written.

▶ Analyze historical narratives to identify the facts the author has provided and to evaluate the credibility of the generalization or interpretation the author has presented on the basis of the evidence he or she has assembled.

▶ Analyze or construct causal analyses taking into account two or more factors contributing to the historical event.

Grades 7-8

Examples of student achievement include:

▶ Determine an author's frame of reference in primary and secondary sources and form analytical questions to examine the data and to determine bias in documents and historical narratives.

▶ Consult multiple sources reflecting differing interpretations of a historic event or individual.

◗ Recognize that historical accounts are subject to change based on newly uncovered records and new interpretations. The publication of government documents and formerly suppressed records (e.g., release of secret treaties and "White Papers" in the post-World War I era and the revelations of Stalinist purges), or changing perspectives on movements, may alter previously accepted historical accounts.

◗ Assess the importance of the individual in history and the importance of individual choices. In assessing the importance of individual action and decision making, for example, students should consider the impact of humanitarian efforts of individuals such as Mother Teresa of Calcutta, or the social consciousness of persons such as Martin Luther King Jr., Jane Addams, or Raul Wallenberg. Students should be able to analyze sources to determine what they reveal about ordinary people as well as recognized leaders and historical events, movements, and trends.

◗ Critically evaluate the evidence presented in both primary and secondary sources and recognize the danger in drawing analogies without considering different circumstances presented by time and place.

Grades 9-12

Examples of student achievement include:

◗ Analyze the motives and interests expressed in both primary and secondary sources and distinguish between accepted historical facts and interpretations.

◗ Compare two or more historical interpretations, differentiate between fact and interpretation, and determine what facts are most significant in the historian's judgment and why. Students should be able to evaluate arguments and arrive at conclusions based on the evidence.

◗ Consider multiple perspectives in interpreting the past and explain how different motives, beliefs, interests, and perspectives influence interpretations of the past.

◗ Evaluate the validity and credibility of historical interpretations, including new or changing interpretations which have developed as new information about the past is uncovered, new voices heard, and new methodologies and interpretations are developed.

◗ Challenge prevailing attitudes of historical inevitability by examining how alternative choices could produce different consequences. Students should understand that options existed in the past and that history is contingent on human agency and individual choices.

◗ Recognize that historical events are the products of deliberate actions or spontaneous responses to given circumstances. Students should understand change and continuity and the dynamics of the interplay of individuals and groups promoting and resisting change.

STANDARD 4

Historical Research Capabilities

Perhaps no aspect of historical thinking is as exciting to students or as productive of their growth in historical thinking as "doing history." Such inquiries can arise at critical turning points in the historical narrative presented in the text. They might be generated by encounters with historical documents, eyewitness accounts, letters, diaries, artifacts, photos, a visit to a historic site, a record of oral history, or other evidence of the past. Worthy inquiries are especially likely to develop if the documents students encounter are rich with the voices of people caught up in the event and sufficiently diverse to bring alive to students the interests, beliefs, and concerns of people with differing backgrounds and opposing viewpoints on the event.

Historical inquiry proceeds with the formulation of a problem or set of questions worth pursuing. In the most direct approach, students might be encouraged to analyze a document, record, or site itself. Who produced it, when, how, and why? What is the evidence of its authenticity, authority, and credibility? What does it tell them of the point of view, background, and interests of its author or creator? What else must they discover in order to construct a useful story, explanation, or narrative of the event of which this document or artifact is a part? What interpretation can they derive from their data, and what argument can they support in the historical narrative they create from the data?

In this process students' contextual knowledge of the historical period in which the document or artifact was created becomes critically important. Only a few records of the event will be available to students. Filling in the gaps, evaluating the records they have available, and imaginatively constructing a sound historical argument or narrative requires a larger context of meaning.

For these purposes, students' ongoing narrative study of history provides important support, revealing the larger context. But just as the ongoing narrative study, supported by but not limited to the textbook, provides a meaningful context in which students' inquiries can develop, it is these inquiries themselves that imbue the era with deeper meaning. Hence the importance of providing students documents or other records beyond materials included in the textbook, that will allow students to challenge textbook interpretations, to raise new questions about the event, to investigate the perspectives of those whose voices do not appear in the textbook accounts, or to plumb an issue that the textbook largely or in part bypassed.

Under these conditions, students will view their inquiries as creative contributions. They will better understand that written history is a human construction, that certain judgments about the past are tentative and arguable, and that historians regard their work as critical inquiry, pursued as ongoing explorations and debates with other historians. By their active engagement in historical inquiry, students will learn for themselves why historians are continuously reinterpreting the past, and why new interpretations emerge not only from uncovering new evidence but from rethinking old evidence in the light of new ideas springing up in our own times. Students then can also see why the good historian, like the good teacher, is interested not in manipulation or indoctrination but in acting as the honest messenger from the past — not interested in possessing students' minds but in presenting them with the power to possess their own.

Students Should Be Able to:

A. **Formulate historical questions** from encounters with historical documents, eyewitness accounts, letters, diaries, artifacts, photos, historical sites, art, architecture, and other records from the past.

B. **Obtain historical data** from a variety of sources, including: library and museum collections, historic sites, historical photos, journals, diaries, eyewitness accounts, newspapers, and the like; documentary films; and so on.

C. **Interrogate historical data** by uncovering the social, political, and economic context in which it was created; testing the data source for its credibility, authority, authenticity, internal consistency and completeness; and detecting and evaluating bias, distortion, and propaganda by omission, suppression, or invention of facts.

D. **Identify the gaps in the available records and marshal contextual knowledge and perspectives of the time and place** in order to elaborate imaginatively upon the evidence, fill in the gaps deductively, and construct a sound historical interpretation.

Grades 5-6

Examples of student achievement include:

▶ Studying historical documents to formulate significant questions such as: Who produced the document? When, how, and why? What does the document tell about the person(s) who created it? What do the students need to find out in order to "tell a story" about the document and the people and events connected with it?

Grades 7-8

Examples of student achievement include:

▶ Formulate questions to guide and focus research.

▶ Draw from a variety of primary and secondary sources, including diaries, letters, periodicals, literature, oral histories, artifacts, art, and documentary photographs and films in historical research.

▶ Interpret the data obtained from historical documents to analyze the historical context in which they were created, and develop a report about it.

▶ Examine historical accounts to determine what voices are missing from narratives; explain reasons for omissions, and challenge generalizations and interpretations in text accounts.

Grades 9-12

Examples of student achievement include:

▶ Consult bibliographical studies to help select appropriate source materials for the research of historical periods, events, or personalities. Encyclopedic endnotes, footnote references, recommended readings in texts and monographs, and bibliographies such as the *Harvard Guide to American History* should be used as an aid in gathering materials for research projects and papers.

▶ Use book reviews and critiques to make choices regarding historical sources and examine references to determine the context in which they were written. Students should, as a matter of habit, cross-reference sources and ask probing questions to determine the authenticity and credibility of references.

S T A N D A R D   5

Historical Issues-Analysis and Decision-Making

Issue-centered analysis and decision-making activities place students squarely at the center of historical dilemmas and problems faced at critical moments in the past and the near-present. Entering into such moments, confronting the issues or problems of the time, analyzing the alternatives available to those on the scene, evaluating the consequences that might have followed those options for action that were not chosen, and comparing with the consequences of those that were adopted, are activities that foster students' deep, personal involvement in these events.

If well chosen, these activities also promote capacities vital to a democratic citizenry: the capacity to identify and define public policy issues and ethical dilemmas; analyze the range of interests and values held by the many persons caught up in the situation and affected by its outcome; locate and organize the data required to assess the consequences of alternative approaches to resolving the dilemma; assess the ethical implications as well as the comparative costs and benefits of each approach; and evaluate a particular course of action in light of all of the above and, in the case of historical issues-analysis, in light also of its long-term consequences revealed in the historical record.

Because important historical issues are frequently value-laden, they also open opportunities to consider the moral convictions contributing to social actions taken. The point to be made is that teachers should not use critical events to hammer home a particular "moral lesson" or ethical teaching. Not only will many students reject that approach; it fails also to take into account the processes through which students acquire the complex skills of principled thinking and moral reasoning. The best approach is to open these issues to analysis grounded in historical evidence and allow a variety of perspectives on the problem to emerge.

Value-laden issues worthy of classroom analysis include not only those irredeemable events in human history from which students can most easily draw clear ethical judgment — the Holocaust, for example, or the Cambodian genocide under the Pol Pot regime. These analyses should also address situations of lasting consequence in which what is morally "right" and "wrong" may not be self-evident. Was it right, for example, for Lincoln, in his Emancipation Proclamation, to free only those slaves behind the Confederate lines? Because of the complicated way values act upon people confronted with the need to decide, the full moral situation in a past event is not always immediately clear. Students should understand, therefore, that their opinions should be held tentative and open to revision as they acquire new insight into these historical problems.

Particularly challenging are the many social issues throughout United States history on which multiple interests and different values have come to bear. Issues of civil rights or equal education opportunity, of the right of choice vs. the right to life, and of criminal justice have all brought such conflicts to the fore. When these conflicts have not been resolved within the social and political institutions of the nation, they have regularly found their way into the judicial system, often going to the Supreme Court for resolution.

As the history course approaches the present era, such inquiries assume special relevance, confronting students with issues that resonate in today's headlines and invite their participation in lively debates, simulations, and Socratic seminars — settings in which they can confront alternative policy recommendations, judge their ethical implications, challenge one another's assessments, and acquire further skills in the public presentation and defense of positions. In these analyses, teachers have the special responsibility of helping students differentiate between (1) relevant historical antecedents, and (2) those that are clearly inappropriate and irrelevant. Students need to learn how to use their knowledge of history (or the past) to bring sound historical analysis to the service of informed decision making.

Students Should Be Able to:

A. **Identify issues and problems in the past** and analyze the interests, values, perspectives, and points of view of those involved in the situation.

B. **Marshal evidence of antecedent circumstances** and contemporary factors contributing to problems and alternative courses of action.

C. **Identify relevant historical antecedents** and differentiate from those that are inappropriate and irrelevant to contemporary issues.

D. **Evaluate alternative courses of action** in terms of ethical considerations, the interests of those affected by the decision, and the long- and short-term consequences of each.

E. **Formulate a position or course of action on an issue** by identifying the nature of the problem, analyzing the underlying factors contributing to the problem, and choosing a plausible solution from a choice of carefully evaluated options.

F. **Evaluate the implementation of a decision** by analyzing the interests it served; estimating the position, power, and priority of each player involved; assessing the ethical dimensions of the decision; and evaluating its costs and benefits from a variety of perspectives.

Grades 5-6

Examples of student achievement include:

▸ Examine proposals for resolving a problem, compare the possible consequences of two or more courses of action, and analyze their effects on various individuals and groups caught up in the situation.

▸ Identify the values and moral convictions of those on different sides of an issue and evaluate some of the long-term as well as immediate consequences of the decisions made.

▸ Apply these same skills to the analysis of a contemporary issue in the students' local community or state which has its roots in past decisions and requires resolution today.

Grades 7-8

Examples of student achievement include:

▸ Identify factors that led to a historical issue, define the problems involved in its resolution, and explain the motives, values, and varying perspectives surrounding the problem. For example, students might investigate background causes that led Alexander II to abolish serfdom in Russia and Lincoln to issue the Emancipation Proclamation. They should explore various attitudes regarding these policy decisions, the factors that led to their enactment, and form warranted value judgments regarding the timing and the scope of these decisions.

▸ Use primary source materials to assume the role of an individual and explain a policy issue from the perspective of that individual within the context of time and place.

‣ Analyze individual decisions and grapple with the personal dilemmas encountered in pursuing a course of action. Students should be able to examine choices such as Susan B. Anthony's decision to vote in the presidential election of 1872, Mohandas Gandhi's decision to organize the 1930 salt march, or Rosa Park's decision to confront Jim Crow laws in Montgomery, Alabama.

‣ Reach value judgments regarding the course of action taken by individuals in history by weighing the influence of attitudes, values, and alternative options of that particular time and place. For example, in analyzing whether delegates at the Philadelphia Convention of 1787 should have taken a firm stand against slavery, thereby confronting threats by South Carolina and Georgia to withdraw support for the Constitution, students should be able to identify the issues involved, compare the alternative perspectives and ethical considerations of the delegates on issues of slavery and union, and assess the compromises reached.

‣ Analyze the historical circumstances and reach warranted ethical judgments concerning such events as Hitler's "final solution" and Pol Pot's "killing fields."

Grades 9-12

Examples of student achievement include:

‣ Analyze value-laden public policy issues by taking into account the social conditions, the interests of the players involved, the values that came into conflict in the situation, and the policies adopted on the issue.

‣ Analyze the decisions leading to events recognized as major turning points in history, compare alternative courses of action, and hypothesize, within the context of the historic period, other possible outcomes. For example, students may debate the alternative actions Britain and France could have taken at Munich given the political situation and diplomatic initiatives of September 1938. Students could focus on opposition to Prime Minister Chamberlain as expressed by Winston Churchill and Clement Attlee through debates in the British House of Commons.

‣ Assess the nonrational, irrational, and the accidental in history and human affairs. In appraising decisions, students should be cautious to avoid present-mindedness by asking whether circumstances evolving in later years necessarily made a decision irrational at the time it was made. (E.g., was Woodrow Wilson's neglect of a youthful Ho Chi Minh's appeal to apply to the French colonies of Southeast Asia the same principle of self-determination that Wilson advocated at Versailles irrational at the time? What were the influences of prevailing early 20th-century attitudes regarding colonialism, diplomatic goals, and confrontation with allies over self-determination for colonies? Students should debate similar issues and assess reactions to given situations in the context of time.)

‣ Debate national and international policy issues and suggest alternative courses of action based on sound reasoning that employs historical analysis and interpretation.

‣ Differentiate appropriate from inappropriate historical analogies by critically assessing the parallels between the current situation and that of the past.

Library of Congress

Ramusio's "Navigationi el viaggi", Mexico City, 1557

CHAPTER 3

United States History Standards for Grades 5-12

Overview of United States History Standards Integrating Historical Thinking and Historical Understandings

In this chapter, the historical understandings of ten eras of United States history are integrated with the five Historical Thinking Standards. An overview of the 31 main understandings is followed by a complete section for each era.

Era 1: Three Worlds Meet (Beginnings to 1620)

Standard 1: The characteristics of societies in the Americas, western Europe, and West Africa that increasingly interacted after 1450

Standard 2: Early European exploration and colonization; the resulting cultural and ecological interactions

Era 2: Colonization and Settlement (1585-1763)

Standard 1: The early arrival of Europeans and Africans in the Americas, and how these people interacted with Native Americans

Standard 2: How political institutions and religious freedom emerged in the North American colonies

Standard 3: How the values and institutions of European economic life took root in the colonies; how slavery reshaped European and African life in the Americas

Era 3: Revolution and the New Nation (1754-1820s)

Standard 1: The causes of the American Revolution, the ideas and interests involved in forging the revolutionary movement, and the reasons for the American victory

Standard 2: How the American Revolution involved multiple movements among the new nation's many groups to reform American society

Standard 3: The institutions and practices of government created during the revolution and how they were revised between 1787 and 1815 to create the foundation of the American political system

Era 4: Expansion and Reform (1801-1861)

Standard 1: United States territorial expansion between 1801 and 1861, and how it affected relations with external powers and Native Americans

Standard 2: How the industrial revolution, the rapid expansion of slavery, and the westward movement changed the lives of Americans and led toward regional tensions

Standard 3: The extension, restriction, and reorganization of political democracy after 1800

Standard 4: The sources and character of reform movements in the antebellum period and what the reforms accomplished or failed to accomplish

Era 5: Civil War and Reconstruction (1850-1877)

Standard 1: The causes of the Civil War

Standard 2: The course and character of the Civil War and its effects on the American people

Standard 3: How various reconstruction plans succeeded or failed

Era 6: The Development of the Industrial United States (1870-1900)

Standard 1: How the rise of big business, heavy industry, and mechanized farming transformed the American peoples

Standard 2: Massive immigration after 1870 and how new social patterns, conflicts, and ideas of national unity developed amid growing cultural diversity

Standard 3: The rise of the American labor movement, and how political issues reflected social and economic changes

Standard 4: Federal Indian policy and United States foreign policy after the Civil War

Era 7: The Emergence of Modern America (1890-1930)

Standard 1: How Progressives and others addressed problems of industrial capitalism, urbanization, and political corruption

Standard 2: The changing role of the United States in world affairs through World War I

Standard 3: How the United States changed from the end of World War I to the eve of the Great Depression

Era 8: The Great Depression and World War II (1929-1945)

Standard 1: The causes of the Great Depression and how it affected American society

Standard 2: How the New Deal addressed the Great Depression, transformed American federalism, and initiated the welfare state

Standard 3: The origins and course of World War II, the character of the war at home and abroad, and its reshaping of the U.S. role in world affairs

Era 9: Postwar United States (1945 to early 1970s)

Standard 1: The economic boom and social transformation of postwar America

Standard 2: The postwar extension of the New Deal

Standard 3: The Cold War and the Korean and Vietnam conflicts in domestic and international politics

Standard 4: The struggle for racial and gender equality and for the extension of civil liberties

Era 10: Contemporary United States (1968 to the present)

Standard 1: Major developments in foreign and domestic policies during the Cold War era

Standard 2: Major social and economic developments in contemporary America

Native Americans Tilling the Soil, by Jacques Le Moyne, Library of Congress

ERA 1

Three Worlds Meet (Beginnings to 1620)

The study of American history properly begins with the first peopling of the Americas some 30,000 years ago. After students learn about the spread of human societies and the rise of diverse cultures in the Americas, they are prepared to delve into a historical convergence of European, African, and Native American peoples, beginning in the late 15th century. In studying the beginnings of American history it is best for students to take a hemispheric approach. This broader context of American history avoids provincialism and drives home the point that the English, as latecomers to the Americas, were deeply affected by what had already occurred in vast regions of the hemisphere.

Although Europeans initiated the changes in the late 1400s that brought about the "great convergence," students will not grasp this collision of cultures without understanding the extensiveness and complexity of the societies of pre-Columbian America and West Africa. Developing an appreciation of these pre-1492 societies will dispel stereotyped images of American Indians and Africans and prepare students for the complexity of the often violent meeting of these three worlds.

By studying the colonization of the Americas to 1620, students will embark upon a continuing theme — the making of the American people. As a people, we were composed from the beginning of several ethnic and racial strains. The consequences of that beginning, both immediate and long-term, were to raise issues and tensions among us that are still unresolved.

By studying early European exploration, colonization, and conquest, students will learn about five long-range changes set in motion by the Columbian voyages. First, the voyages initiated the redistribution of the world's population, with several million Europeans and at least 10-12 million Africans relocating on the west side of the Atlantic and the catastrophic losses suffered by the indigenous peoples. Second, the arrival of Europeans in the Americas led to the rise of the first global empires in world history — empires that for the next four centuries would colonize and Europeanize the world to a considerable degree. Third, the Columbian voyages sparked a commercial expansion in Europe that would hasten the rise of capitalism. Fourth, the voyages led in time to the planting of English settlements where ideas of representative government and religious toleration would grow haltingly and, over several centuries, would inspire similar transformations in other parts of the world. Lastly, Europe's arrival on the west side of the Atlantic gave rise to systems of forced labor in the Americas at a time when slavery and serfdom were waning in Europe.

Overview

Standard 1: The characteristics of societies in the Americas, western Europe, and West Africa that increasingly interacted after 1450

Standard 2: Early European exploration and colonization; the resulting cultural and ecological interactions

STANDARD 1

Students Should Understand: *The characteristics of societies in the Americas, western Europe, and West Africa that increasingly interacted after 1450.*

Students Should Be Able to:

1A Demonstrate understanding of commonalities, diversity, and change in the societies of the Americas from their beginnings to 1620 by:

[5-12] Drawing upon data provided by archaeologists and geologists to explain the origins and migration from Asia to the Americas and contrasting them with Native Americans' own beliefs concerning their origins in the Americas. [**Compare and contrast differing sets of ideas**]

[7-12] Tracing the spread of human societies and the rise of diverse cultures from hunter-gatherers to urban dwellers in the Americas. [**Reconstruct patterns of historical succession and duration**]

[9-12] Comparing and explaining the common elements of Native American cultures such as gender roles, family organization, religion, values, and environmental interaction and their striking diversity in languages, shelter, tools, food, and clothing. [**Analyze multiple causation**]

[7-12] Comparing commonalities and differences between Native American and European outlooks, and values on the eve of "the great convergence." [**Compare and contrast differing sets of ideas and values**]

| Grades 5-6 | Examples of student achievement of Standard 1A include: |

▶ Locate the Bering land bridge and the routes anthropologists believe were taken by Asian people migrating from Siberia and southward and eastward in the Americas during the periods when massive glaciers covered the northern latitudes. Use sources such as Helen Roney Sattler's *The Earliest Americans* to explore various theories regarding the earliest Americans.

▶ Draw upon a variety of works such as *Myths and Legends of the Indian Southwest* by Bertha Dutton and Caroline Olin; *Myths and Legends of the Haida Indians of the Northwest* by Martine Reid; and *Grandfather's Origin Story: The Navajo Indian Beginning* by Richard Redhawk to explain the beliefs concerning the origins of different Indian societies.

▶ Compare how location and physical geography affected food sources, shelter, and cultural patterns of Native American societies such as the Iroquois and Pueblo or Northwest and Southeast Indian societies. Draw evidence from *First Houses: Native American Homes and Sacred Structures* by Jean Guard Monroe and Ray Williamson to explore the differences in shelter and how different Indian societies adapted to the geography of the region in which they lived.

▶ Compare the different ideas that Native Americans and Europeans held about how the land should be used.

▶ Draw upon legends of Hiawatha and historical records of the Iroquois Nation to analyze how the Mohawk, Oneida, Onondaga, Cayuga, and Seneca united to solve conflicts peaceably.

Grades 7-8

Examples of student achievement of Standard 1A include:

▶ Draw upon archaeological sources to construct evidence of the movement of peoples into the Americas.

▶ Construct a map locating representative Native American peoples such as the Mississippian, Aztec, Mayan, Incan, Iroquois, Pueblo, and Inuit societies.

▶ Write a historical narrative illustrating the cultural traditions, gender roles, and patterns of life of a specific Indian society.

▶ Draw upon anthropological and historical data to develop a sound historical argument on such questions as: *Were Native American societies "primitive," as the first Europeans to encounter them believed, or had these societies developed complex patterns of social organization, trading networks, and political culture?*

Grades 9-12

Examples of student achievement of Standard 1A include:

▶ Make connections between the images in Native American origin stories and their beliefs about the peopling of the Americas. *What, for example, do Native American origin stories tell us about Native American values and beliefs? How are symbols in origin stories such as wood, rock, rivers, corn, and squash used to explain migration, settlement, and interactions with the environment? What are their significance to understanding a Native American view of the earth?*

▶ Draw upon Native American and European artifacts, visual sources, oral traditions, journals and historical narratives to compare the diversity of European perceptions of Native Americans. Compare, for example, John White's images of Native Americans with those of Theodore deBry in terms of perceptions of Native Americans. *How do their perceptions differ? What factors might account for the different representations of Native Americans in these images?*

▶ Marshal specific evidence from such Native American societies as the Hopi and Zuni cultures of the Southwest, the Algonkian and Iroquoian cultures of the Northeast Woodlands, and the earlier Moundbuilder and Mississippian cultures of the Ohio and Mississippi valleys to develop a historical argument on such questions as the following: *Were Native American societies such as the Hopi and Zuni different in their agricultural practices, gender roles, and social development from 15th-century peasant communities in Europe? To what extent did the striking differences between Native American societies reflect different phases of the agricultural revolution in the Americas? To what extent did they reflect different geographic environments and resources available to these societies?*

Crescent Books, NY

Students Should Be Able to:

1B Demonstrate understanding of the characteristics of western European societies in the age of exploration by:

5-12 Analyzing how geographical, scientific, and technological factors contributed to the age of exploration. **[Draw upon data in historical maps]**

7-12 Analyzing relationships among the rise of centralized states, the development of urban centers, the expansion of commerce, and overseas exploration. **[Analyze cause-and-effect relationships]**

9-12 Appraising customary European family organization, gender roles, acquisition of private property, relationship to the environment, and ideas about other cultures. **[Examine the influences of ideas]**

| Grades 5-6 | **Examples of student achievement of Standard 1B include:** |

▶ Using literature, investigate stories of the early exploration of the Americas before Columbus. Discuss how myths and legends may have played a role in voyages of exploration using such sources as *Brendan the Navigator: A History Mystery about the Discovery of America* by Jean Fritz.

| Grades 7-8 | **Examples of student achievement of Standard 1B include:** |

▶ Analyze how navigational knowledge and shipbuilding contributed to exploration. *How did the design of caravels help to revolutionize navigation? Why did European exploration occur in the 15th and 16th centuries and rarely in the previous centuries?*

▶ Analyze how their views affected European perspectives of different cultures. *What historical evidence illustrates European attitudes toward property and the environment during the period of exploration and early settlement?*

| Grades 9-12 | **Examples of student achievement of Standard 1B include:** |

▶ Develop a historical argument of the cause-and-effect relationships that stimulated European overseas exploration, considering such factors as the Crusades and Reconquista of Islamic Spain, the rise of cities, the military revolution, the development of strong monarchies, the expansion of intercontinental commerce, and the expansion of scientific, geographic, and technological knowledge.

▶ Analyze representative examples of ideas, art, and literature illustrating the spirit of individualism that sparked overseas exploration. For example: Analyze examples of Renaissance art, such as Michelangelo's painting of the Sistine Chapel or the sculpture David for what it says about the relationship between man and God and the position and power of the individual. Analyze how the character of Caliban and his relationship with Antonio in Shakespeare's *The Tempest* illustrate the prevailing attitude toward cross-cultural contacts with new people — encountering the "other."

Students Should Be Able to:

1C Demonstrate understanding of the characteristics of West African societies in the era of European contact by:

5-12 Describing the physical and cultural geography of West Africa and analyzing its impact on settlement patterns and trade. [**Draw upon data in historical maps**]

5-12 Locating the political kingdoms of Mali, Songhai, and Benin, and urban centers such as Timbuktu and Jenne, and analyzing their importance and influence. [**Analyze cause-and-effect relationships**]

9-12 Describing how family organization, gender roles, and religion shaped West African societies. [**Analyze multiple causation**]

7-12 Appraising the influence of Islam and Muslim culture on West African societies. [**Examine the influence of ideas**]

Grades 5-6

Examples of student achievement of Standard 1C include:

▶ Identify and locate the political kingdoms of Mali, Songhai, and Benin and major urban centers such as Timbuktu and Jenne.

▶ Draw upon stories of Mansa Musa and his great pilgrimage to Mecca in 1324 in order to analyze the great wealth of Mali, its trade in gold and salt, and the importance of its learning center at Timbuktu.

▶ Draw upon West African proverbs, folk tales and artifacts to illustrate and explain traditional family living and gender roles. *How were children taught about expected behavior in traditional West African communities? What were the roles of men and women in their families? How did West African people use local materials to make masks, sculpture and artifacts reflecting their beliefs?*

Grades 7-8

Examples of student achievement of Standard 1C include:

▶ Draw upon historical narratives of Muslim scholars such as Ibn Fadi Allah al-Omari and Ibn Battuta to analyze the achievements and grandeur of Mansa Musa's court, and the social customs and wealth of the kingdom of Mali.

▶ Analyze representative examples of West African art such as terra cotta, wood, and bronze sculpture in order to illustrate West African social relationships and political structures.

▶ Analyze relationships between the geographic features and resources of West Africa and the patterns of settlement and trade that developed between African states, southwestern Asia, and Europe.

Grades 9-12

Examples of student achievement of Standard 1C include:

▶ Describe the major characteristics of African religious practices and explain how they affected child-rearing practices such as naming ceremonies and age groupings; the role of the individual and social relationships; and attitudes toward nature and use of the land.

▶ Develop a historical argument explaining the growing influence of Islam in West Africa. *Why, for example, were merchants and rulers in West Africa likely to adopt Islam? Why was Islam more widespread than Christianity in West Africa? How were West African religious beliefs and practices affected by Islam?*

▶ Draw upon historical narratives of Muslim scholars such as Leo Africanus, Mahmud al-Kati, and Ibn Battuta in order to evaluate the cultural, political and economic life of the African kingdoms of Mali and Songhai.

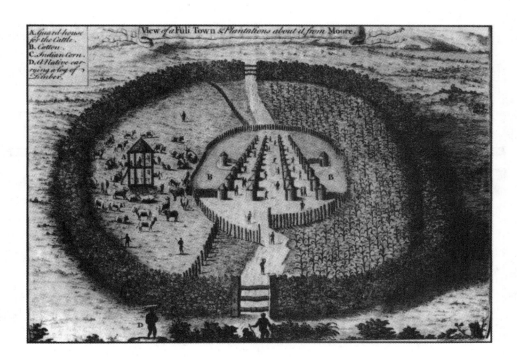

Drawing of a West African Village, Library of Congress

STANDARD 2

Students Should Understand: *Early European exploration and colonization; the resulting cultural and ecological interactions.*

Students Should Be Able to:

2A **Demonstrate understanding of how the stages of European oceanic and overland exploration from 1492 to 1700 occurred amid international rivalries by:**

[5-12] Tracing routes taken by early explorers, from the 15th through the 17th centuries, around Africa, to the Americas, and across the Pacific. [**Draw upon data in historical maps**]

[7-12] Evaluating the significance of Columbus's voyages and his interactions with indigenous peoples. [**Assess the importance of the individual in history**]

[9-12] Appraising the role of national and religious rivalries in the age of exploration and evaluate their long-range consequences. [**Consider multiple perspectives**]

[7-12] Evaluating the consequences of the "Columbian Exchange." [**Hypothesize the influence of the past**]

Grades 5-6

Examples of student achievement of Standard 2A include:

- For major early voyages of exploration, locate the Mediterranean and Atlantic seaports from which they sailed and map the routes each followed.

- Create a time line of European exploration showing names, dates, countries of origin and destinations.

- Compare the perils and problems encountered on the high seas with the fears and superstitions of the time.

- Create "diaries" or role-play answers to such questions as: *What did sailors expect to find when they reached the "Indies"? How did explorers think and feel as they moved across the uncharted seas?*

- Draw evidence from primary sources including Columbus's log, illustrations, maps, and charts to investigate the voyage using such sources as *The Log of Christopher Columbus; First Voyage to America: In the Year 1492, as Copied Out in Brief by Bartholomew Las Casas.*

Grades 7-8

Examples of student achievement of Standard 2A include:

▶ Draw upon evidence from Columbus's journal and other historical sources to appraise his voyages of exploration. *How, for example, did Columbus's description of the peaceful and pleasant nature of the Carib Indians contrast with his treatment of them?*

▶ Analyze the immediate and long-term significance of the Columbian Exchange by developing historical arguments on such questions as: *How did the exchange of food such as maize affect population growth in Europe? How did it lead to the forced relocation and enslavement of Native Americans and Africans in the Americas? How did the spread of diseases affect societies? Were these consequences probable or could they have been avoided, given the state of medical knowledge and the lack of biological immunity of the Amerindian populations to these diseases at the time?*

▶ Explain how religious influences affected colonization in the Americas. *What inferences may be drawn from the establishment of the Spanish St. Augustine south of the French Protestant colonies of Fort Caroline and Charlesfort? Why did the English government promote the activities of "sea dogs" such as Hawkins and Drake?*

Grades 9-12

Examples of student achievement of Standard 2A include:

▶ Contrast the perceptions of Columbus — the man and his exploits — in 1892 and 1992. *What accounts for the changing interpretations of Columbus and his exploits?*

▶ Analyze how religious antagonisms unleashed by the Reformation stimulated overseas expansion by developing historical arguments on such questions as: *How was the Spanish "Black Legend" used to motivate and justify English colonization of North America? To what extent was the "Black Legend" Protestant propaganda? To what extent was it a valid description of the effect of the Spanish conquest?*

▶ Assess the long-range social and ecological impact of the Columbian Exchange in the Americas by developing historical arguments on such questions as: *How did the dandelion, the horse, and the pig bring about changes in the land? What was the significance of the great populations changes, including the forced relocation to the Americas of 10-12 millions of Africans, the migration of several million Europeans, and the decimation of Native American populations through disease? How did sugar connect Caribbean slaves, Indian laborers, and European urban proletarians, and with what consequences for these populations?*

Students Should Be Able to:

2B   Demonstrate understanding of the Spanish conquest of the Americas by:

7-12 Describing the social composition of the early settlers and comparing their motives for exploration and colonization. [**Compare and contrast differing sets of ideas**]

5-12 Explaining and evaluating the Spanish interactions with such people as Aztecs, Incas, and Pueblos. [**Examine the influence of ideas**]

9-12 Describing the evolution and long-term consequences of labor systems such as *encomienda* and slavery in Spanish America. [**Evidence historical perspectives**]

Grades 5-6

Examples of student achievement of Standard 2B include:

◗ Explain Spanish motivations for immigration to the Americas.

◗ Trace and map Spanish exploration in the Americas for the century following Columbus's explorations.

◗ Use adventure stories such as *The King's Fifth* by Scott O'Dell, *Ferdinand Magellan* by Jim Hargrove, and *De Soto, Finder of the Mississippi* by Ronald Syme to examine the exploration and conquest of Spanish America.

◗ Trace the explorations of Cabeza de Vaca and Francisco Vásquez de Coronado across the American Southwest with stories such as *Walk the World's Rim* by Betty Baker.

Grades 7-8

Examples of student achievement of Standard 2B include:

◗ Construct a historical narrative that analyzes the Spanish reasons for establishing footholds in the Americas and the groups that came with the conquistadores. *Why did they include Africans as well as Spaniards, and Catholic missionaries as well as soldiers?*

◗ Draw upon historical narratives and visual data to chronicle the Spanish conquest of the Aztec and Incan empires and develop historical arguments on such questions as: *How were the Spanish able to conquer such great civilizations with limited men and resources? Why was it possible for the Spanish conquistadores to recruit Indian allies to assist in their conquest of the Aztecs? What impact did internal rivalries have on the resistance of the Incas to the Spanish conquest?*

◗ Draw upon historical documents such as Cortés's letters on first viewing Tenochtitlán (Mexico City) to develop historical analyses of such questions as: *How did explorers react to the societies they encountered in Aztec and Incan settlements? What kind of architecture, skills, labor systems, and agriculture did they find in these places?*

Grades 9-12

Examples of student achievement of Standard 2B include:

▶ Draw upon historical records to contrast and explain the Aztec view of the Spanish and the Spanish view of the Aztecs at the time of contact. *What role did religious beliefs play in the perceptions each held of the other?*

▶ Draw evidence from historical monographs to explain how Cortés and Pizarro were able to conquer the Aztecs and Incas. *Why did it seem unlikely that Cortés or Pizarro could succeed? How did the factors of disease, political and ethnic rivalry, succession problems, military strategy, religion, and trickery contribute to Cortés's success? How did they contribute to Pizarro's success?*

▶ Assess the Spanish justification for their treatment of Native Americans by developing historical arguments on such questions as: *What was the background and significance of the* <u>requierimiento</u>? *How did Sepúlveda justify the Spanish treatment of Native Americans — morally, legally, and religiously? How did Las Casas try to refute Sepúlveda's argument? Which argument is more persuasive and why?*

▶ Explain the *encomienda* system and describe the evolution of labor systems within the Spanish empire in the Americas.

▶ Explain the origin and expansion of the African slave trade in the Americas. *Why did African chattel slavery gradually replace Indian labor in the Spanish colonies? How did slavery as practiced in African societies contrast with chattel slavery as it developed in the Americas? What were the consequences for Africans and the Americas of the forced relocation and enslavement of millions of Africans in the Spanish and Portuguese colonies?*

▶ Analyze the social composition of early Spanish settlers in the Americas in terms of age, class, and gender; and describe the long-range consequences for the history of Latin America. *What was the extent of the Spanish empire in North America?*

Bartolome de Las Casas (1474-1566),
Library of Congress

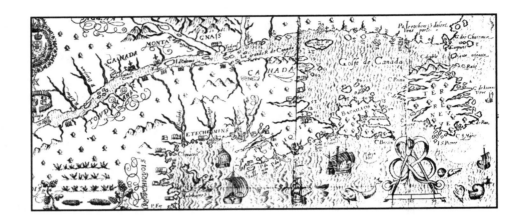

New France, Library of Congress,
Rare Book Division

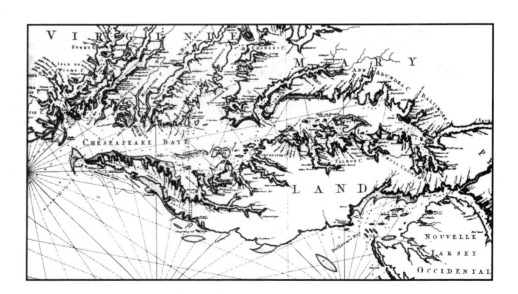

Cheseapeake Bay,
Library of Congress

ERA 2

Colonization and Settlement (1585-1763)

The study of the colonial era in U.S. history is essential because the foundations for many of the most critical developments in our subsequent national history were established in those years. The long duration of the nation's colonial period — nearly two centuries — requires that teachers establish clear themes. A continental and Caribbean approach best serves a full understanding of this era because North America and the closely linked West Indies were an international theatre of colonial development.

One theme involves the intermingling of Native Americans, Europeans, and Africans. Necessarily, this topic must address two of the most tragic aspects of American history: first, the violent conflicts between whites and indigenous peoples, the devastating spread of European diseases among Native Americans, and the gradual dispossession of Indian land; second, the traffic in the African slave trade and the development of a slave labor system in many of the colonies. While coming to grips with these tragic events, students should also recognize that Africans and Native Americans were not simply victims, but were intricately involved in the creation of colonial society and a new, hybrid American culture.

A second theme is the development of political and religious institutions and values. The roots of representative government are best studied regionally, so that students can appreciate how colonizers in New England, the mid-Atlantic, and the South differed in the ways they groped their way toward mature political institutions. In studying the role of religion — especially noteworthy are the foundations of religious freedom, denominationalism, and the many-faceted impact of the Great Awakening — a comparative geographic approach can also be fruitful. Comparison to Dutch, French, and Spanish colonies can be fruitful.

A third theme is the economic development of the colonies through agriculture and commerce. A comparative approach to French, Spanish, Dutch, and English colonies, and a regional approach to the English mainland and West Indian colonies, as part of a developing Atlantic economy, will also be instructive. As in studying politics and religion, students should ponder how economic institutions developed — in ways that were typically European or were distinctively American — and how geographical variations — climate, soil conditions, and other natural resources — helped shape regional economic development.

Overview

Standard 1: The early arrival of Europeans and Africans in the Americas, and how these people interacted with Native Americans

Standard 2: How political institutions and religious freedom emerged in the North American colonies

Standard 3: How the values and institutions of European economic life took root in the colonies; how slavery reshaped European and African life in the Americas

STANDARD 1

Students Should Understand: *The early arrival of Europeans and Africans in the Americas, and how these people interacted with Native Americans.*

Students Should Be Able to:

1A Demonstrate understanding of how diverse immigrants affected the formation of European colonies by:

5-12 Comparing English, French, and Dutch motives for exploration and colonization with those of the Spanish. **[Compare and contrast differing sets of ideas]**

9-12 Comparing the social composition of English, French, and Dutch settlers in the 17th and 18th centuries. **[Interrogate historical data]**

7-12 Tracing the arrival of Africans in the English colonies in the 17th century and the rapid increase of slave importation in the 18th century. **[Reconstruct patterns of historical succession and duration]**

Grades 5-6

Examples of student achievement of Standard 1A include:

▶ Construct a timeline of Spanish, Dutch, French, and English explorations in North America and map the route(s) taken by each.

▶ Draw upon biographies, stories, and historical studies to develop a historical narrative about one of these explorers. *Who sent this expedition? Did the explorer plan to spread his religion? Did those on his expedition plan to find wealth and return home? What were the occupations, social background, and religion of the people on this expedition? What did this expedition achieve? What roles did Africans play in the Spanish overland expeditions?*

▶ Draw upon stories, biographies, ships' passenger lists, and documentary records to analyze and compare the first settlers who established Jamestown, Plymouth, and Philadelphia. *What were their backgrounds, reasons for coming, occupational skills, leadership qualities, and ability to work together? Was it probable these groups would survive their first year?*

▶ Contrast and compare the early English settlements with a Spanish settlement (e.g., St. Augustine or Santa Fe) and a French settlement (e.g., Quebec or New Orleans). *How did the people who came to these settlements differ from those in the English colonies?*

Grades 7-8

Examples of student achievement of Standard 1A include:

▶ Develop a historical argument explaining cause-and-effect relationships on such questions as: *Why did the English wait so long after John Cabot's 1497-98 exploration to establish colonies in the Americas? How did the motives of English settlers compare with the motives of the Spanish, French, and Dutch colonizers in the Americas?*

▶ Draw upon the accounts of such writers as William Bradford *(Of Plymouth Plantation)*, John Winthrop ("A Model of Christian Charity"), and John Smith *(The General History of Virginia)* to compare English motives for colonization and determine if their goals were achieved.

▶ Compare the growth of the European colonies in the two centuries following their founding. *What new groups arrived, voluntarily in the case of European colonists, involuntarily in the case of Africans forced into indentured servitude and slavery? How did the colonies change as their population grew?*

Grades 9-12

Examples of student achievement of Standard 1A include:

▶ Analyze the influence of such factors as the following on the English colonization of the Americas: the enclosure movement and the growth of the poor in cities like London; the accession of Elizabeth I to the throne in 1558; the accounts of Spanish wealth from Mexico and Peru; the accounts of the Spanish "black legend"; the Protestant Reformation; and religious persecution.

▶ Compare these factors with those influencing Spanish, French, and Dutch colonization of the Americas.

▶ Analyze the changing patterns of European immigration and settlement in the Americas in the 17th and 18th centuries by developing a historical narrative on such questions as: *How did the motives of 17th-century Puritans and Quakers differ from those of 18th-century immigrants such as Germans and Scots-Irish? Why did the colonies of New York and Pennsylvania attract the greatest diversity of immigrants and become the most cosmopolitan of the mainland colonies?*

▶ Draw upon historical documents relating to the slave trade and the system of chattel slavery that evolved over the 17th and 18th centuries in order to develop a historical argument on such questions as: *Were there significant differences between slavery in the Spanish Caribbean and New Spain, the French Caribbean and Louisiana, the Dutch West Indies, and the English Caribbean and Chesapeake? Why did Brazil and the West Indies have more enslaved Africans than North America? Which colonies experienced the greatest increase and which experienced the most notable decrease in slave imports between the 17th and 18th centuries, and why?*

Students Should Be Able to:

1B Demonstrate understanding of family life, gender roles, and women's rights in colonial North America by:

`5-12` Explaining how and why family and community life differed in various regions of colonial North America. [**Consider multiple perspectives**]

`7-12` Analyzing gender roles in different regions of colonial North America and how these roles changed from 1600 to 1760. [**Explain historical continuity and change**]

`9-12` Analyzing women's property rights before and after marriage in the colonial period. [**Interrogate historical data**]

Grades 5-6

Examples of student achievement of Standard 1B include:

▶ Draw upon books such as *Everyday Life in Colonial America,* stories, and historical records in order to compare family life in Puritan society with that of other colonial families such as a Pennsylvania Quaker household; a Williamsburg, Virginia, or Philadelphia craftsman's family; a Boston or New York merchant's family; a family on a self-sufficient southern plantation; a farm family, black or white, in tidewater Virginia or backcountry New York; a family in French Quebec or Fort Vincennes; or a family in Spanish Santa Fe or St. Augustine. Analyze how differences in family housing, work, and the roles of men, women, and children reflected differences in family status and wealth, geographic region and resources, prior conditions of indentured servitude or slavery, and ethnic traditions and religious beliefs.

Grades 7-8

Examples of student achievement of Standard 1B include:

▶ Analyze family portraits by such colonial artists as Charles Willson Peale, John Wollaston, Ralph Earl, and John Singleton Copley to determine what the pictures reveal about the relationships of parents and children, and how family and gender roles are reflected in the paintings.

Grades 9-12

Examples of student achievement of Standard 1B include:

▶ Draw evidence from a variety of secondary sources to investigate different patterns of family life in colonial North America. Compare the different ideals of family life among such diverse groups as the New England Puritans, the Virginia aristocracy, the frontier farmers, the Quakers, the Iroquois, the French in Quebec, the Indians of the Southwest, and the Spanish in Santa Fe. *How would you account for the similarities and the differences? How is patriarchy defined? To what extent are the families patriarchal? How were young children treated? Were boys treated differently from girls? What was it like to be a teenager in these different societies? What role did economic interests play in the development of family life and its relationship to the community? To what extent did family roles, values, and structure change during the colonial period?*

▶ Draw upon literary selections, historical documents, and historical accounts to analyze how men's and women's roles and status differed in colonial America. *How, for example, did the following lines in Anne Bradstreet's poem, "The Prologue," illustrate the role of women in colonial Massachusetts?*

> *I am obnoxious to each carping tongue*
> *Who says my hand a needle better fits*

Why were women much more likely than men to be accused of witchcraft during the 17th century? Why, in early Spanish New Mexico, were honor and virtue defined in gender specific terms, with honor viewed as strictly a male attribute and shame viewed as intrinsic to women?

▶ Compare the property rights of single and married women in the English Atlantic seaboard colonies and the Spanish borderlands in the colonial period. *How did the community view single women and grant them property rights? Why did English common law deny married women [femme covert] property rights? How did property settlements on a first marriage differ from those settlements when a widow remarried?*

The Wonders of the Invisible World:

Being an Account of the

TRYALS

O F

𝕾𝖊𝖇𝖊𝖗𝖆𝖑 𝖂𝖎𝖙𝖈𝖍𝖊𝖘,

Lately Excuted in

NEW-ENGLAND:

And of several remarkable.Curiosities therein Occurring.

Together with,

I. Observations upon the Nature, the Number, and the Operations of the Devils.

II. A short Narrative of a late outrage committed by a knot of Witches in *Swede-Land,* very much resembling, and so far explaining, that under which *New-England* has laboured.

III. Some Councels directing a due Improvement of the Terrible things lately done by the unusual and amazing Range of *Evil-Spirits* in *New-England.*

IV. A brief Discourse upon those *Temptations* which are the more ordinary Devices of Satan.

By *COTTON MATHER.*

Published by the Special Command of his EXCELLENCY the Governcur of the Province of the *Massachusetts-Bay* in *New-England.*

Printed first, at *Boston* in *New-England*; and Reprinted at *London,* for *John Dunton,* at the *Raven* in the *Poultry.* 1693.

Cotton Mather's defense of the witchcraft trials, Library of Congress

Students Should Be Able to:

1C Demonstrate understanding of the European struggle for control of North America by:

`7-12` Analyzing relationships between Native Americans and Spanish, English, French, and Dutch settlers. **[Compare and contrast differing values and behaviors]**

`5-12` Comparing how English settlers interacted with Native Americans in New England, mid-Atlantic, Chesapeake, and lower South colonies. **[Consider multiple perspectives]**

`7-12` Analyzing how various Native American societies changed as a result of the expanding European settlements and how they influenced European societies. **[Examine the influence of ideas and interests]**

`7-12` Analyzing the significance of the colonial wars before 1754 and the causes, character, and outcome of the Seven Years War. **[Analyze multiple causation]**

`9-12` Analyzing Native American involvement in the colonial wars and evaluating the consequences for their societies. **[Consider multiple perspectives]**

Grades 5-6

Examples of student achievement of Standard 1C include:

▶ Compare Native American and European views of the land. *How did European beliefs in private property and in their claim to lands that were not "settled" or "improved" differ from Native American beliefs that land was not property, but entrusted by the Creator to all living creatures for their common benefit and shared use?*

▶ Compare William Penn's friendly relations with the Lenni Lenape and Susquehannocks with the wars between the colonial settlers and the Powhatans in Virginia (1622) and the Pequots in Massachusetts (1637). *Was conflict unavoidable in European relationships with the Native Americans? What helped prevent such wars? What contributed to them?*

▶ Compare how Native Americans and European societies in North America were influenced by one another. *In what ways did the early settlers in Massachusetts and Virginia depend on the skills and assistance of Native Americans in order to survive? In what ways did trade benefit Native Americans and Europeans and foster alliances, but also change traditional patterns of Native American life in ways that were harmful?*

▶ Examine the interaction of American Indians and early European settlers through biographies and historical fiction using evidence from such books as *The Double Life of Pocahontas* by Jean Fritz; *The Serpent Never Sleeps: A Novel of Jamestown and Pocahontas* by Scott O'Dell and John Billington; *Friend of Squanto* by Clyde Robert Bulla; *Sign of the Beaver* by Elizabeth Speare; and *Squanto* by Fennie Ziner.

Grades 7-8

Examples of student achievement of Standard 1C include:

▸ Analyze examples of English colonists who opposed prevailing policies toward Native Americans and demonstrated that alternatives to hostility existed. *How did such individuals as Roger Williams, William Penn, and John Eliot differ in their actions toward Native Americans from most of their countrymen and with what results? What explains the generally friendly relations in Rhode Island and Quaker Pennsylvania?*

▸ Develop a historical argument explaining why French relations with the Hurons, Ottawas, and Algonkians were among the friendliest on the continent. *In what ways did the relatively small numbers of French settlers, their dependence on the Indians for trade in furs, and the large presence of French Jesuit priests contribute to peaceable relations?*

▸ Develop a historical argument or debate on the long-term effects of the fur trade, considering for example its destruction of animal life; its disruption of traditional Native American relationships with the environment; and its effects in pitting tribe against tribe as their hunting grounds became depleted and they sought to conquer more distant tribes whose resources had not yet been exhausted. Compare with ways in which changes today can lead to unanticipated results in the depletion of resources and to conflict.

▸ Develop a historical narrative, news report to a Boston, London, or Paris newspaper, or a "You Are There" dramatic interview to recreate the events culminating in the English victory over the French in the Seven Years War. *Why was this war and its outcome significant?*

Grades 9-12

Examples of student achievement of Standard 1C include:

▸ Draw upon a variety of historical narratives, travel accounts, and visual sources to compare the diversity of Native American interactions with Spanish, English, French, and Dutch settlers. *How did the experiences of Native American societies in the interior differ from those who lived in coastal regions? How did they benefit from trade? How did trade alter their way of life and disrupt their societies?*

How did Native American societies such as the Pueblos, Catawbas, Iroquois, and Lenni Lenape respond to European land hunger and expansion? Analyze Pontiac's speech to the French on the reasons for making war in 1763, and compare his reasons with those of Opechancanough in 1622 and Metacomet (King Philip) in 1676. Explain the background and consequences of the Pueblo revolts of 1680 and 1696. Analyze the reasons for and results of the mission system in the Southwest and California.

▸ Analyze how the European wars for control of North America between 1675 and 1763 pitted the English, French, and Spanish against one another and allowed the Iroquois League, the Creek, and the Cherokee nations to strengthen their own position by expertly playing off European nations against one another in return for their assistance.

▸ Compare these wars with the events and consequences of the Seven Years War. *What was the significance of the Peace of Paris in ending European rivalry for control of North America? What options were left to Native Americans, now faced with a tide of settlers heading over the Alleghenies and without the assistance of French allies defending these same lands against English encroachment?*

STANDARD 2

Students Should Understand: *How political institutions and religious freedom emerged in the North American colonies.*

Students Should Be Able to:

2A Demonstrate understanding of the rise of individualism, the roots of representative government, and how political rights were defined by:

5–12 Analyzing how the rise of individualism affected the ideal of community. [**Assess the importance of the individual**]

7–12 Explaining how the growth of individualism challenged European ideas of hierarchy and deference and contributed to the idea of participatory government. [**Examine the influence of ideas**]

7–12 Compare how early colonies were established and governed. [**Compare and contrast differing sets of ideas, behaviors, and institutions**]

7–12 Explaining the concept of the "rights of Englishmen" and the impact of the English Civil War and the Glorious Revolution on the colonies. [**Hypothesize the influence of the past**]

9–12 Analyzing how gender, property ownership, religion, and legal status affected political rights. [**Analyze cause-and-effect relationships**]

| Grades 5-6 | Examples of student achievement of Standard 2A include: |

▶ Draw upon stories of the arrival of the Pilgrims at Plymouth and the Mayflower Compact in order to analyze the significance of this document in proclaiming the right of self-government. *How did this Compact reflect the Pilgrims' self-government of their church? Why was the Compact important in establishing a precedent for self-government in New England?*

▶ Explore how different colonies define the right to vote or hold office. *Why were women not permitted to vote?*

| Grades 7-8 | Examples of student achievement of Standard 2A include: |

▶ Analyze how the following contributed to the concept of "the rights of Englishmen": Magna Carta, English common law, and the English Bill of Rights (1689).

▶ Evaluate to what degree colonial society was democratic in practice. *How were political rights affected by gender, property ownership, religion, and legal status? What were the religious requirements for voting? Why did they exist? Why were Jews and Catholics not allowed to vote?*

▶ Analyze what the following quotation from an 18th-century New Yorker tells us about changing values and the growth of prosperity in colonial America. *"The only principle of life propagated among the young people is to get money, and men are only esteemed according to what they are worth, that is, the money they are possessed of."*

▶ Develop a historical argument on the question whether Benjamin Franklin's thirteen virtues in his formula for moral perfection in his *Autobiography* represented a change in values from the ideals of Puritan New England. Or similarly, assess his proverbs relating to the acquisition of wealth, such as: *"Sloth makes all things difficult but industry all easy"; "It is hard for an empty sack to stand upright"; "time lost is never found again."*

Grades 9-12   Examples of student achievement of Standard 2A include:

▶ Draw upon such documents as the Mayflower Compact (1620), the Fundamental Orders of Connecticut (1639), the Massachusetts Body of Laws and Liberty (1641), the New Jersey Laws, Concessions, and Agreements (1677), and the Pennsylvania Frame of Government (1701) to explain the growth of early representative government and institutions in the colonies. *Did geography and demography have an impact on the different forms of government in colonial America? How did Pennsylvania's fluid social organization and Virginia's more rigid social hierarchy affect representative government in the two colonies?*

▶ Analyze how institutions such as the Virginia House of Burgesses, the county court system, parish vestries, congregational organization of churches, the Massachusetts General Court, and the New England town meeting contributed to the growth of representative government in the colonies. *How did such institutions promote the practice of "actual" as opposed to "virtual" representation? How democratic were such institutions in practice? Who could vote? Why did Jefferson call the New England town meeting "the wisest invention ever devised by the wit of man for the perfect exercise of self-government"?*

▶ Develop a historical argument on the question whether the political settlements of the Glorious Revolution expanded "the rights of Englishmen" in the colonies, or led to the establishment of more centralized administration and imperial control. *Was Leisler's Rebellion in New York a democratic uprising? Was it inspired by ethnic hostility? Explain.*

▶ Using selections from primary sources such as John Winthrop's *History of New England* and Thomas Jefferson's "Letters to His Daughters," explain why women were not allowed to vote even if they held property and met religious requirements.

▶ Analyze how the Puritan beliefs in a covenant community and support of communal ideals compared with the acquisitive and individualistic values associated with the early Chesapeake colonies. *To what extent did values in New England and Chesapeake colonies shape different societies?*

▶ Analyze how Puritan leaders in the 17th century might have appraised the spirit of individualism professed in Benjamin Franklin's *Autobiography* and *Poor Richard's Almanack.*

▶ Develop a historical argument about whether such factors as the abundance of land, devotion to private property, and the growth of individualism and a competitive entrepreneurial spirit in 18th-century colonial America challenged European ideas of hierarchy and deference and contributed to the idea of participatory democracy.

Students Should Be Able to:

2B Demonstrate understanding of religious diversity in the colonies and how ideas about religious freedom evolved by:

9-12 Describing religious groups in colonial America and the role of religion in their communities. [**Consider multiple perspectives**]

5-12 Explaining how Puritanism shaped New England communities and how it changed during the 17th century. [**Compare and contrast differing sets of ideas, values, and institutions**]

7-12 Tracing and explaining the evolution of religious freedom in the English colonies. [**Reconstruct patterns of historical succession and duration**]

9-12 Explaining the impact of the Great Awakening on colonial society. [**Examine the influence of ideas**]

Grades 5-6

Examples of student achievement of Standard 2B include:

- Explain why the Puritans came to America, seeking a place to practice their religion.

- Draw upon stories such as Elizabeth Speare's *The Witch of Blackbird Pond,* historical documents such as Eleazar Moody's *The School of Good Manners* (1772), pictures of hornbooks, replicas of *The New England Primer* (1727), family portraits, and other historical records in order to create historical narratives, reenactments, or illustrations of children's roles in Puritan families and compare with their own lives today. *What religious beliefs and values were families trying to instill in their children? Why were children taught to read at an early age and apprenticed at age 13 to friends or relatives? How did the skills and values taught to boys and girls reflect the gender roles they were expected to assume as adults?*

- Examine opposition of dissenters to King James I as reflected in historical fiction such as *The House of Stink Alley* by F. N. Monjo.

Grades 7-8

Examples of student achievement of Standard 2B include:

- Draw upon historical records in order to analyze and debate the confrontation between Thomas Leverett and Anne Hutchinson at her trial and the justice of her banishment from the Massachusetts Bay Colony. *Did Anne Hutchinson violate Puritan mores? Was she justified in pursuing her acts of civil disobedience? Were the colonial officials justified in banishing her for her beliefs and actions?*

- Compare the treatment of dissenters in various colonies such as Puritan Massachusetts, Anglican Virginia, and Quaker Pennsylvania. *Why did Puritans immigrate in search of religious freedom and then deny it to others? What did Roger Williams mean by separation of church and state? Do we have the same meaning of separation of church and state today?*

- Draw evidence from biographies of Roger Williams, Anne Hutchinson, William Penn, and Cecilius Calvert on religious dissenters in the English colonies.

▶ Use simulations such as American History Re-creations to reenact the trial of Anne Hutchinson. Evaluate the classroom simulation comparing the outcome to the historical record of the trial.

| Grades 9-12 |

Examples of student achievement of Standard 2B include:

▶ Draw upon such sources as John Winthrop's "A Model of Christian Charity," John Milton's *Paradise Lost*, Increase Mather's "Predestination and Human Exertion" Michael Wigglesworth's "The Day of Doom," and the poetry of Anne Bradstreet and Edward Taylor in order to analyze the major tenets of Puritanism.

▶ Analyze how these tenets of faith shaped the social, political, and religious life of the Puritan colony.

▶ Draw upon such records as the *Trial of Anne Hutchinson at Newton* and the banishment of Roger Williams from Massachusetts in order to develop a historical argument or debate on such questions as: *How did Roger Williams and Anne Hutchinson justify their actions? Why did Puritans object to their ideas and behavior? Did Hutchinson threaten gender and hierarchy roles? How was the treatment of the two dissenters different? Was their treatment justified?*

▶ Analyze the reasons for the gradual decline of Puritanism in the later part of the 17th century, and explain its enduring legacy in the national character.

▶ Analyze how the presence of diverse religious groups in the English colonies such as Quakers, Catholics, Jews, Huguenots, and German Pietists contributed to the evolution of religious freedom. *Why did Roger Williams support the separation of church and state? What were the reasons for passage of the Maryland Act of Toleration in 1649? Why does the Pennsylvania Frame of Government (1701) guarantee religious freedom?*

▶ Explore the Great Awakening as the first American mass movement. Draw upon such sources as Jonathan Edwards's sermon, "Sinners in the Hands of an Angry God" and on historical accounts of the Great Awakening in order to create a historical argument agreeing or disagreeing with the statement: *The Great Awakening was a major influence in changing traditional relationships between rulers and the ruled and in the development of American "republicanism" and the nation's "civil religion."*

▶ Explain the major tenets of Puritanism such as predestination, the covenant of works, the covenant of grace, and the doctrine of sanctification; and demonstrate how these beliefs shaped the Puritan colony.

Edward Hicks (1780-1849), Peaceable Kingdom, Courtesy of National Gallery of Art, Washington, D.C.

Students Should Be Able to:

2C Demonstrate understanding of political conflicts in the colonies by:

`7-12` Explaining the social, economic, and political tensions that led to violent conflicts between the colonists and their governments. [**Examine the influence of ideas**]

`9-12` Explaining how the conflicts between legislative and executive branches contributed to the development of representative government. [**Analyze cause-and-effect relationships**]

Grades 5-6

Examples of student achievement of Standard 2C include:

Not appropriate at this grade level

Grades 7-8

Examples of student achievement of Standard 2C include:

▶ Explain how political, geographic, social, and economic tensions caused Bacon's Rebellion and the Paxton Boys Massacre.

▶ Develop a historical argument on questions such as: *To what extent were these rebellions justifiable attempts of the people to change their government's policies? To what extent were they lawless attempts to overthrow legitimate governments? Did Bacon's Rebellion lead to greater or less democracy in Virginia?*

Grades 9-12

Examples of student achievement of Standard 2C include:

▶ Analyze the factors behind Bacon's Rebellion to illustrate the conflicts between the underrepresented backwoodsmen and the privileged tidewater planters. Compare with the ethnic and class tensions behind Leisler's Rebellion in colonial New York and with later conflicts of the Carolina Regulators and Pennsylvania Paxton Boys, involving similar grievances and tensions. *To what extent are the causes of Bacon's Rebellion, Leisler's Rebellion, and the revolts of the Carolina Regulators and Pennsylvania Paxton Boys similar? How are they different? How do historians view the significance of Bacon's Rebellion for race and class relations in the South? Do you agree?*

▶ Analyze how the conflict between the lower houses of colonial legislatures and the governors over such items as "control of the purse" contributed to the development of representative government. *Did conflicts over "control of the purse" cause lower houses of assembly to view themselves increasingly as a "miniature House of Commons?" How did these conflicts affect their view of sovereignty and what was the significance of these developments?*

▶ Explain the meaning and analyze the accuracy of the following statement: *"The Virginia Governor had power on paper, but the real power of government was with the Council and the House of Burgesses." How did the governor's power depend upon the ruling elite? Was this true in Massachusetts and New York? Did power in the Virginia colony shift from the Council to the Burgesses? If so, when and why?*

S T A N D A R D   3

Students Should Understand: *How the values and institutions of European economic life took root in the colonies; how slavery reshaped European and African life in the Americas.*

Students Should Be Able to:

3A Demonstrate understanding of colonial economic life and labor systems in the Americas by:

7-12 Analyzing mercantilism and explaining how it influenced patterns of economic activity. [**Analyze cause-and-effect relationships**]

5-12 Identifying the major economic regions in the Americas and explaining how labor systems shaped them. [**Utilize visual and mathematical data**]

9-12 Explaining the development of an Atlantic economy in the colonial period. [**Reconstruct patterns of historical succession and duration.**]

Grades 5-6	**Examples of student achievement of Standard 3A include:**

▶ Develop a historical map of the colonies by researching and locating (by symbols) the crops, animal products, minerals, and other natural resources found in New England, the Middle Atlantic, and southern colonies.

▶ Develop a map of economic relationships between the colonies, the Caribbean Islands, and the home country by locating major ports and shipping lanes between them.

Grades 7-8	**Examples of student achievement of Standard 3A include:**

▶ Analyze the advantages and disadvantages of mercantilism for both the mother country and its colonies.

▶ Compare the regions that produced sugar, rice, tobacco, timber, coffee, grains, fish, and minerals, and consider their value to the mother country.

Grades 9-12	**Examples of student achievement of Standard 3A include:**

▶ Drawing upon a variety of data relating to overseas trade between European countries and their American colonies, including statutory measures like the Navigation Acts, reports of colonial merchants and government officials, and graphic sources illustrating economic developments, analyze the advantages and disadvantages of mercantilism for both the mother country and its colonies. *How did the accumulation of gold and silver in its American colonies affect the Spanish economy? How did it promote further colonization? How was mining organized?*

▶ Compare the regions producing sugar, rice, tobacco, timber, coffee, grains, fish, and minerals, and evaluate their importance in terms of overseas colonization. *Which areas of the Americas became the most valuable colonies? Which areas exhibited the greatest imperial conflict? Why? How did climate and soil conditions affect the development of "money crops" in various regions? How did the economic development of French, English, and Spanish colonies differ?*

▶ Analyze the evolution of the Atlantic economy and describe the developing trade patterns. *To what extent was there a "triangular trade" and how significant was it?*

Courtesy of Arents Collection,
New York Public Library

. A

TREATISE

ON THE

CULTURE

OF THE

TOBACCO PLANT;

WITH THE

Manner in which it is usually CURED.

ADAPTED TO

NORTHERN CLIMATES,

AND

DESIGNED FOR THE USE OF THE

LANDHOLDERS of GREAT-BRITAIN.

TO WHICH ARE PREFIXED,

Two PLATES OF THE PLANT AND ITS FLOWERS.

By JONATHAN CARVER, Esq.

Author of TRAVELS through the interior Parts of
NORTH-AMERICA.

LONDON:
Printed for the AUTHOR,
And sold by J. JOHNSON, in St. Paul's Church-yard.
1779.

Students Should Be Able to:

3B Demonstrate understanding of economic life and the development of labor systems in the English colonies by:

`5-12` Explaining how environmental and human factors accounted for differences in the economies that developed in the colonies of New England, in mid-Atlantic, Chesapeake, and lower South. [**Compare and contrast differing behaviors and institutions**]

`7-12` Analyzing how the early Navigation Acts affected economic life in the colonies. [**Marshal evidence of antecedent circumstances**]

`7-12` Comparing the characteristics of free labor, indentured servitude, and chattel slavery. [**Compare and contrast different sets of ideas**]

`9-12` Explaining the shift from indentured servitude to chattel slavery in the southern colonies. [**Challenge arguments of historical inevitability**]

Grades 5-6

Examples of student achievement of Standard 3B include:

▶ Draw upon historical stories and other descriptions of colonial economic life in various regions, and compare the likenesses and differences in the work people did, the crops they grew, and the environmental conditions that supported their activities.

▶ Compare and contrast family farming in New England with plantation life in the Chesapeake and with small yeoman farming in the southern piedmont.

▶ Develop a product map showing the New England merchants' trading triangle and the goods and people regularly transported between the English colonies, West Indies, Africa, and Great Britain.

▶ Examine stories such as *If You Lived in Colonial Times* by Ann McGovern, *How the Colonists Lived* by David McKay, and *Colonial Living* by Edwin Tunis to build an understanding and appreciation of life in colonial America.

▶ Examine labor patterns that emerged in the colonies. Drawing upon stories and diaries, describe the differences between free labor, indentured servitude, and slavery. Chart the rights, obligations, and opportunities for people under each form of labor. *Why did colonists bring more people to work the land? What was the hope of indentured people when they contracted to come to the colonies? What did chattel slavery mean for the Africans who were forced to come to work in the colonies?*

Grades 7-8

Examples of student achievement of Standard 3B include:

▶ Analyze how climate, land fertility, water resources, and access to markets affected economic growth in different regions.

▶ Explain the reasons for the passage of the early Navigation Acts and their relation to mercantilism.

▶ Draw evidence from historical fiction such as *Calico Bush* by Rachel Field and *Master Entrick* by Michael Mott to investigate the hardships of indentured servitude.

▶ Explain why indentured servitude was more prevalent in the mid-Atlantic, Chesapeake, and southern colonies. Describe the typical terms of a contract for an indentured servant. *What is the reason for the headright system and why does it decline?*

▶ Examine laws enacted in Virginia and Maryland that helped institutionalize slavery. *What rights were taken away from enslaved Africans? What restrictions were placed on white-black relations? How was slavery made perpetual and hereditary?*

Grades 9-12

Examples of student achievement of Standard 3B include:

▶ Analyze how climate, land fertility, and access to markets affected economic growth in the English West Indies and in the English North American colonies. *Which of the English colonies were most valuable to the mother country? Why? What factors accounted for the higher death rate among white settlers in the West Indian, Chesapeake, and southern colonies compared to the New England and Middle colonies in the colonial period? What were some of the major consequences of such developments?*

▶ Analyze the reasons for passage of the Navigation Acts and explain how they reflected traditional mercantile values. *To what extent did the Navigation Acts promote and retard economic growth in the colonies? To what extent were they obeyed?*

▶ Draw upon historical evidence to trace the gradual emergence of chattel slavery in Virginia and Maryland in the 17th century and compare historical interpretations concerning its origin and development.

▶ Differentiate between free labor and chattel slavery, and explain why neither provided a viable and effective alternative for labor in the Chesapeake colonies in the period before 1675. *How did the headright system and indentured servitude provide a better alternative for labor in the first half of the 17th century? Why did the increased life expectancy of indentured servants contribute to the transition to chattel slavery after 1660? How did laws enacted in the Chesapeake colonies institutionalizing slavery differ from laws regulating indentured servitude?*

Students Should Be Able to:

3C Demonstrate understanding of African life under slavery by:

5-12 Analyzing the forced relocation of Africans to the English colonies in North America and the Caribbean. [**Evidence historical perspectives**]

7-12 Analyzing how African Americans drew upon their African past to develop a new culture. [**Consider multiple perspectives**]

9-12 Assessing the contribution of enslaved and free Africans to economic development in different regions of the American colonies. [**Assess the importance of the individual in history**]

7-12 Analyze overt and passive resistance to slavery. [**Compare and contrast differing values, behaviors, and institutions**]

Grades 5-6

Examples of student achievement of Standard 3C include:

▶ Draw evidence from sources such as *A Slaver's Log Book: Twenty Years' Residence in Africa* by Theophile Conneau and *The Slave Ship* by Emma Sterne to examine stories of the slave trade.

▶ Trace the movement of enslaved Africans to different parts of the Caribbean and North America. *What was meant by the "middle passage"?*

▶ Draw upon stories and narratives such as *Africa Remembered: Narratives by West Africans from the Era of the Slave Trade* edited by Philip Curtin, and slave narratives in *America's Children: Voices from the Past* edited by Matthew Downey to describe chattel slavery.

▶ Drawing upon music, literature, stories such as the Brer Rabbit folktales and art, describe the influence of African heritage on slave life in the colonies. *How did enslaved Africans draw upon their heritage in art, music, childrearing activities, and values to draw strength to cope with slavery and develop a strong culture in an unfamiliar land?*

Grades 7-8

Examples of student achievement of Standard 3C include:

▶ Develop a chart that illustrates the contribution of African slaves. Identify crops cultivated in West Africa that were introduced in the Carolinas.

▶ Describe the variety of measures used to resist slavery and discuss their effectiveness. *How did forms of resistance vary depending on the region and the slave's gender or age?*

▶ Investigate slave rebellions in colonial America such as New York, 1712 and 1740, and the Stono Rebellion in South Carolina in 1739. *What caused these rebellions? What were the results of them?*

▶ Draw evidence from primary sources such as *The Interesting Narrative of the Life of Olaudah Equiano or Gustavus Vasa, Written by Himself* to examine the "middle passage."

Grades 9-12

Examples of student achievement of Standard 3C include:

▶ Drawing upon the account of Olaudah Equiano, evaluate conditions faced by enslaved Africans and how survivors coped with the brutality of bondage.

▶ Investigate religious practices, dances, songs, holistic medicine, work chants, cuisine, and marriage and burial ceremonies to determine the degree to which African Americans retained and transmitted their cultural heritage.

▶ Identify crops cultivated in West Africa that were introduced in the Carolinas and evaluate the contributions of African slaves to rice cultivation and cattle raising in South Carolina. *How did the sickle cell enable Africans to work in the Carolina lowlands more effectively than whites?*

▶ Compare slavery and slave resistance in different parts of the Americas. *How did slavery differ in Spanish America and British America? How did it differ in urban and plantation areas? Why were there more slave revolts in South America than in North America?*

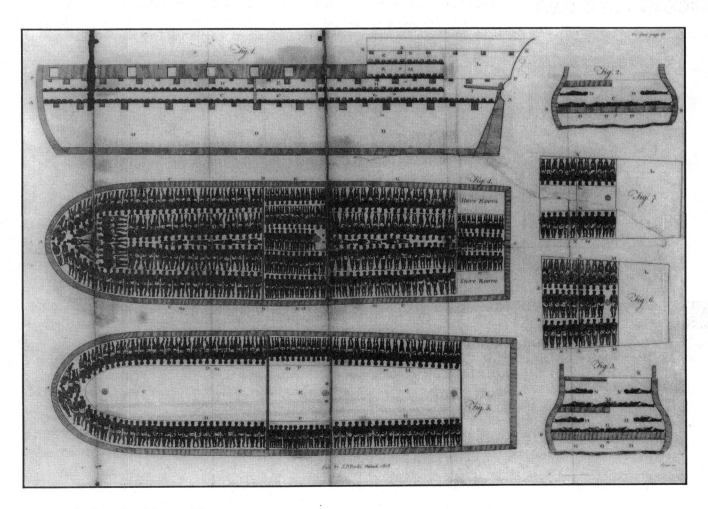

Diagram of a slave ship, Library of Congress

ERA 3

Revolution and the New Nation (1754-1820s)

The American Revolution is of signal importance in the study of U.S. history. First, it severed the colonial relationship with England and legally created the United States. Second, the revolutionary generation formulated the political philosophy and laid the institutional foundations for the system of government under which we live. Third, the revolution was inspired by ideas concerning natural rights and political authority that were transatlantic in reach, and its successful completion affected people and governments over a large part of the globe for many generations. Lastly, it called into question long-established social and political relationships — between master and slave, man and woman, upper class and lower class, officeholder and constituent, and even parent and child — and thus demarcated an agenda for reform that would preoccupy Americans down to the present day. In thinking about the causes and outcomes of the American Revolution, students need to confront the central issue of how revolutionary the Revolution actually was. In order to reach judgments about this, they necessarily will have to see the Revolution through different sets of eyes — enslaved and free African Americans, Native Americans, white men and women of different social classes, religions, ideological dispositions, regions, and occupations.

Students can appreciate how agendas for redefining American society in the postwar era differed by exploring how the Constitution was created and how it was ratified after a dramatic ideological debate in virtually every locale in 1787-88. While broaching the Constitution of 1787 and the Bill of Rights as the culmination of the most creative era of constitutionalism in American history, students should also ponder the paradox that the Constitution sidetracked the movement to abolish slavery that had taken rise in the revolutionary era. Nor should they think that ratification of the Constitution ended debate on governmental power; rather, economic, regional, social, and ideological tensions spawned continuing debates over the meaning of the Constitution.

In studying the postrevolutionary generation, students can understand how the embryo of the American two-party system took shape, how political turmoil arose as Americans debated the French Revolution, and how the Supreme Court rose to a place of prominence. Politics, political leadership, and political institutions have always bulked large in the study of this era, but students will also need to understand other less noticed topics: the military campaigns against Native American nations; the emergence of free black communities; and the democratization of religion.

Overview

Standard 1: The causes of the American Revolution, the ideas and interests involved in forging the revolutionary movement, and the reasons for the American victory

Standard 2: How the American Revolution involved multiple movements among the new nation's many groups to reform American society

Standard 3: The institutions and practices of government created during the revolution and how they were revised between 1787 and 1815 to create the foundation of the American political system

Boston Massacre Engraving,
by Paul Revere
From The American Revolution
by John Grafton, c.1975,
by Dover Publications, Inc.

STANDARD 1

Students Should Understand: *The causes of the American Revolution, the ideas and interests involved in forging the revolutionary movement, and the reasons for the American victory.*

Students Should Be Able to:

1A Demonstrate understanding of the causes of the American Revolution by:

5-12 Explaining the consequences of the Seven Years War and the overhaul of English imperial policy following the Treaty of Paris in 1763, demonstrating the connections between the antecedent and consequent events. [**Marshal evidence of antecedent circumstances**]

5-12 Comparing the arguments advanced by defenders and opponents of the new imperial policy on the traditional rights of English people and the legitimacy of asking the colonies to pay a share of the costs of empire. [**Consider multiple perspectives**]

5-12 Reconstructing the chronology of the critical events leading to the outbreak of armed conflict between the American colonies and England. [**Establish temporal order**]

7-12 Analyzing the connection between political and religious ideas and economic interests in bringing about revolution. [**Consider multiple perspectives**]

9-12 Reconstructing the arguments among Patriots and Loyalists about independence and drawing conclusions about how the decision to declare independence was reached. [**Consider multiple perspectives**]

| **Grades 5-6** | **Examples of student achievement of Standard 1A include:** |

▶ Identify such major consequences of the Seven Years War as the English victory, the removal of the French as a contending power in North America, and the reduced need of the colonists for protection by the mother country.

▶ Select in chronological order and explain the major events leading to the outbreak of conflict at Lexington and Concord.

▶ Create historical arguments or narratives explaining at least one reason why the English Parliament felt it was justified in taxing the colonies to help pay for a war fought in their defense and at least one reason why the colonists, claiming their rights as Englishmen, challenged the legitimacy of the new taxes as "taxation without representation."

| **Grades 7-8** | **Examples of student achievement of Standard 1A include:** |

▶ Assemble the evidence, including the consequences of the Seven Years War, England's new imperial policy and the voices of such resistance leaders as John Adams, Thomas Jefferson, John Dickinson, Thomas Paine, Patrick Henry, and Samuel Adams, and construct a sound historical argument on such questions as:

Was it reasonable for the English to tax the colonists to help pay for a war fought in their defense? Were the American colonists justified in their resistance to England's new imperial policies?

▶ Explain the divisions in the colonies over these issues by comparing the interests and positions of Loyalists and Patriots from different economic groups such as northern merchants, southern rice and tobacco planters, yeoman farmers, and urban artisans.

▶ Marshal historical evidence including events leading up to "the shot heard 'round the world" and develop a historical argument on such questions as the following: *Was the outbreak of conflict at Lexington and Concord probable? Could any action at that point have prevented war with England?*

Grades 9-12

Examples of student achievement of Standard 1A include:

▶ Draw upon the arguments advanced by opponents and defenders of England's new imperial policy in order to construct a sound historical argument or narrative on such questions as: *Were the arguments against parliamentary taxation a legitimate and constitutional defense of the historic and traditional rights of Englishmen under common law, or were they merely a defense for tax evasion? Was the British decision to station troops in the colonies at the end of the Seven Years War designed to defend the colonies or did it reflect a conscious decision to keep contentious and expansionist colonists under control?*

▶ Draw upon evidence of the mounting crisis as well as the efforts in Parliament and in the colonies to prevent a rupture with the mother country in order to construct a sound historical narrative or argument on such questions as: *Was the break with England avoidable? Could decisions on either side, other than those which were taken, have changed the circumstances leading to the escalation of the crisis and the outbreak war?*

▶ Drawing upon ideas of religious groups such as Virginia Baptists, mid-Atlantic Presbyterians, and millennialists, assess how religion became a factor in the American Revolution.

▶ Construct a historical narrative analyzing the factors which explain why a person chose to be a Loyalist or a Patriot. *Why did approximately one-third of the colonists want to remain neutral? Did economic and social differences play a role in how people chose sides? Explain.*

▶ Marshal evidence to explain how a Loyalist and a Patriot would view each of the following: The Tea Act of 1773, the Boston Tea Party, the "Intolerable" Acts, the cause of the skirmish at Lexington Green. *How might a Loyalist have rewritten the natural rights theory of the Declaration of Independence? How might a Loyalist have answered the charges in the Declaration of Independence?*

Students Should Be Able to:

1B **Demonstrate understanding of the principles articulated in the Declaration of Independence by:**

[5-12] Explaining the major ideas expressed in the Declaration of Independence and their sources. [**Marshal evidence of antecedent circumstances**]

[7-12] Demonstrating the fundamental contradictions between the ideals expressed in the Declaration of Independence and the realities of chattel slavery. [**Consider multiple perspectives**]

[9-12] Drawing upon the principles in the Declaration of Independence to construct a sound historical argument regarding whether it justified American independence. [**Interrogate historical data**]

[9-12] Comparing the Declaration of Independence with the French Declaration of the Rights of Man and Citizen and constructing an argument evaluating their importance to the spread of constitutional democracies in the 19th and 20th centuries. [**Compare and contrast differing sets of ideas**]

Grades 5-6

Examples of student achievement of Standard 1B include:

‣ Define the terms in the Declaration of Independence, including "all men," "created equal," "endowed by their Creator," "unalienable rights," "life, liberty, and the pursuit of happiness," "just powers," and "consent of the governed."

‣ Explain why Jefferson wrote the Declaration of Independence, what its signers risked in putting their names to the document, and what its consequences were for the newly declared nation.

‣ Draw evidence from books such as *Fourth of July Story* by Alice Dalgliesh, and *Give Us Liberty: The Story of the Declaration of Independence* by Helen Peterson to explain the ideas expressed in the Declaration of Independence.

Grades 7-8

Examples of student achievement of Standard 1B include:

‣ Explain the major principles set forth in the Declaration of Independence including the basic rights of all people; the source of those rights; the purpose of government; the source of its just powers in the consent of the governed; and the right of the people to alter or abolish a government "destructive of those ends."

‣ Explain the historical antecedents of the Declaration of Independence in key ideas of Enlightenment thought; in traditions of English common law, the English Bill of Rights, and the Glorious Revolution; and in the traditions of natural law and the Judeo-Christian heritage which hold all persons to be of equal worth before God and before the state.

‣ Identify and analyze the fundamental contradictions between the institution of chattel slavery and the ideals expressed in the Declaration of Independence by formulating sound arguments in response to such questions as: *What rights, claimed by the Declaration of Independence to be the inalienable rights of all men, were denied to those held in slavery? Could such contradictions be justified?*

▶ Draw evidence from biographies to examine the lives of individuals who were in the forefront of the struggle for independence such as Sam Adams, Thomas Paine, Mercy Otis Warren, and Ebenezer MacIntosh.

Grades 9-12

Examples of student achievement of Standard 1B include:

▶ Compare the ideas of the Declaration of Independence with those of John Locke in *Two Treatises on Government. How are they different? Similar? Why does Jefferson use the phrase "the pursuit of happiness" instead of "property"? What did Jefferson mean by "the pursuit of happiness"?*

▶ Draw upon the principles in the Declaration of Independence to construct a sound historical argument regarding whether or not it justified American independence.

▶ Compare and evaluate the arguments in letters, speeches, and other documents from advocates and opponents of slavery from different regions of the country, reflecting their perspectives on the ideals of the Declaration of Independence. *How did pro-slavery Americans justify their defense of slavery with their espousal of inalienable rights to freedom? How did enslaved Africans employ revolutionary ideals to obtain their freedom?*

▶ Compare the Declaration of Independence with the French Declaration of the Rights of Man and Citizen, and construct a sound historical argument evaluating their importance to the spread of constitutional democracies in the 19th and 20th centuries. *How have the ideas that inspired the American and French revolutions influenced the 20th-century revolutions in Mexico, Russia, China, Cuba, and Vietnam? How have Americans viewed these modern revolutions?*

Signing the Declaration of Independence, Dover Publications

Students Should Be Able to:

1C Demonstrate understanding of the factors affecting the course of the war and contributing to the American victory by:

5-12 Analyzing the character and roles of the military, political, and diplomatic leaders who helped forge the American victory. [**Assess the importance of the individual**]

5-12 Comparing and explaining the different roles and perspectives in the war of men and women including white settlers, free and enslaved African Americans, and Native Americans. [**Examine the influence of ideas**]

9-12 Analyzing the problems of financing the war and dealing with wartime inflation, hoarding, and profiteering. [**Identify issues and problems in the past**]

7-12 Explaining the American victory. [**Analyze multiple causation**]

| **Grades 5-6** | **Examples of student achievement of Standard 1C include:** |

▶ Reconstruct the chronology of the course of the war as it moved from the North in 1775-78 to the South in 1778-81, climaxing at Yorktown.

▶ Create a time line recording the major developments of the war from its outbreak at Lexington and Concord in 1775 to the Battle of Yorktown in 1781.

▶ Identify and compare the leadership roles of at least two major political, military, and diplomatic leaders such as George Washington, Benjamin Franklin, Thomas Jefferson, John Adams, Samuel Adams, John Hancock, and Richard Henry Lee.

▶ Draw upon evidence from books such as *Jump Ship to Freedom, My Brother Sam is Dead,* and *War Comes to Willy Freeman* by James Collier and Christopher Collier and *Johnny Tremain* by Esther Forbes to determine how war affected the lives of people.

| **Grades 7-8** | **Examples of student achievement of Standard 1C include:** |

▶ Analyze the major campaigns in the Revolutionary War and assess the leadership of both American and British military leaders.

▶ Analyze the varied responses of Native American nations to the American Revolution using the Iroquois and Cherokee as case studies. Construct a historical narrative examining the dilemma of establishing alliances or remaining neutral. *Why did both the British and Americans seek alliances with Indian nations? What were Mohawk chief Joseph Brant's reasons for supporting Britain after the Oswego Council (1777)? What impact did the war have on the Iroquois confederation? On the Cherokee?*

▶ Examine the Revolutionary War from the African American perspective and construct persuasive arguments or broadsides to enlist support for either the British or the Patriot cause. *What was the impact of Lord Dunmore's proclamation? Why did free blacks and slaves join the Patriots during the war? On what grounds did they base their appeals for freedom during and immediately after the conflict?*

▶ Construct an argument assessing the comparative advantages and disadvantages of such efforts to finance the Revolutionary War as taxing Americans, borrowing from foreign nations, confiscating goods and requiring services needed by the military, printing unbacked paper money, and repudiating debts.

Grades 9-12

Examples of student achievement of Standard 1C include:

▶ Draw upon diaries, letters, and historical stories to construct a narrative concerning how the daily lives of men, women, and children were affected by such wartime developments as the participation of men and women in the front lines; the need for women and children to assume men's roles in managing farms and urban businesses; the physical devastation caused by the fighting; the occupation and plunder of the cities by the British troops; and the economic hardship and privation caused by the war.

▶ Construct a sound historical argument concerning the significance of the leadership traits and contribution of at least one of the major political, military, and diplomatic leaders of the war and hypothesize how the war might have been affected had this individual not been on the scene.

▶ Explain why the Battle of Saratoga has been considered the turning point of the Revolutionary War. *How did Benjamin Franklin use the battle to gain French aid? How important was French aid during the war?*

▶ Construct a position paper or historical narrative analyzing to what extent the American Revolution was a civil war as well as a war for national independence. *How does the battle at King's Mountain illustrate the civil war aspect of the Revolution?*

▶ Draw evidence from a variety of sources to explain how guerrilla warfare as well as conventional warfare was an aspect of the American Revolution. *Which was more important to the American victory?*

▶ Explain the factors that helped to produce the Treaty of Paris. *Was the treaty a military or a diplomatic victory? Why?*

Molly Pitcher taking her husband's place in battle. With permission from Dover Publications

Students Should Be Able to:

1D Demonstrate understanding of how American relations with European powers affected the character and outcomes of the American Revolution by:

`5-12` Analyzing United States relationships with France, Holland, and Spain during the Revolution and the contributions of each European power to the American victory. [**Analyze cause-and-effect relationships**]

`7-12` Analyzing the terms of the Treaty of Paris, and their implications for U.S. relationships with Native Americans and with the European powers that continued to hold territories and interests in North America. [**Consider multiple perspectives**]

Grades 5-6

Examples of student achievement of Standard 1D include:

▸ Assess the importance of Benjamin Franklin's negotiations with the French government and of French aid to the Americans by constructing historical arguments on such questions as: *Could the underfinanced and undermanned Americans have defeated the most powerful military force in the Western world without French aid? What might have happened if the French army and navy had not been available to assist Washington at Yorktown?*

▸ Specify the terms of the Treaty of Paris and locate on a map the territorial changes agreed upon in the treaty.

Grades 7-8

Examples of student achievement of Standard 1D include:

▸ Compare and contrast the interests, goals, and actions of France, Holland, and Spain in responding to American requests for assistance in their war with England.

▸ Develop a historical argument assessing the contributions to the American victory of such Europeans as the Marquis de Lafayette, Pierre de Beaumarchais, Baron Friedrich Wilhelm von Steuben, Baron Johann de Kalb, Thaddeus Kosciusko, Count Casimir Pulaski, and others.

▸ Assess the position of the Native Americans at the close of the war. *What were their prospects, given the terms of the Treaty of Paris, which granted to the Americans sole rights to negotiate with them? How did white land hunger, which had contributed to the tensions between the colonists and England over the Proclamation of 1763, express itself after the war?*

Grades 9-12

Examples of student achievement of Standard 1D include:

▸ Explain how American diplomatic initiatives and the contributions of European military leaders affected the character and outcome of the American Revolution. Construct a historical argument agreeing or disagreeing with the statement: "The American Revolution succeeded because of a very small cadre of patriots, the intervention of foreign governments like France and Spain, and supreme good luck."

▶ Examine how the self-interests of France and Spain differed from the national interests of the United States. *What did France expect in return for its military and financial assistance to the United States during the Revolutionary War? What did Spain hope to get as a result of its war against Britain?*

▶ Compare how the terms of the Treaty of Paris and the national boundaries it specified affected economic and strategic interests of the United States, Native American nations, Spain, England, and France. *What was the economic impact of the loss of trade with the British West Indies following the American Revolution? What boundaries remained in dispute after the Treaty of Paris? To what extent did the Treaty of Paris address issues of importance to the Indians? What was the impact of the Treaty of Fort Stanwix (1784) with the Iroquois and the Treaty of Hopewell with the Cherokee following the Revolution? What benefits could Indian allies of the United States expect to gain from their support?*

▶ Describe the boundary dispute between the United States and Spain resulting from the Treaty of Paris of 1783. Explain why the Jay-Gardoqui Treaty of 1786 resulted in regional economic conflict in the new nation.

▶ Construct a dialogue between an Indian leader and George Washington at the end of the war regarding how a long-standing conflict between their peoples might be resolved.

Portrait by Alonzo Chappel of Marie Joseph Paul Yves Roch Gilbert du Motier, Marquis de Lafayette. From The American Revolution *by John Grafton, c.1975, by Dover Publications, Inc.*

STANDARD 2

Students Should Understand: *How the American Revolution involved multiple movements among the new nation's many groups to reform American society.*

Students Should Be Able to:

2A Demonstrate understanding of the revolution's effects on social, political, and economic relations among different social groups by:

`7-12` Comparing the reasons influencing many whites, African Americans, and Native Americans to remain loyal to the British during the American Revolution and the consequences for each of the American victory. [**Consider multiple perspectives**]

`5-12` Comparing to what extent the revolutionary goals of different groups were achieved and how the Revolution altered social, political, and economic relations among them. [**Compare and contrast differing values, behaviors, and institutions**]

`7-12` Analyzing the revolutionary hopes of enslaved and free African Americans, the reformist calls for the abolition of slavery during the revolution, and the gradual postrevolutionary abolition of slavery in the northern states. [**Examine the influence of ideas**]

`7-12` Analyzing the ideas on which women drew in arguing for new roles and rights; the conventions of the 18th century that limited their aspirations and achievements; and the extent to which women were successful in gaining their rights after 1776. [**Examine the influence of ideas**]

`9-12` Explaining the contributions of African American leaders in the early republic and the importance of the African American institutions developed in the free black communities of the North. [**Assess the importance of the individual**]

Grades 5-6

Examples of student achievement of Standard 2A include:

▶ Compare the effects of the American victory on at least two of the following groups: small farmers; wealthy merchants; women who had contributed to the war effort; newly freed African Americans who had fought on the American or the English side; Native Americans who had fought on the American or the English side.

▶ Construct biographical sketches of individuals such as Abigail Adams, Mercy Otis Warren, and Phyllis Wheatley using such sources as *Rebellion's Song* by Melissa Stone.

Grades 7-8

Examples of student achievement of Standard 2A include:

▶ Interpret documentary evidence from diaries, letters, and journals to construct sound historical arguments, debates, or narratives on such issues as the following: *Were women justified in seeking new roles and rights in American society? To what extent were they influenced by such revolutionary ideals as liberty, equality and the right to representation? To what extent were they constrained by the social conventions of the 18th century?*

▶ Draw upon evidence from biographies and other historical sources to construct sound historical assessments of the contributions of such former slaves as Prince Hall, Paul Cuffe, Richard Allen, and Absalom Jones, who worked to improve the social, economic, and community life of newly freed African Americans

▶ Construct historical arguments in the form of balance sheets, debates, or narratives which marshal historical evidence on such questions as: *To what extent were the revolutionary goals of those who supported the Revolution achieved? What were the goals of those who remained loyal to the English (Loyalists, Native Americans, and many African Americans), and what were the consequences for them of the American victory?*

▶ Examine the views of young people regarding life during the revolutionary era through a variety of historical fiction and primary source collections such as *Becoming American: Young People in the American Revolution*, edited by Paul Zall.

Grades 9-12

Examples of student achievement of Standard 2A include:

▶ Develop a sound historical argument concerning the degree to which the interests of such groups as enslaved and free African Americans and Native Americans were advanced or retarded by the American victory. *How did farmers, merchants, and artisans fare as a result of the American Revolution?*

▶ Draw upon biographies and other historical data to evaluate the importance of African American leaders in the early republic and of the institutions developed in the free black communities of the North in order to overcome the obstacles they faced in racial discrimination in the North and fierce resistance to the antislavery movement in the South. *What was the role of African American churches in building strong communities among free blacks in the North?*

▶ Draw upon arguments such as those offered by Abigail Adams's letters to John Adams (1776), Mary Wollstonecraft's *Vindication of the Rights of Women* (1792) and Judith Sargeant Murray in "The Gleaner" (1798) to analyze how women's quest for new roles and rights for their gender continued to evolve, the extent to which they were successful in gaining new educational and political rights in the years following 1776, and the degree to which they were able to enter the public realm.

". . . Remember the Ladies, and be more generous and favourable to them than your ancestors. Do not put such unlimited power into the hand of the husbands. Remember all Men would be tyrants if they could. If particular care and attention is not paid to the ladies we are determined to foment a Rebellion, and will not hold ourselves bound by any laws in which we have no voice, or representation . . ."

LETTER FROM ABIGAIL ADAMS TO JOHN ADAMS, 1776

S T A N D A R D   3

Students Should Understand: *The institutions and practices of government created during the revolution and how they were revised between 1787 and 1815 to create the foundation of the American political system.*

Students Should Be Able to:

3A Demonstrate understanding of government-making, at both national and state levels by:

[5-12] Analyzing the arguments over the Articles of Confederation. [**Examine the influence of ideas**]

[9-12] Comparing at least two state constitutions and explaining why they differed. [**Analyze multiple causation**]

[7-12] Assessing the accomplishments and failures of the Continental Congress. [**Evaluate major debates among historians**]

[7-12] Assessing the importance of the Northwest Ordinance. [**Interrogate historical data**]

Grades 5-6

Examples of student achievement of Standard 3A include:

▶ Construct an explanation of how the thirteen colonies settled the question of governing themselves after declaring their independence from England.

▶ Compare and explain the powers apportioned to the states and to the Continental Congress under the Articles of Confederation.

▶ Map the cession of western lands by various states to the national government.

Grades 7-8

Examples of student achievement of Standard 3A include:

▶ Develop a historical argument assessing the long-term importance of the Northwest Ordinance of 1787 in providing for the development of new states, restrictions on slavery, provisions for public education, and "the utmost good faith" clause for dealing with the Native Americans in the Northwest Territory.

▶ Analyze the issue of the western lands dispute by constructing sound historical arguments or narratives on such questions as: *Were states whose original charters had not granted them western lands justified in demanding that all western lands be ceded to the central government before they would sign the Articles of Confederation? Was the sale of these western lands important for a central government?*

▶ Assess the comparative accomplishments and failures of the national government under the Articles of Confederation, and their contributions to the call for a constitutional convention to revise the Articles of Confederation. Debate the proposition: *"The Articles of Confederation was an effective government."*

Grades 9-12

Examples of student achievement of Standard 3A include:

▶ Draw upon specific provisions in any two state constitutions in order to demonstrate various applications of 18th-century republicanism such as virtue in government, balancing the interests of different social groups, service to the common good, representation, separation of powers, judicial independence, and the legitimacy of slavery. Analyze factors contributing to the differences in the selected state constitutions.

▶ Weigh historical evidence and construct a sound argument, debate, or narrative which evaluates the accomplishments and failures of the Continental Congress and Articles of Confederation. *How effective was the Continental Congress in waging war with Britain and negotiating diplomatic alliances with European powers? How difficult was it to reach an agreement on conflicting state claims to western lands? How successfully did the Continental Congress deal with Indian-white relations?*

▶ Formulate historical questions assessing the importance of the Northwest Ordinance based on a careful study of the document. *To what extent were the first two articles of the Northwest Ordinance a precursor to the Bill of Rights? How revolutionary was the antislavery clause of the Northwest Ordinance? Under the Ordinance, what was the status of free blacks in the territory? What was the "utmost good faith clause"? To what extent was it enforced? How did the Land Ordinance of 1785 and the Northwest Ordinance of 1787 promote public education? How did these ordinances lead to the opening of the West? What was their impact on Native Americans in the Old Northwest?*

Cartoon by Benjamin Franklin, Dover Publications

Students Should Be Able to:

3B Demonstrate understanding of the issues involved in the creation and ratification of the United States Constitution and the new government it established by:

5-12 Analyzing the factors involved in calling the Constitutional Convention, including Shays's Rebellion. [**Analyze multiple causation**]

7-12 Analyzing the alternative plans considered by the delegates and the major compromises agreed upon to secure the approval of the Constitution. [**Examine the influence of ideas**]

9-12 Analyzing the fundamental ideas behind the distribution of powers and the system of checks and balances established by the Constitution. [**Examine the influence of ideas**]

9-12 Comparing the arguments of Federalists and Anti-Federalists during the ratification debates and assess their relevance in late 20th-century politics. [**Hypothesize the influence of the past**]

Grades 5-6

Examples of student achievement of Standard 3B include:

▶ Draw upon a variety of historical sources such as paintings, biographies of major delegates, and narratives of the Constitutional Convention to construct a description of who the delegates were and why they were assembled in Philadelphia.

▶ Role-play a session at the Philadelphia Convention in which representatives of large and small states debated the Virginia and New Jersey plans. Draw evidence from sources such as *If You Were There When They Signed the Constitution* by Elizabeth Levy. *Why did the large states support the Virginia Plan? What was the Connecticut Compromise?*

▶ Compare the interests of those delegates who opposed and those who defended slavery, and explain the consequences of the compromises over slavery.

▶ Apply their understanding of the Constitutional separation of powers and system of checks and balances by constructing a flowchart, diagram, or narrative demonstrating the checks each branch of government can exert on the other two.

▶ Use historical fiction such as *The Winter Hero* by Christopher Collier and James Collier to gain an understanding of the importance of Shays's Rebellion.

Grades 7-8

Examples of student achievement of Standard 3B include:

▶ Identify the issues involved in Shays's Rebellion and construct a sound historical argument, from the viewpoint of the debtor class or wealthy creditors, on such questions as: *Were the ordinary farmers who followed Daniel Shays justified in invoking revolutionary rights of petition and taking extralegal action to obtain redress of their grievances? To what extent did the grievances of the debtor class and the fears of wealthy creditors contribute to the national call for a constitutional convention?*

▶ Draw upon their understandings of the great debates and the compromises achieved by the delegates in order to construct a sound historical argument or narrative on questions such as the following: *Within the context of the late 18th century, were the compromises reached by the delegates reasonable? Were the slavery compromises necessary in order to obtain approval of the Constitution? What might the consequences have been had the antislavery delegates remained firm in their resolve?*

Grades 9-12

Examples of student achievement of Standard 3B include:

▶ Develop a sound historical narrative explaining the source and nature of the basic principles behind the separation of powers and the system of checks and balances established by the Constitution.

▶ Develop a sound historical argument on such questions as: *To what extent were the compromises reached in the Constitutional Convention the result of 18th-century republican ideals held by the delegates and to what extent were they the result of deep-rooted economic and political interests of the regions they represented?*

▶ Compare and analyze the major arguments for and against the Constitution of 1787 in leading Federalist and Anti-Federalist writings and major ratification debates.

▶ Analyze the differences between leading Federalists and Anti-Federalists in terms of their background, service during the Revolution, and political experience, and develop a historical argument concerning how these influences shaped their positions on such issues as individual rights, republican government, federalism, separation of powers, and popular sovereignty.

▶ Analyze a recent presidential election to demonstrate what elements of Anti-Federalist thought surfaced in party platforms, state initiatives, and candidate speeches and assess the relevance of Anti-Federalist ideas in late 20th-century politics.

An engraving of the inauguration of George Washington, Federal Hall, New York. Library of Congress

Students Should Be Able to:

3C Demonstrate understanding of the guarantees of the Bill of Rights and its continuing significance by:

5-12 Analyzing the significance of the Bill of Rights and its specific guarantees. [**Examine the influence of ideas**]

9-12 Analyzing whether the Alien and Sedition Acts (1798) threatened those rights and the issues they posed in the absence of judicial review of acts of Congress. [**Evaluate the implementation of a decision**]

9-12 Analyzing issues addressed in recent court cases involving the Bill of Rights to assess their continuing significance today. [**Identify relevant historical antecedents**]

Grades 5-6

Examples of student achievement of Standard 3C include:

▶ Develop sound arguments explaining and illustrating the importance of at least three guarantees in the Bill of Rights.

▶ Construct an InfoCube using art reproductions, photographs, or cartoons to illustrate the relevance of the Bill of Rights in today's society.

Grades 7-8

Examples of student achievement of Standard 3C include:

▶ Specify and explain the importance of the basic guarantees incorporated in the Bill of Rights. *Which do you feel is the most important guarantee? Why?*

▶ Draw evidence from primary and secondary sources to explain why the Anti-Federalists argued for the incorporation of a Bill of Rights in the Constitution. *What did they mean by a Bill of Rights? Were the Anti-Federalist suggestions incorporated into the Bill of Rights?*

▶ Construct classroom learning stations or collages incorporating illustrations and short quotations to examine the historical context and contemporary application of the Bill of Rights. Draw evidence from sources such as the Center for Civic Education's *We the People* and *With Liberty and Justice for All*.

Grades 9-12

Examples of student achievement of Standard 3C include:

▶ Draw evidence from "Federalist 84," James Madison's letter to Thomas Jefferson (October, 1788), Jefferson's response, and selections from the Anti-Federalist Papers to explain the arguments presented in the debate over whether there was a need for a Bill of Rights. *Was a Bill of Rights necessary? Why or why not?*

▶ Draw upon historical data and the Bill of Rights to construct a sound historical argument on such questions as: *Were the Alien and Sedition acts of 1798 and the arrest and imprisonment of critics of the Adams administration such as Benjamin Franklin Bache and Matthew Lyon violations of the First Amendment or were they justified by the crises confronting the new nation? Might these events have taken a different turn if the 1803 principle of judicial review had been developed at that time?*

▶ Using historical data and the First Amendment to the Bill of Right, analyze the reasons why the Alien and Sedition Acts were passed and appraise their significance. *To what extent were the Alien and Sedition Acts a violation of the Bill of Rights? How did the Federalist party justify the need for the acts? Why did they feel it did not violate the Bill of Rights? How did they affect the growth of the Democratic-Republican Party? Were the Virginia and Kentucky Resolutions opposed to the restriction of rights under the Alien and Sedition Acts or were they concerned about the nature of federalism? Explain.*

Matthew Lyon brawling in the House of Representatives with a congressman from Connecticut. Library of Congress

Students Should Be Able to:

3D Demonstrate understanding of the development of the first American party system by:

`9-12` Explaining the development of the two-party system, although political factions were widely deplored. [**Analyze multiple causation**]

`5-12` Comparing the leaders and the social and economic composition of each party. [**Compare and contrast differing personalities, behaviors, and institutions**]

`7-12` Comparing the different views of the two parties on the central economic and foreign policy issues of the 1790s. [**Compare and contrast differing sets of ideas**]

Grades 5-6

Examples of student achievement of Standard 3D include:

▶ Construct a project in the form of a classroom newspaper, skit, or role-play activity which examines the positions of Alexander Hamilton and Thomas Jefferson on a major issue confronting the Washington administration.

▶ Draw upon historical evidence and fictional accounts of the Whiskey Rebellion such as *Beyond the Allegheny* by Betty Koch to describe the issues which impacted the lives of farmers in western Pennsylvania.

Grades 7-8

Examples of student achievement of Standard 3D include:

▶ Identify the central economic issues of the 1790s on which people with varying economic interests and regional ties held different views, and construct an argument regarding how these differences contributed to the development of the Federalists and the Democratic-Republicans.

▶ Prepare a list of probing questions to determine the policies advocated by leaders of the Federalist and Democratic-Republican parties, and through a "meeting of the minds" or "point counter-point" format debate the effectiveness of their positions on prominent issues.

▶ Analyze the social and economic bases of the two emerging political parties.

▶ Evaluate the role of ordinary people in the Whiskey Rebellion and in demonstrations against Jay's Treaty. *What were the causes of the Whiskey Rebellion? How were the demonstrations against the whiskey tax similar to those of the revolutionary period against British taxation? What were the differences? Why did western farmers object to the Jay Treaty?*

▶ Discuss the bitterly fought presidential election of 1800, including Adams's appointment of "midnight judges." *What were the issues in the election of 1800? During the campaign why was Jefferson accused of advocating anarchy and destroying Christian principles? Was Adams's appointment of Federalist judges in the last days of his administration appropriate?*

Grades 9-12

Examples of student achievement of Standard 3D include:

▶ Draw upon historical data disclosing the viewpoints of different constituencies in the North, South, and West concerning Hamilton's plans for promoting the economic development of the new nation. Construct a historical argument or debate in defense or opposition to Hamilton's plans from the viewpoint of several of these regional constituencies.

▶ Draw upon historical documents such as Jefferson's critique of Hamilton's economic program, Patrick Henry's "Resolution on the Assumption of State Debts," and the Hamilton-Jefferson disagreement on the constitutionality of the Bank of the United States. *What was the nature of the objections to Hamilton's financial plan? On what grounds did Hamilton use the "necessary and proper" clause of Article I, Section 8 of the Constitution to argue for the establishment of a national bank? How did Jefferson use the same clause to argue that a federally funded bank was unconstitutional? Who would benefit from the Bank of the United States? Who would benefit from funding the debt at par value?*

▶ Explain how differences concerning support for the French Revolution, foreign policy issues (such as the Gênet affair, the Jay and Pinckney treaties, the XYZ Affair, the undeclared war with France), and immigration contributed to the emergence of an organized opposition party led by Jefferson and Madison.

▶ Examine the social and economic make-up of the membership of the Federalist and Democratic-Republican parties in the 1790s. *To what extent does the social and economic status of the leadership of each of the two parties reflect their membership? Who would be most likely to support the Federalists? The Democratic-Republicans?*

▶ Analyze the factors which led to the Whiskey Rebellion and evaluate the following quotations from two political antagonists?

"An insurrection was announced and proclaimed and armed against, but could never be found." Thomas Jefferson

Suppressing the rebellion "will do us a great deal of good and add to the solidity of everything in this country." Alexander Hamilton

Was the government overreacting to the "Whiskey Rebels" or was the rebellion a threat to the security of the nation? Why or why not? Was the Whiskey Rebellion a confrontation between "haves" and "have-nots?" Compare the grievances of the "Whiskey Rebels" to those of the Regulators, Paxton Boys, and Shaysites.

Students Should Be Able to:

3E Demonstrate understanding of the development of the Supreme Court's powers and significance from 1789 to 1820 by:

7-12 Appraising the significance of John Marshall's precedent-setting decisions in establishing the Supreme Court as an independent and equal branch of the U.S. government. [**Assess the importance of the individual**]

9-12 Tracing the evolution of the Supreme Court's powers during the 1790s and early 19th century and analyzing its influence today. [**Explain historical continuity and change**]

Grades 5-6
Examples of student achievement of Standard 3E include:

Not appropriate for this grade level.

Grades 7-8
Examples of student achievement of Standard 3E include:

▶ Identify the powers and responsibilities of the Supreme Court set forth in Article III of the Constitution and in the Judiciary Act of 1789 which confers the power of judicial review of acts of state governments.

▶ Discuss why *Marbury* v. *Madison* is considered a landmark decision of the Supreme Court.

▶ Compare the power and significance of the Supreme Court in 1800 and 1820. *How did Chief Justice Marshall contribute to the growth of the Court's importance in relationship to the other two branches of the federal government?*

Grades 9-12
Examples of student achievement of Standard 3E include:

▶ Review *Marbury* v. *Madison* (1803) and at least one other major case such as *Fletcher* v. *Peck* (1810), *Dartmouth College* v. *Woodward* (1819) or *Gibbons* v. *Ogden* (1824) in order to construct a sound historical argument concerning how Chief Justice Marshall's decisions established important legal precedents and strengthened the role of the Supreme Court as an equal branch of government.

▶ Draw evidence from Marshall's decision in *McCulloch* v. *Maryland* to construct an argument or historical narrative appraising the position of the national government vis-à-vis state governments. *To what extent does McCulloch v. Maryland strengthen the powers of the national government? How does the decision impact the interpretation of the Constitution?*

▶ Draw upon the evidence about the operations and decisions of the Supreme Court before 1800 and the Marshall Court to explain changes in the stature and significance of the federal judiciary.

Students, West Milford Township, New Jersey. Photograph by John Jordan

ERA 4

Expansion and Reform (1801-1861)

The new American republic prior to the Civil War experienced dramatic territorial expansion, economic growth, and industrialization. The increasing complexity of American society, the growth of regionalism, and the cross-currents of change that are often bewildering require the development of several major themes to enable students to sort their way through the six decades that brought the United States to the eve of the Civil War.

One theme is the vast territorial expansion between 1800 and 1861, as restless white Americans pushed westward across the Appalachians, then across the Mississippi, and finally on to the Pacific Ocean. But students also need to study how white Americans, animated by land hunger and the ideology of "Manifest Destiny," forced the removal of many Indian nations in the Southeast and Old Northwest, acquired a large part of Mexico through the Mexican-American War, and engaged in abrasive racial encounters with Native Americans, Mexicans, Chinese immigrants, and others in the West.

A second theme confronts the economic development of the expanding American republic — a complex and fascinating process that fed growing regional tensions. In the North, the first stage of industrialization brings students face to face with the role of technology in historical change and how economic development has had profound environmental effects. In studying the rise of immigrant-filled cities, the "transportation revolution," the creation of a market system, and the proliferation of family farming in newly opened territories, students will appreciate how Tocqueville might have reached the conclusion that the Americans seemed at one time "animated by the most selfish cupidity; at another by the most lively patriotism." In studying the expanding South, students must understand the enormous growth of slavery as an exploitive and morally corrupt economic and social system; but they should also comprehend how millions of African Americans struggled to shape their own lives as much as possible through family, religion, and resistance to slavery.

A third theme can be organized around the extension, restriction, and reorganization of political democracy after 1800. The rise of the second party system and modern interest-group politics mark the advent of modern politics in America. However, students will see that the evolution of political democracy was not a smooth, one-way street as free African Americans were disenfranchised in much of the North and women's suffrage was blocked.

Connected to all of the above is the theme of reform, for the rapid transformation and expansion of American society brought forth one of the greatest bursts of reformism in American history. Emerson captured the vibrancy of this era in asking, "What is man born for but to be a reformer." Students will find that the attempts to complete unfinished agendas of the revolutionary period and new reforms necessitated by the rise of factory labor and rapid urbanization are all predecessors of social movements — such as the civil rights movement and feminism — that are still part of our contemporary society.

Overview

Standard 1: United States territorial expansion between 1801 and 1861, and how it affected relations with external powers and Native Americans

Standard 2: How the industrial revolution, the rapid expansion of slavery, and the westward movement changed the lives of Americans and led toward regional tensions

Standard 3: The extension, restriction, and reorganization of political democracy after 1800

Standard 4: The sources and character of reform movements in the antebellum period and what the reforms accomplished or failed to accomplish

Map of Louisiana and Mexico, Library of Congress

S T A N D A R D   1

Students Should Understand: *United States territorial expansion between 1801 and 1861, and how it affected relations with external powers and Native Americans.*

Students Should Be Able to:

1A Demonstrate understanding of the international background and consequences of the Louisiana Purchase, War of 1812, and the Monroe Doctrine by:

`5-12` Analyzing Napoleon's reasons for selling Louisiana to the United States. [**Draw upon the data in historical maps**]

`7-12` Comparing the arguments advanced by Democratic Republicans and Federalists regarding the acquisition of Louisiana. [**Compare and contrast differing sets of ideas**]

`9-12` Analyzing the consequences of the Louisiana Purchase for United States politics, economic development, and race relations, and describing its impact on Spanish and French inhabitants. [**Explain historical continuity and change**]

`7-12` Identifying the origins and explaining the provisions of the Monroe Doctrine. [**Examine the influence of ideas**]

`7-12` Comparing President Madison's reasons for declaring war in 1812 and the sectional divisions over the war. [**Formulate a position or course of action on an issue**]

`9-12` Assessing the interests and actions of Native Americans in the war. [**Consider multiple perspectives**]

| Grades 5-6 | **Examples of student achievement of Standard 1A include:** |

▶ Identify the boundaries of United States and French territorial claims in the Western Hemisphere in 1801 and compare with the boundaries of the U.S. following the Louisiana Purchase. *Why did Napoleon agree to sell the Louisiana territory to the United States?*

▶ Draw upon children's literature that chronicles the Lewis and Clark expedition using such sources as *Bold Journey: West with Lewis and Clark* by Charles Bohner, *Streams to the River, Rivers to the Sea* by Scott O'Dell, and *Sacagawea: Indian Interpreter to Lewis and Clark* by Marion Marsh Brown.

▶ Draw upon journals, maps, stories, and other historical records to assess the influence of such explorers and mountain men as Zebulon Pike, John C. Frémont, Jedediah Smith, James Beckwourth, and Kit Carson. *Would the development of the United States have been different if these men had not blazed the trails and provided the information used by the thousands of settlers who moved west?*

▶ Draw upon maps of the Western Hemisphere showing territories held by Spain, France, Britain, and Russia in 1800 and locate the nations which declared their independence by 1823. *How did President Monroe propose to deal with attempts by Europe to reestablish their control in the hemisphere?*

◗ Develop a historical argument whether or not the War of 1812 helped to unite the new nation. *Why did New Englanders oppose the war? Why did the War Hawks want to move against Native Americans in the Northwest Territory? Was the war a "Second War for Independence," a war of expansion, or a war for maritime rights?*

◗ Assume the role of a young adult during the War of 1812, and through a diary or journal write firsthand accounts of memorable events during the conflict. *How would a British soldier, Shawnee, or Creek report on these same events?*

Grades 7-8

Examples of student achievement of Standard 1A include:

◗ Draw upon geographic data, European diplomacy, and black rebellion in Haiti in order to construct a historical argument in the form of "balance sheets," debates, or partisan newspapers assessing the case for and against the acquisition of Louisiana. *Why did Jefferson believe that the Louisiana Purchase provided the opportunity for an "Empire of Liberty?" Why did Senator Samuel White (Delaware) refer to the Louisiana Purchase as "the greatest curse that could befall us?" What were the advantages and disadvantages of doubling the territorial holdings of the United States?*

◗ Draw upon evidence from the diaries of Lewis and Clark to construct a historical narrative assessing the importance of the newly acquired Louisiana Territory and analyze the effects of the expedition. *Why is it considered one of the most successful scientific expeditions in United States history? How did it contribute to friendly relations with Native Americans in the region? What were its long-term effects?*

◗ Construct a historical argument from the perspective of Native Americans on the impact of territorial expansion. *How did the acquisition of the Louisiana Territory affect Native Americans in the region?*

◗ Place the Monroe Doctrine in its historical context and explain its major provisions and significance. *Why did President Monroe feel a need to issue the Monroe Doctrine? How was it a departure from earlier foreign policy? What was its historical significance? What is its impact today?*

◗ Explain the diplomatic problems facing the U.S. as a result of the renewal of English-French hostilities, including their seizure of American ships, English impressment of American sailors into the English navy, and economic losses in trade.

◗ Analyze the causes of the War of 1812 by drawing upon evidence from a variety of primary sources, including excerpts from Henry Clay's speeches, President Monroe's declaration of war, and Congressional debates. *Why did the War Hawks want to move against Native Americans in the Northwest Territory? Was the war a "Second War for Independence," a war of expansion, or a war for maritime rights?*

◗ Use Tecumseh's speeches in recruiting Indian allies between 1809 and 1811 to illustrate the Native American perspective on the encroachment of white settlers on tribal lands. Explain the interests and actions of Native Americans in different regions of the country in the war. *Why did Tecumseh join with the British during the War of 1812? What did he hope to achieve by an English victory?*

Grades 9-12

Examples of student achievement of Standard 1A include:

▸ Assemble evidence on such matters as the black rebellion in Haiti, French losses in the Santo Domingo campaign, pending hostilities with Great Britain, and American opponents to French designs on New Orleans in order to create a "position paper" or argument such as French Minister Talleyrand might have developed in 1803 to advise Napoleon to sell all of Louisiana to the United States.

▸ Assemble the evidence and develop a historical narrative on such questions as: *How did Jefferson, a strict constructionist, devotee of limited government, and frugality in terms of government spending, justify the purchase of Louisiana? On what grounds did many New England Federalists justify their opposition to the purchase? What were the consequences of the Louisiana Purchase in terms of economic development, slavery, and politics?*

▸ Draw on historical sources, maps, and documents in order to analyze the three major provisions of the Monroe Doctrine and their significance. *To what extent was the major purpose of the Monroe Doctrine to protect the newly won independence of Latin American states or to serve notice of U.S. expansionist intentions in the hemisphere? Why did the U.S. and other countries ignore the provisions of the Monroe Doctrine for so long? Does the U.S. emphasize the Monroe Doctrine today in world affairs?*

▸ Analyze the responses of Jefferson and Madison to impressment and the harassment of U.S. shipping prior to the outbreak of the War of 1812. *How effective were the Embargo Act, Macon's Bill No. 2, and the Nonintercourse Act? What was the domestic political and economic impact of the Embargo Act? Why was it repealed?*

▸ Create a historical argument that explains the opposing positions of congressmen from Pennsylvania, the South, and the West in supporting the war resolution of June 3, 1812, and those from New England and the other mid-Atlantic states in voting against it, though President Madison's war message focused on the maritime issues most directly affecting their interests.

▸ Compare the interests of Native Americans and white settlers of the Northwest Territory in the war, taking into account such factors as the impact of the Land Ordinance of 1785, the Northwest Ordinance of 1787, the Treaty of Greenville (1795), Tecumseh's appeal for a great Indian confederation, and the situation created by Indian defeat at Kithtippecanoe (1811). *What did Native Americans hope to gain from the war by joining the British? How did Indian support for Britain feed war fever? Why did the Cherokee remain neutral? What were the reasons the Red Stick Creeks fought? Why did the Cherokee join General Jackson against the Creeks at Horseshoe Bend? What were the consequences of the war for Indian nations in the Northwest and South?*

▸ Analyze reasons for dissent during the War of 1812. Draw data from the Hartford Convention resolutions to explain New England's resentment of the war. *If the War of 1812 was fought to guarantee rights on the "high seas," as Madison maintained, why did New England oppose the war? Were the proposed constitutional amendments reasonable? How do the sectional interests expressed at the Hartford Convention compare with those of the Kentucky and Virginia Resolutions of 1798? Why was the Hartford Convention considered the death-knell of the Federalist party?*

Students Should Be Able to:

1B Demonstrate understanding of federal and state Indian policy and the strategies for survival forged by Native Americans by:

`7-12` Comparing the policies toward Native Americans pursued by presidential administrations through the Jacksonian era. [**Compare and contrast differing sets of ideas**]

`9-12` Comparing federal and state Indian policy and explaining Whig opposition to the removal of Native Americans. [**Consider multiple perspectives**]

`5-12` Analyzing the impact of the removal and resettlement on Native Americans such as the Cherokee and the Choctaw. [**Evidence historical perspectives**]

`7-12` Explaining and evaluating the various strategies of Native Americans such as accommodation, revitalization, and resistance. [**Compare and contrast differing sets of ideas, values, and behaviors**]

| **Grades 5-6** | **Examples of student achievement of Standard 1B include:** |

- On a map, identify (1) the original lands in the Old Northwest Territory occupied by the Shawnee, Miami, and Pottawatomie, and (2) the Seminole, Creek, Cherokee, Chickasaw, and Choctaw nations of the Southeast.

- Draw upon stories and historical accounts of such leaders as Tecumseh, the Prophet, and Black Hawk in order to develop a historical narrative, news report, or story of the Native American efforts to hold on to their lands, resist government policies of removal, and return to the ways of their ancestors.

- Examine personal stories of the Trail of Tears using such sources as *Only the Names Remain: The Cherokee and the Trail of Tears* by Alex Bealer, and *Yunini's Story of the Trail of Tears* by Ada Loomis Barry.

| **Grades 7-8** | **Examples of student achievement of Standard 1B include:** |

- Draw upon evidence from biographies and other historical sources to appraise the survival strategies employed by Native Americans such as John Ross, Speckled Snake, Red Eagle (William Weatherford), Sequoyah, Tenskwatawa (the Shawnee Prophet), Tecumseh, Osceola, and Black Hawk.

- Draw upon the Cherokee Nation and Worcester cases before the U.S. Supreme Court in order to compare state and federal policy toward Native Americans. *What were Georgia's apparent motives in passing laws governing the Cherokees? How did Georgia respond to the Marshall Court's decisions in the two cases? What factors contributed to President Jackson's opposition to the Court's decisions?*

- Construct a historical narrative or simulated journal account of Cherokee removal from the perspective of Native Americans. In developing the narrative, draw upon both primary and secondary sources, such as Reverend Jones's eyewitness account of the Cherokee removal, Speckled Snake's response to President Jackson's removal policy, George Harkins's farewell letter, and Robert Lindneux's 1942 painting, *The Trail of Tears*.

▶ Use a physical map of the United States to compare the topography and climate of Cherokee and Choctaw lands in the southeastern United States with resettlement areas in western Arkansas and eastern Oklahoma. *How did the geography of the two regions differ? How would the region's topography, climate, and resources affect Cherokee and Choctaw societies?*

▶ Draw evidence from historical fiction such as *In the Shadow of the Wind* by Luke Wallin, *Sequoyah and the Cherokee Alphabet* by Robert Cwiklik, and *No Resting Place* by William Humphrey to examine accounts of the removal of the Creek and Cherokee to Oklahoma in the 1830s.

▶ Examine the Black Hawk War and federal and state removal policies in the Old Northwest. Compare the removal of Indians of the Old Northwest to that of the Cherokees and Choctaws of the Southeast.

Grades 9-12

Examples of student achievement of Standard 1B include:

▶ Analyze the U.S. government's changing policies toward Native Americans from an assimilationist strategy in the early 19th century to removal and isolation after 1825. *Were the policies of Indian removal announced by President Monroe in his last annual message (December 1824) and implemented by Andrew Jackson the result of Jeffersonian paternalism toward Native Americans or a decided reorientation of U.S. policy? Did Northerners, Southerners, and Westerners agree in regard to policy toward Native Americans or were there clear-cut sectional and/or political differences? How, for example, did northern Whigs respond to removal, and why?*

▶ Compare and evaluate the arguments in favor of removal advanced by President Andrew Jackson in his second annual message and the arguments against removal advanced by Native American leaders such as Chief John Ross in his 1836 message to Congress. *Why did Jackson, who was determined to force South Carolina's "nullifiers" to comply with the "law of the land," refuse to enforce the Supreme Court's decision in the Worcester case on the state of Georgia?*

▶ Using selections from primary and secondary sources, including articles from the *Cherokee Phoenix*, describe Cherokee values, their integration of European culture, and their resistance to removal. *How do stories regarding the sacrifices on the "Trail of Tears" help one understand Cherokee adaptation and resistance? How do the Cherokee define law, property rights, heroism, and freedom?*

Sequoyah (c. 1770-1843) after a painting attributed to C. B. King, Bureau of Ethnology, Smithsonian Institution, reproduced from the Dictionary of American Portraits, Dover Publications, 1967

Students Should Be Able to:

1C Demonstrate understanding of the ideology of Manifest Destiny, the nation's expansion to the Northwest, and the Mexican-American War by:

7-12 Explaining the economic, political, racial, and religious roots of Manifest Destiny and analyzing how the concept influenced the westward expansion of the nation. [**Examine the influence of ideas**]

7-12 Explaining the diplomatic and political developments that led to the resolution of conflicts with Britain and Russia in the period 1815-1850. [**Formulate a position or course of action on an issue**]

9-12 Analyzing United States trading interests in the Far East and explaining how they influenced continental expansion to the Pacific. [**Analyze cause-and-effect relationships**]

5-12 Comparing and explaining President James K. Polk's resolution of the Oregon dispute with Great Britain and his initiation of war with Mexico. [**Challenge arguments of historical inevitability**]

5-12 Explaining the causes of the Mexican-American War, the sequence of events leading to the outbreak of hostilities, and the provisions and consequences of the Treaty of Guadalupe Hidalgo. [**Analyze multiple causation**]

9-12 Analyzing Mexican perspectives on the Mexican-American War. [**Consider multiple perspectives**]

Grades 5-6

Examples of student achievement of Standard 1C include:

▶ Draw upon stories and biographies of Stephen F. Austin, Davy Crockett, Jim Bowie, and Sam Houston and maps of North America in the 1820s to develop a historical explanation of why Mexico invited Americans to settle in Texas; the conflict that developed when Mexico outlawed slavery and settlement in the territory; and the Texas rebels' victory and declaration of independence following their initial defeat at the Alamo.

▶ Draw evidence from historical novels such as *The Far Battleground* by F. M. Parker and *The Dunderhead War* by Betty Baker to investigate personal stories of the Mexican-American War. Analyze the annexation of Texas by the United States and the invasion of Mexico by U.S. troops, which led to war with Mexico. *Was the war justified? What might have happened if Mexican officials had agreed to negotiate with President Polk's ambassador? What else could Polk have done to prevent the war? What could the Mexican government have done?*

▶ Analyze why the people known as "expansionists" believed that it was the nation's destiny to stretch "from sea to shining sea." *How did that belief lead to war with Mexico? How did it lead to settlement of the Oregon dispute with Great Britain and the acquisition of the Oregon territory? How might life be different in Mexico and in the U.S. today if these lands had not become part of the United States?*

Grades 7-8

Examples of student achievement of Standard 1C include:

▶ Draw upon documents such as John O'Sullivan's editorial (1845) and Major Auguste Davezac's speech of 1846, and the lithographs of Currier & Ives, *Westward the Course of Empire,* and John Gast's *America's Progress* to construct a historical narrative explaining the ethos of Manifest Destiny and its appeal to 19th-century American industrial workers and small farmers.

◆ Interpret documentary evidence from maps, political speeches, diaries, and letters to construct sound historical arguments, debates, or narratives on such questions relating to the Mexican-American War as: *What role did the annexation of Texas and the American desire for California play in leading to the outbreak of war between Mexico and the United States? Was the war justified? On what grounds did such critics as Abraham Lincoln, Frederick Douglass, and Henry David Thoreau oppose the war? On what grounds did supporters of President Polk's policies justify going to war? In what ways did the terms of the Treaty of Guadalupe Hidalgo reflect the spirit of Manifest Destiny?*

◆ Identify the issues surrounding the controversy over Oregon and evaluate Polk's campaign slogan "54° 40' or fight." *How practical was Polk's call for annexation of the entire Oregon Territory? Would it have been realistic for the United States to conduct a war over disputed territories with Mexico and Great Britain simultaneously? To what extent was the negotiated treaty of 1846 a satisfactory solution to interested parties in the United States and Great Britain?*

Grades 9-12

Examples of student achievement of Standard 1C include:

◆ Develop a historical narrative explaining the 19th-century belief in Manifest Destiny. Study such factors as: (a) John Winthrop's vision of a "City Upon a Hill" and the subsequent Protestant belief in the divine mission of the U.S. to build a model Christian community; (b) the emphasis on millennialism during the Second Great Awakening; (c) the belief in Republicanism — in a nation of independent and virtuous citizens and in the necessity for obtaining additional territory to ensure social and economic opportunity for a growing population; (d) the desire to prevent potential foreign enemies from gaining control of adjacent areas and to control the Pacific coast with its good harbors for the profitable China trade; (e) the belief in America's duty to uplift the "backward" and "less civilized" peoples in the West.

◆ Contrast Mexican and American perspectives on the Alamo. Assess the treatment of Mexicans and Cherokees loyal to the Texan revolution in the Lone Star Republic prior to 1846.

◆ Draw upon evidence such as President James K. Polk's diplomatic correspondence with Mexican officials and American officials such as Thomas Larkin, John C. Frémont, and James Slidell, Polk's War Message and the timing of its delivery, Senator Thomas Corwin's speech against the war in the Senate on February 11, 1847, and the ensuing debate in Congress in order to develop a historical argument concerning the extent to which Polk bore responsibility for initiating war with Mexico, and whether the war was justified.

◆ Analyze the terms of the Treaty of Guadalupe Hidalgo and assess its impact on Mexico and on the U.S. *How did Mexican perspectives on the war differ from the perspective of those in the U.S. who supported the war and its outcomes? Why did the U.S. Senate reject the land grant provisions in Article 10? How did the treaty affect relations with Native Americans in the Mexican cession? What have been its lasting consequences for the U.S.? For Mexico?*

STANDARD 2

Students Should Understand: *How the industrial revolution, the rapid expansion of slavery, and the westward movement changed the lives of Americans and led toward regional tensions.*

Students Should Be Able to:

2A Demonstrate understanding of how the factory system and the transportation and market revolutions shaped regional patterns of economic development by:

5-12 Explaining the major technological developments which revolutionized land and water transportation and analyzing how they transformed the economy, affected international markets, and affected the environment. [**Analyze cause-and-effect relationships**]

7-12 Evaluating national and state policies regarding a protective tariff, a national bank, and federally funded internal improvements. [**Examine the influence of ideas**]

7-12 Explaining how economic policies related to expansion served different regional interests and contributed to growing political and sectional differences in the antebellum era. [**Compare and contrast differing sets of ideas**]

9-12 Comparing how patterns of economic growth and recession affected territorial expansion and community life in the North, South, and West. [**Analyze cause-and-effect relationships**]

7-12 Analyzing how the factory system affected gender roles and changed the lives of men, women, and children. [**Analyze cause-and-effect relationships**]

7-12 Evaluating the factory system from the perspectives of owners and workers and assessing its impact on the rise of the labor movement in the antebellum period. [**Consider multiple perspectives**]

Grades 5-6

Examples of student achievement of Standard 2A include:

▶ Draw upon stories, paintings, folk songs, and picture books such as *The Erie Canal* by Peter Spier to compare transport by wagon, flatboat, and clipper ship before the invention of the steam locomotive with rail and steamboat travel afterwards.

▶ Draw upon illustration, historical accounts, and biographies of such individuals as Samuel Slater, Robert Fulton, Eli Whitney, Samuel B. Morse, John Deere, and Cyrus McCormick in order to create a time line or historical narrative identifying and explaining the importance of such inventions as the spinning jenny, the steam locomotive, the steamboat, and the telegraph.

▶ Examine historical maps locating the Erie Canal, the other canals developed after 1825, and the railroads built by 1860. *How were the lives of people changed as travel became faster and the cost of shipping goods cheaper?*

▶ Draw upon historical paintings, stories, and other records to compare the lives of farm children and urban children. *How were their lives different? Why were there no laws to prevent child labor and to guarantee all children an education? Why was Horace Mann's crusade for free public education for all children important at this time?*

▶ Use sources such as *Mill* by David Macaulay and *A Gathering of Days: A New England Girl's Journal, 1830-1832* by Joan Blost to examine life in New England milltowns in the early 1800s.

Grades 7-8

Examples of student achievement of Standard 2A include:

▶ Draw from primary and secondary sources, such as diaries, interviews, art reproductions, and biographies to compare the effect of technological developments on business owners, farmers, and workers in different regions.

▶ Draw upon data from maps and historical research to develop a historical argument or debate on whether the federal government should invest in internal improvements. *What was the nature of the controversy surrounding internal improvements? Are there parallels in the controversies over "public" investment in the national infrastructure today?*

▶ Construct a narrative which marshals historical evidence on such questions as: *Should the federal government impose protective tariffs? Do tariffs promote or hinder commercial development? To what extent did economic issues intensify political and sectional differences in the antebellum era?*

▶ Draw from primary and secondary sources such as diaries, interviews with factory workers, paintings and lithographs, literature (such as Charles Dickens's *American Notes*), and letters written by New England farm girls working in the mills at Lowell, Massachusetts, to construct a journal illustrating the impact of the factory system upon the lives of working men, women, and children.

▶ Construct historical arguments in the form of "balance sheets," debates, or narratives which marshal historical evidence on the advantages and disadvantages of the factory system from the opposing viewpoints of owners and laborers. *To what extent did the factory system create wealth and improve the lives of Americans? To what extent did it stimulate the rise of the labor movement? In what has been called the "age of the common man," to what extent was social mobility improving and to what extent were class distinctions narrowing?*

▶ Examine personal stories as revealed in *The Mill Girls: Lucy Larcom, Harriet Hanson Robinson, and Sarah G. Bagley* by Bernice Selden and fictional accounts such as *A Spirit to Ride the Whirlwind* by Athena Lord to explore child labor in the New England mills.

Grades 9-12

Examples of student achievement of Standard 2A include:

▶ Compare and analyze the advantages and disadvantages of a protective tariff, a national bank, internal improvements at federal expense, and a cheap price for the sale of western lands to residents of the North, South, and West. *How did such issues affect regional interests and the growth and development of political parties during the period?*

▶ Draw upon Andrew Jackson's veto of the bank recharter bill on July 10, 1832, and the opposition to it in order to construct a sound historical argument on whether or not the veto served the national interest.

▶ Construct an argument explaining how one of the following Supreme Court cases promoted the market revolution: *Fletcher* v. *Peck* (1810), *McCulloch* v. *Maryland* (1819), *Dartmouth College* v. *Woodward* (1819), *Gibbons* v. *Ogden* (1824), *Charles River Bridge* v. *Warren Bridge* (1837).

▶ Draw upon a variety of historical and statistical data to analyze the causes and results of the onset of depression in 1819, 1837, and 1857.

▶ Using paintings from the Hudson River School and writings by Henry Thoreau and Ralph Waldo Emerson, analyze their reaction to the impact of industrialization on the environment. *How did Asher Brown Durand and artists of the Hudson River school view nature and the American land? How did Henry David Thoreau's* Walden *express skepticism over the disruption of nature by the machine?*

▶ Analyze the growth and spread of the factory system in New England and compare the early "piece work" and "putting out" systems with the factory system of production. *How did the transformation from household to factory labor erode the earlier artisan tradition, impose a new industrial discipline on the workforce, and affect the lives of men, women, and children? How did workers respond to the changes? How did the development of interchangeable parts by such inventors as Eli Whitney and Samuel Colt and the machine tool industry contribute to American economic growth in the antebellum era?*

▶ Construct a historical narrative using selections from a variety of primary and secondary sources to analyze reasons for the strikes at Lowell in 1834 and 1836. *How did women use community bonds to mobilize protest in times of crisis? Did the Lowell example influence others? How did immigration affect labor organization in the New England mills?*

▶ Compare the pattern of economic development in the different regions and explain why the North became increasingly associated with industry and finance, the South with plantations and subsistence farms, and the Northwest with family farms, meatpacking and food processing, and the manufacture of agricultural machinery. *What impact did the transportation revolution have on the pattern of economic development in each region? What was its impact on Native Americans?*

▶ Analyze labor conflict during the antebellum period (such as the Lowell strike of 1834, the textile strikes in Rockdale, Pennsylvania, in 1836 and 1842, and the Lynn, Massachusetts, shoemakers' strike in 1860). *How did the perspectives of industrial workers and employers differ? What were the goals of the unions, and how did such groups as owners and managers, state and federal governments, and political parties respond to the workers' demands? How did ethnic, religious, and racial tensions divide the working classes, and what effect, if any, did such conflicts have on the emergence of a unified labor movement?*

Students Should Be Able to:

2B Demonstrate understanding of the first era of American industrialization by:

`5-12` Identifying and explaining the factors that caused rapid urbanization and comparing the new industrialized centers with the old commercial cities. [**Explain historical continuity and change**]

`7-12` Analyzing how rapid urbanization, immigration, and industrialization disrupted the social fabric of early 19th-century cities. [**Analyze cause-and-effect relationships**]

`7-12` Explaining the growth of free African American communities in the cities and analyzing the rise of white racial hostility. [**Examine the influence of ideas**]

`9-12` Comparing popular and high culture in the growing cities. [**Compare and contrast differing sets of ideas**]

Grades 5-6

Examples of student achievement of Standard 2B include:

▶ Analyze historical maps in order to compare the location and size of cities before and after the development of the canals and railroads. *Why did the growth of transportation after 1820 spur the development of cities? Why were so many immigrants coming to America and settling in the cities?*

▶ Draw upon diaries, stories, pictures, newspaper advertisements, historic sites, and records to compare city life between 1840 and 1850 with city life today. Develop a historical argument on such questions as: *Would life in a city of that time have been more or less satisfying than life in a city today? What advantages and disadvantages would urban dwellers have known in jobs, housing, urban crowding, relations among groups (ethnic, racial, religious), attitudes toward immigrants, the availability of schools, public services, health, safety, and cultural activities? How successfully did people deal with urban problems compared with today?*

Grades 7-8

Examples of student achievement of Standard 2B include:

▶ Identify the major cities of the United States in 1800 and compare their size with large urban centers in 1860. Construct a sound historical narrative explaining the forces that caused urbanization. *What accounted for increased emigration from Europe and for the growth of free black communities in the North? To what extent were cities able to meet the demands and problems caused by rapid growth? What issues facing today's cities are similar to those of the mid-19th century?*

▶ Draw upon historical evidence from biographies and other historical sources to construct sound historical assessments of the contributions of individuals such as Benjamin Banneker, Prince Hall, Richard Allen, and Absalom Jones to free black communities. *What explains the growing white hostility they faced in the cites, particularly among new immigrants? How did the African American communities respond?*

Grades 9-12

Examples of student achievement of Standard 2B include:

▸ Draw on a variety of historical sources such as city directories, maps, old city plans, photographs, and newspapers in order to analyze the factors that led to the rapid growth of northern, southern, and western cities such as Boston, New York, Philadelphia, Baltimore, Charleston, New Orleans, Chicago, Cincinnati, Salt Lake City, and San Francisco, or smaller cities such as Paterson (N.J.), Rochester (N.Y.), Lexington (Ky.), and Fall River and Lowell (Mass.).

▸ Draw on several examples of urban conflict in the period 1830-1861 in order to analyze the factors contributing to tensions in cities during the period. *What was the social composition of the city's population in terms of ethnicity, religion, class, and race? Were there discernible differences in terms of where people lived and worked in the city? What were some of the major problems facing the city in the period? Were cities less violent places to live in the mid-19th century than they are today?*

▸ Draw on such sources as the *Dictionary of African American Biography* to explain how former slaves like Richard Allen, Peter Williams, Prince Hall, and Absalom Jones gained their freedom, became instrumental leaders of the burgeoning African American communities in northern cities, and advanced the interests and rights of African Americans.

▸ Explain the appeal of novels, the popularity of the theater for all classes, the minstrel shows, and P.T. Barnum's "American Museum." *Why did the sentimental novels appeal to women? How was Shakespeare transformed by the popular theater? How was P.T. Barnum's "American Museum" different from other museums? Why did it attract large crowds?*

Bells governed the mill worker's day as indicated in a time table of the Lowell Mills, September, 1853. Museum of Textile History, North Andover, MA

Students Should Be Able to:

2C Demonstrate understanding of the rapid growth of slavery after 1800 and how African Americans coped with the "peculiar institution" by:

`5-12` Explaining how the cotton gin and the opening of new lands in the South and West led to the advance of "King Cotton" and to the increased demand for slaves. [**Analyze cause-and-effect relationships**]

`9-12` Analyzing the argument that the institution of slavery retarded the emergence of capitalist institutions and values in the South. [**Evaluate major debates among historians**]

`5-12` Describing the plantation system and the roles of the owner and his family, of hired white workers, and of enslaved African Americans. [**Compare and contrast differing values, behaviors, and institutions**]

`7-12` Identifying the various ways in which African Americans resisted the conditions of their enslavement and analyzing the consequences of violent uprisings. [**Analyze cause-and-effect relationships**]

`7-12` Evaluating how enslaved African Americans used religion and family to create a viable culture to ameliorate the effects of slavery. [**Obtain historical data**]

Grades 5-6

Examples of student achievement of Standard 2C include:

▶ Draw upon historical accounts, diaries, narratives by freed slaves, stories, and other records to compare life among the poor yeomen farm families of the South with life on the southern plantations. *How did life differ for poor farm families (free black and white) of the South, the families of plantation owners, and the enslaved men, women, and children who labored in the great houses, in skilled crafts, and in the fields?*

▶ Draw upon stories such as *The People Could Fly* and Virginia Hamilton's "Carrying the Running Aways," biographies of Harriet Tubman, and the *Autobiography of Frederick Douglass* to develop a historical narration, dramatic reading, or mural depicting the experiences of those who resisted slavery by escaping, the courage of those who helped them, and the terrible costs of being caught.

▶ Draw from children's literature such as the novel *Nightjohn* by Gary Paulsen to examine the human impact of slavery.

▶ Use children's stories such as *Brady* by Jean Fritz, *Drinking Gourd* by Jeanette Winter, *Runaway to Freedom* by Barbara Smucker, and *Get on Board: The Story of the Underground Railroad* by Jim Haskins to examine personal experiences of men and women involved in the Underground Railroad.

Grades 7-8

Examples of student achievement of Standard 2C include:

▶ Analyze the impact of the invention of the cotton gin on the maintenance and spread of slavery.

▶ Construct a historical narrative, graph, or illustrative chart which explains roles and responsibilities of different classes and genders in the plantation system. *How did the plantation system affect family life of slaveholders and of the enslaved? To what extent was the plantation a "self-contained" world?*

▶ Draw upon sources such as slave songs, black spirituals, folklore, and narratives and testimony of freed slaves in order to describe the ways in which enslaved Africans survived an oppressive regime, forged their own culture, and resisted slavery.

▶ Draw from a variety of historical sources such as diaries, autobiographies, court records, handbills and reward posters, folk tales, and political tracts such as David Walker's *Appeal* and Henry Garnet's *Address to the Slaves of the United States of America* to evaluate the effectiveness of various methods of passive and active resistance to slavery. *What factors contributed to the failure of slave conspiracies and revolts such as those of Gabriel Prosser, Denmark Vesey, and Nat Turner? Was passive resistance to slavery a more effective response?*

▶ Use personal accounts of the exploits of individuals such as Henry "Box" Brown, Frederick Douglass, and Harriet Tubman in escaping slavery.

Grades 9-12

Examples of student achievement of Standard 2C include:

▶ Draw upon economic data and historical maps in order to document the expansion of the cotton kingdom between 1801 and 1861, and explain the impact of such factors as the invention of the cotton gin and the opening of new lands in the South and the West.

▶ Develop a historical argument on such questions as: *How did slavery affect the South's economy? How did slavery affect the development of a middle class in the South? What was the extent of slave ownership in the South? Why did many non-slaveholding whites support slavery? Was slavery profitable?*

▶ Draw on a variety of historical and literary sources such as autobiographies, diaries, newspapers, and other periodicals to analyze the plantation system and the consequences for southern society of a hierarchical system based on paternalism and slave labor.

▶ Analyze the major causes and consequences of the conspiracies led by Gabriel Prosser (Virginia, 1800) and Denmark Vesey (South Carolina, 1822), and Nat Turner's rebellion(Virginia, 1831). *What did these events signify about the view of slavery held by those who were enslaved? Why did Nat Turner's rebellion create such widespread consternation throughout the South in particular? What kinds of restrictions on slaves and free blacks were instituted by most southern states in the aftermath of Turner's insurrection?*

▶ Debate why so few church leaders and nonslaveholders in the South spoke out against the internal slave trade that separated countless brothers, sisters, parents, and children.

Students Should Be Able to:

2D Demonstrate understanding of the settlement of the West by:

5-12 Explaining the lure of the West while comparing the illusions of migrants with the reality of the frontier. [**Examine the influence of ideas**]

7-12 Analyzing cultural interactions among diverse groups in the trans-Mississippi region. [**Consider multiple perspectives**]

9-12 Assessing the degree to which political democracy was a characteristic of the West, and evaluating the factors influencing political and social conditions on the frontier. [**Differentiate between historical facts and historical interpretations**]

7-12 Examining the origins and political organization of the Mormons, explaining the motives for their trek west, and evaluating their contributions to the settlement of the West. [**Evidence historical perspectives**]

| Grades 5-6 | **Examples of student achievement of Standard 2D include:** |

▶ Locate and compare the overland trails west to Santa Fe, Oregon, Salt Lake, and California; the trail north from Mexico; and the water routes around the Horn and by way of Panama to California. Draw upon pioneer journals, letters and diaries, newspaper advertisements, paintings and literature to develop a diary, reenact events, or illustrate episodes on the trails.

▶ Analyze why various groups undertook hazardous journeys to the West on the basis of books for young adults such as *Westering* by Alice Putnam, *Beyond the Divide* by Kathryn Lasky, *On to Oregon!* by Honore Morrow, and *Walking up a Rainbow* by Theodore Taylor. *What were the hazards they endured? What goals did they hope to achieve? How accurate are these fictionalized accounts of the journey west?*

▶ Identify Joseph Smith and Brigham Young and explain why the Mormons headed west.

▶ Analyze these great movements of settlers from the perspective of Native Americans on the plains and in California and from the perspective of Mexicans already living in these territories. *How did earlier peaceful relations of Native Americans with the settlers change as more and more newcomers arrived, bringing diseases, killing the buffalo, and upsetting their way of life? What was the cost to Mexican rancheros of California and New Mexico, who lost most of their land grants to Americans following the Mexican Cession?*

| Grades 7-8 | **Examples of student achievement of Standard 2D include:** |

▶ Draw evidence from contemporary periodicals, diaries, journals, folklore, music, and art to compare the dream of a western utopia with the realities of everyday life on the frontier. *How did the image of the West depicted in popular folklore differ from everyday life on the frontier?*

▶ Draw upon evidence from a variety of sources including biographies and historical novels to explain the interaction of different cultural groups in the West. *To what extent were the motives for settlement in the West similar among different groups of people? What factors brought people together in a cooperative spirit? What factors caused disagreements and open conflicts?*

▶ Draw upon a variety of primary and secondary sources including diaries, journals, biographies, and the art of C.C.A. Christensen, to construct a historical narrative explaining the founding of the Church of Latter Day Saints, the struggles that led Mormons to establish communities in Utah, and their contributions to settlement of the West. *What religious practice set Mormons apart from other religious communities? How were the Mormons able to turn the desert region of the Salt Lake basin into thriving farms? To what extent do we benefit from these contributions today?*

▶ Use novels such as *West against the Wind* by Liza Ketchum Murrow to trace the personal story of a family moving west.

Grades 9-12

Examples of student achievement of Standard 2D include:

▶ Describe the cultural characteristics of such diverse groups in the trans-Mississippi West as Chinese, Lakota, Comanche, Zuni, Métis, and Hispanics.

▶ Assemble the evidence and prepare a narrative analyzing one example of cultural conflict between different peoples and societies in the Cis-Mississippi or Trans-Mississippi West in the period 1801-1861. *What arguments did white settlers in the West advance to expropriate Native American lands? What factors contributed to the disunity of the Plains Indians? What obstacles did they pose to white expansion? What conflicts arose between Hispanic and Anglo settlers in the Southwest and California and between Anglo and Chinese settlers in California?*

▶ Analyze the impact of the Second Great Awakening and religious revivals of the early 19th century on Joseph Smith and his followers in the "burned over district" of western New York. *How did Mormons' beliefs differ from the major Protestant denominations? Why were the Mormons persecuted and forced to migrate westward? How did the Mormon political organization, settlement pattern around the Great Salt Lake, and relations with Native Americans differ from others in the West?*

▶ Analyze the debate among historians over the Frederick Jackson Turner thesis on "The Significance of the Frontier in American History." *Was political democracy characteristic of the West? What effect did frontier conditions have on Mexican Americans in New Mexico and California? How were gender roles defined in the West? If the West was a "crucible for democracy," why did so many western states in the 1840s and 1850s initiate laws prohibiting the immigration of free blacks?*

▶ Using diaries and letters of women in the West, describe the roles they played, the hardships they faced, and the importance of family ties in the development of the West. *How were gender roles defined in the West? Did gender roles differ among different cultural groups?*

STANDARD 3

Students Should Understand: *The extension, restriction, and reorganization of political democracy after 1800.*

Students Should Be Able to:

3A Demonstrate understanding of the changing character of American political life in "the age of the common man" by:

`7-12` Relating the increasing popular participation in state and national politics to the spreading idea that adult white males were entitled to political participation. **[Identify relevant historical antecedents]**

`7-12` Explaining the contradictions between the movement for universal white male suffrage and the disenfranchisement of free African Americans. **[Evaluate the implementation of a decision]**

`7-12` Analyzing the influence of the West on the heightened emphasis on equality in the political process. **[Analyze cause-and-effect relationships]**

`9-12` Explaining the combination of sectional, cultural, economic, and political factors that contributed to the formation of the Democratic, Whig, and "Know-Nothing" parties. **[Analyze multiple causation]**

`9-12` Evaluating the importance of state and local issues, the rise of interest-group politics, and the style of campaigning in increasing voter participation. **[Compare and contrast differing sets of ideas]**

`5-12` Explaining why the election of Andrew Jackson was considered a victory for the "common man." **[Assess the importance of the individual in history]**

`7-12` Analyzing how Jackson's veto of the U.S. Bank recharter and his actions in the nullification crisis contributed to the revolt against "King Andrew" and the rise of the Whig party. **[Analyze cause-and-effect relationships]**

Grades 5-6

Examples of student achievement of Standard 3A include:

▶ Draw evidence from journals, diaries, and caricatures of President Jackson's inauguration to explain why his administration is said to have supported the interests of the "common man." *What do stories of the inaugural parties and open house at the White House tell about Jackson and the people who supported him? What was the "spoils system"? Was Jackson interested in providing the "common man" the opportunities to serve in government?*

▶ Explain the "King Andrew the First, Born to Rule" cartoon. *What are the symbols used in the cartoon? Why is Jackson pictured as a king standing on the Constitution? What does the cartoonist say about Jackson? Who would be most likely to support this view of Jackson? Is it an accurate picture of the Jackson presidency?*

Grades 7-8

Examples of student achievement of Standard 3A include :

▶ Construct a historical narrative that examines the changes in electoral qualifications of adult white males. *What accounts for changes in state policies regarding voter qualifications? What impact did these changes have on local, state, and national elections? To what extent did the style of political campaigns change with the increase of voter participation and the rise of regional interest groups? Why were women excluded from electoral reforms?*

▶ Draw upon the arguments used to support universal white male suffrage to illustrate the paradox in continued disenfranchisement of free African American males. *What arguments were made to justify white male suffrage? Why were these same arguments not applied to free African Americans in most northern states?*

▶ Draw from primary and secondary sources including letters, speeches, and biographies, to construct a historical narrative or oral presentation evaluating the influence of the West and western politicians in supporting equality of opportunity.

▶ Construct a historical argument evaluating opposing views on Jackson's position on the bank recharter and nullification issues. *What were the political motives behind proponents and opponents of the U.S. Bank recharter? Was Jackson's position on the bank a reflection of the will of the "common man?" Was Jackson or Calhoun more in line with the principles of Jefferson and Madison during the nullification crisis? What might have happened if South Carolina had succeeded in nullifying the tariff?*

Grades 9-12

Examples of student achievement of Standard 3A include:

▶ Interpret data presented in political maps of the United States and voting data for the 1800, 1832, and 1852 elections in order to support a sound historical argument on such questions as: *Which states and sections experienced the most significant growth in population and electoral votes in the period 1800-1832 and 1832-1852? Why? What factors account for the changing percentage of total white male population voting in the presidential elections of 1800, 1832, and 1852?*

▶ Analyze how George Caleb Bingham's paintings *Verdict of the People* and/or *County Election Number Two* reflect the changing character of American politics between the first and second party systems.

▶ Analyze how the selection of candidates by the political parties and the style of political campaigns changed in the 1830s and 1840s. *How did such changes influence regional interest group politics and affect the turnout of voters?*

▶ Interpret documentary evidence such as party platforms, political speeches, broadsides, and cartoons between 1820 and 1852 to illustrate how major political parties, such as the National Republicans, Democrats, Whigs, and "Know-Nothings," stood on paramount issues of the day.

▶ Analyze how Jackson's actions in the bank war and the nullification controversy affected voters supporting the Democratic party and contributed to the rise of the Whig party.

Students Should Be Able to:

3B Demonstrate understanding of how the debates over slavery influenced politics and sectionalism by:

5-12 Explaining the Missouri Compromise and evaluating its political consequences. **[Identify issues and problems in the past]**

7-12 Explaining how tariff policy and issues of states' rights influenced party development and promoted sectional differences in the antebellum period. **[Analyze cause-and-effect relationships]**

7-12 Analyzing how the debates over slavery — from agitation over the "gag rule" of the late 1830s through the war with Mexico — strained national cohesiveness and fostered rising sectionalism. **[Compare and contrast differing sets of ideas]**

Grades 5-6

Examples of student achievement of Standard 3B include:

▶ Explain the Missouri Compromise. On a map of the United States, draw the Missouri Compromise line and compare the land areas open to slavery to those in which slavery was prohibited.

▶ List the issues which divided the North and South before the Civil War. *What compromises would you propose to settle the differences?*

Grades 7-8

Examples of student achievement of Standard 3B include:

▶ Construct a historical argument or conduct a debate supporting or opposing the Missouri Compromise of 1820. *Why was there such bitter argument over the admission of Missouri to the Union? Why did the Missouri Compromise fail to resolve the debate over slavery? Was the compromise over the admission of Missouri an appropriate response? How would you have proposed to solve the problem?*

▶ Devise simulated political platforms reflecting the position of Whigs and Democrats on important issues in 1832. *What party positions had special appeal to different sections of the country? What platform issues would have special appeal to different regions?*

▶ Assemble evidence from various sources to construct a historical narrative or position paper on the impact of the debate over slavery from the late 1830s to the Compromise of 1850. *Why did certain states oppose the Wilmot Proviso? Should slavery or involuntary servitude have been permitted in territory acquired after the war with Mexico? Did Congress have the constitutional right to interfere with slavery in states where it was established? Did Congress have the right to prohibit slavery in the territories? To what extent did questions such as these inflame sectional interests?*

Grades 9-12

Examples of student achievement of Standard 3B include:

▶ Analyze the issues created by the Missouri controversy which Thomas Jefferson characterized as "a firebell in the night," sounding for him the death knell of the Union. *How did the free white male population of the South compare to that of the North in 1800, 1820, and 1840? What political dividend did the slave states gain as a result of the three-fifths rule in 1800, 1820, and 1840? How did southern spokesmen attempt to compensate for the minority status of the South's political position in the House of Representatives vis-à-vis the North in the period 1819 to 1845? How did Calhoun's argument in favor of a "concurrent majority" attempt to deal with this imbalance?*

What was the constitutional and legal argument asserting that Congress had the right to exclude slavery in a territory? What was the constitutional and legal argument asserting that Congress did not have the right to exclude slavery in a territory? How was the Missouri controversy finally resolved and with what results?

▶ Draw on a variety of historical sources and documents in order to analyze the reasons why the Mexican War strained national cohesiveness and fostered intraparty squabbles and sectional conflict. *Which policy, "free soil" as outlined in the Wilmot Proviso or Lewis Cass's espousal of "popular sovereignty," best served the interests of the United States? How did the outcome of the Mexican War exacerbate sectional tensions? How did "Barnburners" differ from "Hunkers?" How did "Conscience Whigs" differ from "Cotton Whigs?" What was the basis for the Free Soil party? What did all of this indicate about the impact of the Mexican War on politics?*

▶ Draw on historical data to contrast the positions of northern antislavery advocates and southern proslavery spokesmen on the issues of race, chattel slavery, wage slavery, the nature of the Union, and states' rights. Then develop a sound historical argument explaining how such differences undermined national political parties in the antebellum period, and with what consequences for national unity.

▶ Draw upon evidence for the major sectional issues, debates, and compromises over slavery between 1819 and 1857 in order to construct a historical argument or debate the question: *Was the rupture of the Union and eventual civil war probable or could it have been avoided?*

"There shall be neither slavery nor involuntary servitude in the said territory, otherwise than in punishment of crimes whereof the party shall have been duly convicted . . ."

NORTHWEST ORDINANCE, ARTICLE 6, 1787

"That, as an express and fundamental condition to the acquisition of any territory from the Republic of Mexico by the United States, by virtue of any treaty which may be negotiated between them, and to the use by the Executive of the moneys herein appropriated, neither slavery nor involuntary servitude shall ever exist in any part of said territory, except for crime, whereof the party shall first be duly convicted."

WILMOT PROVISO, 1846

STANDARD 4

Students Should Understand: *The sources and character of reform movements in the antebellum period and what the reforms accomplished or failed to accomplish.*

Students Should Be Able to:

4A Demonstrate understanding of the abolitionist movement by:

7-12 Analyzing the impact of the Haitian Revolution and the ending of the foreign slave trade on African Americans. [**Examine the influence of ideas**]

7-12 Analyzing the changing ideas about race and nationality, and assessing the influence of proslavery and antislavery ideologies. [**Analyze cause-and-effect relationships**]

7-12 Explaining the fundamental beliefs of abolitionism and comparing the antislavery positions of the "immediatists" and "gradualists" within the movement. [**Consider multiple perspectives**]

9-12 Comparing the positions of African American and white abolitionists on the issue of the African American's place in society. [**Compare and contrast differing sets of ideas and values**]

Grades 5-6

Examples of student achievement of Standard 4A include:

▶ Develop a biographical sketch of one of the major African American or white leaders of the abolitionist movement. *What did the leader work to accomplish? Why was he or she important and why do we remember this leader today?*

▶ Compare the arguments of those who opposed and those who defended slavery.

▶ Draw upon literature and slave narratives, such as "Carrying the Running Aways" by Virginia Hamilton, in order to analyze the great risks and heroism of those who fled to freedom in the North and of those who helped them escape by means of the Underground Railroad.

Grades 7-8

Examples of student achievement of Standard 4A include:

▶ Draw upon historical accounts of the Denmark Vesey conspiracy in order to construct a historical narrative examining the influence of the Republic of Haiti on slavery in the United States. Consider such factors as: *Why did southern political leaders oppose Haitian independence? What influence did the Haitian Revolution have on African Americans?*

▶ Draw upon primary and secondary sources to compare arguments used to defend slavery in the 18th and 19th centuries. *How did the arguments change over time? What accounts for this change?*

▶ Interpret documentary evidence from abolitionist literature and biographical studies to construct a historical narrative, debate, or persuasive argument which illustrates and compares different viewpoints in the abolitionist movement. *Were the fundamental beliefs of abolitionists consistent with the Constitution? Did abolitionists advocate the fundamental equality of African Americans? To what extent did abolitionists agree on strategies to end slavery? What were the issues that divided the abolitionists? Why did William Lloyd Garrison and Frederick Douglass reject the goals of the American Colonization Society? How did Quaker abolitionists such as Benjamin Lundy respond to David Walker's* Appeal?

Grades 9-12

Examples of student achievement of Standard 4A include:

▶ Draw on the arguments of southern spokesmen such as John C. Calhoun, Thomas R. Dew, George Fitzhugh, and James H. Hammond, in order to prepare a legal brief defending chattel slavery from the perspectives of the 19th-century southern slaveholder. *What arguments did southern spokesmen advance to defend the institution of slavery as a positive good? Why did Fitzhugh believe chattel slavery to be superior to the "wage slavery" of the North?*

▶ Draw upon historical evidence of the growing hostility toward free blacks in the antebellum North in order to develop a historical argument explaining the following statement by Alexis de Tocqueville: "The Negro is free, but he can share neither the rights, nor the pleasures, nor the labor, nor the afflictions, nor the tomb of him whose equal he has been declared to be; and he cannot meet him upon fair terms in life or in death." Consider such evidence as the laws enacted by several northern states barring the immigration of free blacks, the urban anti-black riots in northern cities such as Philadelphia and Cincinnati, and Pennsylvania's 1837 state constitution denying the vote to African Americans. Consider in what specific ways many of the restrictions on free African Americans in the North and South during the antebellum era violated the Constitution.

▶ Analyze the ways in which leaders such as Paul Cuffe, Frederick Douglass, Henry Highland Garnet, Harriet Tubman, William Still, Sojourner Truth, and David Walker fought for the rights of their fellow African Americans.

▶ Draw on such sources as *Notable American Women, The Dictionary of American Biography*, and *The Dictionary of African-American Biography* in order to contrast the positions of African American abolitionists and white abolitionists on the issue of the African American's place in American society. *How did the strategies of abolitionist leaders differ? What were the major differences between "immediatists" and "gradualists?" To what extent did black and white abolitionists cooperate, and what was their view of each other? What forces and arguments did the abolitionists confront in the North and the South?*

Students Should Be Able to:

4B Demonstrate understanding of how the Second Great Awakening, transcendentalism, and utopianism affected reform by:

`5-12` Explaining the importance of the Second Great Awakening and assessing the importance of its principal leaders. [**Examine the influence of ideas**]

`7-12` Assessing the impact of the Second Great Awakening on antebellum issues such as public education, temperance, women's suffrage, abolition, and commercialization. [**Analyze cause-and-effect relationships**]

`7-12` Analyzing ideas concerning the individual, society, and nature expressed in the literary works of major transcendentalists. [**Examine the influence of ideas**]

`9-12` Identifying the major utopian experiments and analyzing the reasons for their formation. [**Consider multiple perspectives**]

`7-12` Examining the relevance of the Great Awakeners' ideas for contemporary American society. [**Hypothesize the influence of the past**]

Grades 5-6 | Examples of student achievement of Standard 4B include:

▶ Draw upon stories and historical accounts in order to describe and explain the great religious revival that swept across the nation in the early 19th century. *What was it like to attend one of the great camp meetings that drew thousands of people to hear such famous preachers as Charles Finney and Peter Cartwright? What was their message? Why did they believe that if each individual took responsibility for living a good life, all of society could be better? How did the Second Great Awakening influence reform movements?*

Grades 7-8 | Examples of student achievement of Standard 4B include:

▶ Assess the importance of the revivalist spirit of the Second Great Awakening and explain its impact on American society by constructing a historical narrative or argument on such questions as: How did the Second Great Awakening advance social reform? What was the significance of Charles Finney's statement: *"Away with the idea that Christians can remain neutral and keep still, and yet enjoy the . . . blessings of God"*?

▶ Drawing from current social issues and contemporary reform movements, assess the relevance of the Second Great Awakening in contemporary society.

▶ Draw upon the literary works and actions of such major Transcendentalists as Emerson, Thoreau, and Whitman in order to develop a historical narrative or argument on such questions as: *Why were the Transcendentalists and their themes of self-reliance, optimism, concern for nature, and social equality popular at this time? To what extent did they reflect the spirit of early 19th-century Americans? To what extent did they influence American ideals and social reform?*

▶ Compile a 20th-century version of *The Dial* which applies the philosophy of Transcendentalism to contemporary issues.

▶ Construct an evaluative chart listing major utopian communities of the era and their objectives, and appraising the degree of success in attaining their goals.

▶ Analyze why utopian communities sprang up in such numbers in these years. *What does the popularity of utopian communities tell you about early 19th-century society?*

Grades 9-12

Examples of student achievement of Standard 4B include:

▶ Draw on historical sources to analyze the impact of the Second Great Awakening on the following reform movements: public education, temperance, women's suffrage, and abolitionism. *What were the major goals and ideology of Great Awakening leaders such as Charles Finney and what was his impact on ordinary people? How did the belief in individual responsibility for salvation and millennialism influence the reform movements? What was the role of moral suasion, social control, and compromise in the particular reform movement?*

▶ Draw on examples of the work of Transcendentalists such as Ralph Waldo Emerson, Henry David Thoreau, Theodore Parker, Bronson Alcott, and Margaret Fuller in order to examine their views concerning individualism, society, the nature of good and evil, authority, tradition, and reform; and compare their ideas with those of evangelical Protestants such as Charles Finney and Lyman Beecher. *What were the similarities and differences in their respective views on the role of the individual and the nature of reform? How were the views of Nathaniel Hawthorne and Herman Melville different from those of the Transcendentalists?*

▶ Draw on a variety of historical sources to describe the origin, beliefs, approximate size, and significance of one of the following utopian communities: the Shakers; the Oneida community; New Harmony; and Charles Fourier's utopian socialist communities. *How was the community similar or different from the Transcendentalists in terms of the rights of the individual, the relationship between the individual and the community, and the nature of society?*

Frances Wright (1795-1852), social reformer. Engraving by J. C. Buttre, reproduced from the Dictionary of American Portraits, *published by Dover Publications, 1967*

Students Should Be Able to:

4C Demonstrate understanding of changing gender roles and the roles of different groups of women by:

`9-12` Comparing gender roles in the North, South, and West in the antebellum period. [**Compare and contrast differing values**]

`5-12` Analyzing the roles of women in the reform movements of education, abolition, temperance, and women's suffrage. [**Examine the influence of ideas**]

`7-12` Comparing the changing roles of women of different racial, regional, and social groups and their involvement in the reform movements of the antebellum era. [**Compare and contrast differing sets of ideas**]

`7-12` Analyzing the goals of the 1848 Seneca Falls "Declaration of Sentiments" and evaluating its impact on society. [**Reconstruct the literal meaning of a historical passage**]

`9-12` Evaluating the links between the antebellum women's movement for equality and 20th-century feminism. [**Hypothesize the influence of the past**]

Grades 5-6

Examples of student achievement of Standard 4C include:

▶ Draw upon biographies, stories, history books, and encyclopedias to create a historical narrative, mural, or diary depicting the struggles and contributions of one of the women who was prominent in the reform movements of the antebellum era.

▶ Analyze why some women sought the vote.

▶ Create a speech, newspaper editorial, "letter to the editor" for a classroom newspaper, or a role play reenacting the struggle for one of the reforms women sought at that time: the vote for women, temperance, free public education, and the abolition of slavery.

▶ Draw upon children's stories such as *Bloomers!* by Rhoda Blumberg to investigate how fashion became involved in the movement for women's rights.

Grades 7-8

Examples of student achievement of Standard 4C include:

▶ Draw upon evidence from biographies, speeches, journals, and caricatures to evaluate the leadership role women played in major reform movements of the period. *Who were the women who helped various reform movements and utopian communities during this era? How did the public at large view women who held leadership roles? What is meant by the "cult of domesticity"? Did it prevent women from taking a more active role in society? What is the status of the "cult of domesticity" in society today?"*

▶ Drawing from historical evidence, evaluate the Seneca Falls "Declaration of Sentiments" as a response to the inequities of the period. *How effective was the use of the language in the Declaration of Independence in expressing the sentiments of women? How successful were women in gaining a redress of these grievances? If*

Elizabeth Cady Stanton were alive today, would she construct a new "Declaration of Sentiments"? If so, what would she list as major grievances?

▶ Utilize books for young adults such as *Mother, Aunt Susan, and Me* by William Jacobs to examine the efforts to gain equal rights for women.

Grades 9-12

Examples of student achievement of Standard 4C include:

▶ Draw on biographical, historical, and literary sources to examine the pivotal contribution of women in the reform movements of the antebellum period: *What were the contributions of Catharine Beecher, Emma Willard, and Mary Lyon in education? Of Dorothea Dix, Fanny Wright, Margaret Fuller, and Amelia Bloomer in social welfare? Of Angelina and Sarah Grimké, Sojourner Truth, Harriett Beecher Stowe, Harriet Tubman, and Prudence Crandall in abolitionism?*

▶ Utilizing such sources as diaries, letters, newspaper accounts, and reminiscences, compare gender roles in different geographical regions and across class, ethnic, racial, and religious lines in the antebellum period. *How did gender roles change in the antebellum period, and how did such changes affect different classes of men and women? Under what circumstances was the notion of "separate spheres" challenged?*

▶ Compare the Seneca Falls "Declaration of Sentiments" (1848) with the Declaration of Independence, noting the similarities and differences in language and style. *Why did Elizabeth Cady Stanton model the "Declaration of Sentiments" after the Declaration of Independence? What specific political, social, economic, and legal grievances are outlined in the document? What objectives for women were included in the twelve resolutions at the end of the "Declaration of Sentiments"?*

▶ Analyze the connection between the evangelical movement and the idea of southern womanhood. *To what extent did southern women endorse the "Declaration of Sentiments?"*

▶ Compare the women's struggle of the early 19th century with women's status today. *Have the goals and objectives presented in the "Declaration of Sentiments" now been achieved? In what respects was the antebellum women's movement similar to and different from 20th-century feminism?*

"We hold these truths to be self-evident: that all men and women are created equal; that they are endowed by their Creator with certain inalienable rights; that among these are life, liberty, and the pursuit of happiness. . ."

DECLARATION OF SENTIMENTS,
SENECA FALLS, NEW YORK, 1848

Teacher Gloria Sesso with students, Half Hollow Hill High School East, New York

ERA 5

Civil War and Reconstruction (1850-1877)

The Civil War was perhaps the most momentous event in American history. The survival of the United States as one nation was at risk, and on the outcome of the war depended the nation's ability to bring to reality the ideals of liberty, equality, justice, and human dignity.

The war put constitutional government to its severest test as a long festering debate over the power of the federal government versus state rights reached a climax. Its enormously bloody outcome preserved the Union while releasing not only four million African Americans but the entire nation from the oppressive weight of slavery. The war can be studied in several ways: as the final, violent phase in a conflict of two regional subcultures; as the breakdown of a democratic political system; as the climax of several decades of social reform; and as a pivotal chapter in American racial history. In studying the Civil War, students have many opportunities to study heroism and cowardice, triumph and tragedy, and hardship, pain, grief, and death wrought by conflict. Another important topic is how the war necessarily obliged both northern and southern women to adapt to new and unsettling situations.

As important as the war itself, once the Union prevailed, was the tangled problem of Reconstruction. Through examining the 13th, 14th, and 15th amendments — a fundamental revision of the Constitution — students can see how African Americans hoped for full equality. They can assess the various plans for Reconstruction that were contested passionately. The retreat from Radical Reconstruction — the first attempt at establishing a biracial democracy — should be of concern to all students. They should learn how southern white resistance and the withdrawal of federal supervision resulted in the "redemption" of the South through the disfranchisement of African Americans, the end of their involvement in Reconstruction state legislatures greater racial separation, the rise of white intimidation and violence, and the creation of black rural peonage.

Balancing the success and failures of Reconstruction should test the abilities of all students. Too much stress on the unfinished agenda of the period can obscure the great changes actually wrought. The legacies of the era of war and reconstruction needs to be considered with reference to the North and West as well as the South.

Overview

Standard 1: The causes of the Civil War

Standard 2: The course and character of the Civil War and its effects on the American people

Standard 3: How various reconstruction plans succeeded or failed

STANDARD 1

Students Should Understand: *The causes of the Civil War.*

Students Should Be Able to:

1A **Demonstrate understanding of how the North and South differed and how politics and ideologies led to the Civil War by:**

[7-12] Identifying and explaining the economic, social, and cultural differences between the North and the South. [**Compare and contrast differing values and institutions**]

[9-12] Analyzing the reasons for the disruption of the second American party system in the 1850s and explaining how they led to the ascent of the Republican party. [**Analyze multiple causation**]

[7-12] Explaining how events after the Compromise of 1850 contributed to increasing sectional polarization. [**Analyze cause-and-effect relationships**]

[7-12] Analyzing the importance of the "free labor" ideology in the North and its appeal in preventing the further extension of slavery in the new territories. [**Examine the influence of ideas**]

[5-12] Explaining the causes of the Civil War and evaluating the importance of slavery as a principal cause of the conflict. [**Compare competing historical narratives**]

[7-12] Charting the secession of the southern states, explaining the process and reasons for secession. [**Analyze cause-and-effect relationships**]

Grades 5-6	**Examples of student achievement of Standard 1A include:**

▶ Locate northern and southern states on a map, describe their geographic features and resources, and compare northern industries and agricultural products with those in the South.

▶ Draw upon letters, stories, and pictures to describe views held by people in the largely rural South with its agricultural economy and slavery and the industrial North, with its industry and small family farms.

▶ Draw upon accounts such as Gwen Everett's *John Brown, One Man against Slavery,* Ann Turner's *Nettie's Trip to the South,* and the writings of Frederick Douglass, Harriet Beecher Stowe, and William Lloyd Garrison to explain the growing influence of abolitionists. Develop a skit or create InfoCubes of family life and children's roles under slavery.

Grades 7-8

Examples of student achievement of Standard 1A include:

▶ Construct a balance sheet identifying the social and economic differences between the North and the South on the eve of the Civil War. *How did the free labor system of the North differ from that of the South? To what extent did the different social and economic convictions contribute to tension between the North and the South?*

▶ Construct a time line listing the events from the Compromise of 1850 through John Brown's raid on Harper's Ferry, and write a persuasive speech, create simulated newspaper editorials, or prepare a position paper for a debate in order to clarify sectional issues surrounding these events.

▶ Interpret documentary evidence from a variety of sources to construct an argument which marshals historical evidence on such questions as: *To what extent was slavery the primary cause of the Civil War? What other issues led to the conflict?*

▶ Appraise the effectiveness of President Buchanan's leadership during the secession crisis and compare it with that of President Lincoln.

Grades 9-12

Examples of student achievement of Standard 1A include:

▶ Examine the political and sectional conflicts over slavery and compare how the Missouri Compromise, Wilmot Proviso, Kansas-Nebraska Act, and the Dred Scott case polarized the North and South. *How did the advocates of each position justify their point of view? What were the advantages and disadvantages of each position? Why? Was secession inevitable following passage of the Kansas-Nebraska Act?*

▶ Analyze the Supreme Court's decision in *Dred Scott* v. *Sandford* (1857). Compare the main points of the Court's decision presented by Chief Justice Taney with Justice Benjamin Curtis's dissent. *How do the issues and the arguments of this case reflect the controversy over slavery that led to the Civil War?*

▶ Analyze the party platforms in the election of 1860 and the reasons why people voted as they did. *Was the Republican party platform and Lincoln's election a real threat to southern states' rights?*

▶ Contrast the leadership of President Buchanan and President Lincoln during the secession crisis. *Might Buchanan have avoided a more serious crisis had he adopted sterner measures following South Carolina's decision to secede? Is it justifiable to call Lincoln "the railsplitter who split the nation"? Should he have supported the Crittenden Compromise? Should he have attempted to supply Fort Sumter? How did Lincoln's First Inaugural Address reflect both a "carrot and stick approach" to southerners?*

▶ Analyze the southern justification for secession. *How did southerners use the Declaration of Independence to support their position? What areas of the South remained bastions of Unionism throughout the war?*

▶ Construct an argument or debate using historical evidence to support or reject the following proposition: *The Civil War was an unavoidable result of sectional differences.*

STANDARD 2

Students Should Understand: *The course and character of the Civil War and its effects on the American people.*

Students Should Be Able to:

2A **Demonstrate understanding of how the resources of the Union and Confederacy affected the course of the war by:**

7-12 Comparing the human resources of the Union and the Confederacy at the beginning of the Civil War and assessing the tactical advantages of each side. [**Utilize visual and mathematical data**]

5-12 Identifying the innovations in military technology and explaining their impact on humans, property, and the final outcome of the war. [**Utilize visual and mathematical data**]

5-12 Evaluating how political, military, and diplomatic leadership affected the outcome of the war. [**Assess the importance of the individual in history**]

7-12 Evaluating provisions of the Emancipation Proclamation, Lincoln's reasons for issuing it, and its significance. [**Examine the influence of ideas**]

9-12 Describing the position of the major Indian nations during the Civil War and explaining the effects of the war upon these nations. [**Reconstruct patterns of historical succession and duration**]

Grades 5-6

Examples of student achievement of Standard 2A include:

▶ Explain how the military leaders and resources of the Union and the Confederacy affected the course and outcome of the Civil War. Compare population, armies, and leaders of the Confederacy with those of the Union at the beginning of the war.

▶ Draw upon historical accounts, diaries, literature, and songs to describe conditions in the Confederacy and Union.

▶ Explain why the Civil War is called the "first modern war." Illustrate innovations such as: communication by telegraph, extended railroad lines, observation balloons, ironclad ships, submarines, repeating and breechloading arms. *Did the new technology give the soldiers a better chance in battle? Did technological innovations make war more devastating?*

▶ Explain the reasons why Abraham Lincoln issued his wartime Emancipation Proclamation. Describe public reaction to it in the North and South.

▶ Locate and label major areas of combat on a historical map. Explore local resources for Civil War history, battle sites, memorabilia, and first-hand accounts. Plan a hypothetical "class trip" and map a selected route of one of the military campaigns.

Grades 7-8

Examples of student achievement of Standard 2A include:

▶ Draw upon statistical information from charts and graphs, topographic maps, and other historical sources to construct arguments that compare the economic, technological, and human resources of the Union with those of the Confederacy.

▶ Draw upon Stephen Crane's *Red Badge of Courage* and Michael Shaara's *The Killer Angels,* paintings, photographs, art prints, biographies, and historical narratives in order to evaluate the importance of military technology and to appraise its effect on combatants.

▶ Construct a historical narrative explaining how major battles contributed to the outcome of the war.

▶ Analyze the Emancipation Proclamation and assess its impact on the outcome of the Civil War. *What were President Lincoln's reasons for issuing the Emancipation Proclamation? Did the Emancipation Proclamation affect the foreign recognition of the Confederacy?*

Grades 9-12

Examples of student achievement of Standard 2A include:

▶ Draw on a variety of biographical and historical accounts in order to contrast the wartime leadership of Jefferson Davis and Abraham Lincoln and prepare a sound historical narrative explaining the importance of presidential leadership in the outcome of the war. *How did their leadership styles contrast? Did Davis's military experience make a difference in his leadership? How did Lincoln's sense of humor and pragmatism affect his leadership? Which men exemplified better presidential leadership?*

▶ Analyze the reasons for the impact of the Emancipation Proclamation in transforming the goals of the Civil War. *How did the Emancipation Proclamation transform the goals of the Civil War? How does A.E. Lamb's painting,* The Emancipation Proclamation *portray the theme of the proclamation?*

▶ Explain the meaning of the Gettysburg Address and analyze its significance as one of the most effective political speeches in our nation's history. *What did Lincoln say the Declaration of Independence meant? Did Lincoln change the meaning of the Declaration or explain its true vision? How did Lincoln relate the Constitution to the Declaration?*

▶ Explain how the "hammering campaigns" of Generals Grant and Sherman affected the outcome of the war. *Did the South's emphasis on the eastern theater doom the Confederacy? What was the impact of the Civil War on the trans-Mississippi West?*

▶ Draw upon historical sources in order to assess the varied Native American responses to the Civil War. *How were Native Americans in the West affected by the Civil War? What were the internal conflicts among the "Five Civilized Tribes" regarding their support for the Union or Confederacy? What were the long-term consequences for them once the North emerged victorious?*

Students Should Be Able to:

2B Demonstrate understanding of the social experience of the war on the battlefield and homefront by:

`7-12` Comparing the motives for fighting and the daily life experiences of Confederate with those of white and African American Union soldiers. **[Evidence historical perspectives]**

`9-12` Analyzing the reasons for the northern draft riots. **[Analyze multiple causation]**

`9-12` Evaluating the need for the Union to curb wartime civil liberties. **[Consider multiple perspectives]**

`5-12` Comparing women's homefront and battlefront roles in the Union and the Confederacy. **[Compare and contrast differing sets of ideas]**

`5-12` Explaining the effects of the Civil War on civilians and identifying the human costs of the war in the North and the South. **[Evidence historical perspectives]**

Grades 5-6

Examples of student achievement of Standard 2B include:

▶ Explain how the Civil War changed the lives of American women, men, and children by comparing personal accounts, letters, and photographs. Use resources such as Virginia Hamilton's *The People Could Fly*; Patricia Lee Gauch's *Thunder at Gettysburg, A Child's Account of the Battle of Gettysburg*; and F. N. Monjo's *The Vicksburg Veteran*.

▶ Draw from diaries, letters, and stories about the lives of women like Clara Barton, Harriet Tubman, and Rose Greenhow to show how the war affected the lives of women. *What responsibilities did women take on at home during the war? What role did women play on the battlefield?*

▶ Explain the motives of fighting men in the Civil War by examining documentary and literary accounts such as Milton Meltzer's *The Black Americans: A History in Their Own Words* and novels by Peter Burchard such as *Jed, The Deserter, North by Night*, and *Bimby*. *What reasons might have been given by Confederate or Union soldiers for fighting in the Civil War? What were the motives of African American soldiers? Why were African American soldiers in special danger during the war?*

Grades 7-8

Examples of student achievement of Standard 2B include:

▶ Use historical fiction such as *The Slopes of War* by N.A. Perez, *Thunder on the Tennessee* by Clifton Wisler, *Rifles for Watie* by Harold Keith, and *The 290* by Scott O'Dell to compare the experiences of Union and Confederate soldiers. *How were the motives that compelled Union and Confederate soldiers similar or different? To what extent did these motives change as the war progressed?*

▶ Use biographies and visual depictions of battles such as the Kurz and Allison prints of Fort Wagner and Fort Pillow to compare the experiences of African American and white Union soldiers. Draw upon excerpts from the movie *Glory* and books such as *Between Two Fires: Black Soldiers in the Civil War* and *Which Way*

Freedom by Joyce Hansen to appraise the contributions of African American soldiers during the war.

▶ Draw upon historical evidence to construct a narrative illustrating different perspectives on conscription during the Civil War and Union provisions for avoidance of service. *What alternatives to the draft, if any, were opened to conscientious objectors such as Quakers or members of the Shaker communities? What policy should be taken today towards conscientious objectors?*

▶ Drawing upon a variety of sources including letters, biographies, and visuals, construct a skit or oral presentation which accurately evaluates the role and contribution of women on both sides of the conflict.

▶ Explain the effects of divided loyalties during the Civil War using historical fiction such as *Hew Against the Grain* by Betty Sue Cummings and *Across Five Aprils* by Irene Hunt.

Grades 9-12

Examples of student achievement of Standard 2B include:

▶ Drawing on a variety of historical sources, develop a historical narrative analyzing the treatment of African American soldiers in the Union army and Confederacy during the Civil War. *How was the concept of liberty viewed by African Americans? How did Confederate leaders determine to deal with African American soldiers? What happened to African American Union soldiers at Fort Pillow? What reasons account for the decision to differentiate between soldiers' pay for white troops and African American soldiers in the Union Army before June 1864?*

▶ Analyze the causes and consequences of the New York City draft riots in July 1863 and the irony of African Americans fighting for liberty and democracy at Fort Wagner a few days after the outbreak of violence against blacks in New York City. *How did city officials respond to the riots? How did the federal government respond? What do the riots reveal about support for the Union's war objectives in 1863? Why were African American males so often targeted by rioters?*

▶ Interpret documentary evidence from a variety of sources reflecting differing perspectives to construct a historical argument or debate on such questions as: *What circumstances would justify a restriction of civil liberties? Was President Lincoln justified in suspending the writ of habeas corpus during the war?*

▶ Using diaries and letters, explain the roles of women on the home front and battle front during the Civil War. *What new occupations were open to women during the war? To what extent did the war change gender roles and traditional attitudes toward women in the work force? How did the actions of Clara Barton, Belle Boyd, Rose Greenhow, and Harriet Tubman affect the war?*

▶ Using diaries, paintings, photographs, statistics, and newspaper articles, explain the human costs of the war. *How did photographs of death and destruction affect people of the North? Of the South? What do the paintings of Winslow Homer say about courage and leadership during the Civil War?*

S T A N D A R D   3

Students Should Understand: *How various reconstruction plans succeeded or failed.*

Students Should Be Able to:

3A Demonstrate understanding of the political controversy over Reconstruction by:

7–12 Contrasting the Reconstruction policies advocated by Lincoln, Andrew Johnson, and sharply divided Congressional leaders, while assessing these policies as responses to changing events. [**Evaluate the implementation of a decision**]

7–12 Analyzing the escalating conflict between President Johnson and Republican legislators, and explaining the reasons for and consequences of Johnson's impeachment and trial. [**Consider multiple perspectives**]

5–12 Explaining the provisions of the 14th and 15th amendments and the political forces supporting and opposing each. [**Consider multiple perspectives**]

7–12 Evaluating why the Republican party abandoned African Americans in the South and analyzing the causes and consequences of the Compromise of 1877. [**Analyze cause-and-effect relationships**]

9–12 Analyzing the role of violence and the tactics of the "redeemers" in regaining control over the southern state governments. [**Interrogating historical data**]

| **Grades 5-6** | **Examples of student achievement of Standard 3A include:** |

▶ Use resources such as photographs, narratives, and literature such as Zachary Kent's *The Surrender at Appomattox Court House* to describe the end of the Civil War and demobilization of the armies.

▶ Compare the leadership abilities of Presidents Lincoln and Johnson. *How did the two men differ? What was the effect of Lincoln's assassination on the nation? Why was Andrew Johnson impeached?*

▶ List the basic provisions of the 13th, 14th, and 15th amendments. *How were the lives of African American freedmen changed by these amendments? Did they obtain the rights and freedoms promised to them? How did the Ku Klux Klan attempt to block these rights?*

| **Grades 7-8** | **Examples of student achievement of Standard 3A include:** |

▶ Identify and analyze the fundamental differences in the Reconstruction plans advocated by President Lincoln, Congressional leaders, and President Johnson as a background to creating the students' own position paper or editorial, advising and justifying their recommendation for a Reconstruction policy.

▶ Construct a historical narrative explaining how President Johnson's resistance to Congressional authority led to his impeachment. *How did Congress respond to President Johnson's attempts to control Reconstruction policy? To what extent did*

President Johnson's personality play a role in the conflict with "Radical" Republicans? What was the Tenure of Office Act and how did it play a role in the impeachment of Andrew Johnson?

▶ Explain the basic principles incorporated in the Reconstruction amendments and examine different perspectives on the effectiveness of these constitutional amendments. *What was the intent of these amendments? How did African American freedmen experience change following these amendments? How did southern "Redeemers" restrict the civil rights of African Americans?*

▶ Construct a historical argument, debate, or narrative which appraises the Compromise of 1877 from the perspectives of African Americans, southern political leaders, and northern Republicans. *Was the compromise an effective way to end the political stalemate over the election of 1876? To what extent did the Compromise of 1877 abandon reconstruction goals? What were the long-range consequences of the Compromise of 1877?*

Grades 9-12

Examples of student achievement of Standard 3A include:

▶ Compare the Lincoln, Johnson, and Radical Republican plans for Reconstruction. *How did each plan view secession, amnesty and pardon, and procedure for readmission to the Union? How did the issue of Federalism influence the debate over Reconstruction policy? How did President Andrew Johnson's personality and character affect relationships with congressional leaders, particularly Radical Republicans, in the period 1865-1868? Were the Radical Republicans motivated by genuine humanitarian concerns or crass political ones for maintaining control over the government?*

▶ Evaluate the reasons the Republicans used in wanting to impeach Andrew Johnson. *Were the reasons in violation of the Constitution? Were they justified? What would have been the change in American government if the Republicans had succeeded in convicting Andrew Johnson and removing him from office?*

▶ Construct a historical narrative analyzing the meaning and intent of the 14th and 15th amendments. *How is citizenship being defined? Why were the clauses of "equal protection of the laws" and "due process" included? Which group of Republicans felt that the 14th and 15th amendments were necessary? Were they necessary? Explain. Why is the word "male" used for the first time in the Constitution in the 15th Amendment? Why were women excluded in the amendment?*

▶ Analyze how violence helped to produce the Compromise of 1877 and the consequences of the compromise on the South. *How did southerners justify the origin of the Ku Klux Klan? How was the Ku Klux Klan a form of "guerrilla warfare"? Why did northern Republicans and congressional leaders abandon African Americans in the 1870s? Would you agree or disagree that the Compromise of 1877 made the end of the Civil War a draw rather than a victory for the North?*

Students Should Be Able to:

3B Demonstrate understanding of the Reconstruction programs to transform social relations in the South by:

`7-12` Explaining the economic and social problems facing the South and appraising their impact on different groups of people. [**Evidence historical perspectives**]

`5-12` Evaluating the goals and accomplishments of the Freedmen's Bureau. [**Hold interpretations of history as tentative**]

`9-12` Describing the ways in which African Americans laid the foundation for the modern black community during Reconstruction. [**Hypothesize the influence of the past**]

`7-12` Analyzing how African Americans attempted to improve their economic position during Reconstruction and explaining the factors involved in their quest for landownership. [**Analyze multiple causation**]

Grades 5-6

Examples of student achievement of Standard 3B include:

▶ Interpret diaries, letters, journals, biographies, and cartoons to describe how the Union victory and emancipation changed life in the South during Reconstruction. *What did defeated Confederate soldiers find when they returned home? What were the needs of nearly four million African American freed men and women?*

▶ Examine ways in which former slaves organized into communities to improve their position in American society. *Why were former slaves eager to build schools and get an education? How important were the black churches in working to improve the condition of African Americans in the South? How did they work together to obtain land? Why did some move to the North and West after the Civil War?*

▶ Explain the goals of the Freedmen's Bureau and give examples of how people from the North traveled south to help with Reconstruction. *What was the most important need the Freedmen's Bureau faced?*

Grades 7-8

Examples of student achievement of Standard 3B include:

▶ Compare the economic base of the South before and after the Civil War.

▶ Interpret documentary evidence from diaries, letters, journals, and biographies in order to construct a historical narrative, examining the problems facing different groups of people in the South at the close of the war.

▶ Draw from a variety of historical sources, including diaries and journals of administrators and participants, to evaluate the successes and failures of the Freedmen's Bureau. *What were the goals of the Freedmen's Bureau? To what extent were the services of the Freedmen's Bureau offered to southern poor whites? How did the Freedmen's Bureau propose to deal with abandoned land in the South? To what extent was the policy effective? What political, economic, and social factors hindered the success of the Freedmen's Bureau?*

▶ Formulate examples of historical contingency by explaining how different choices regarding land redistribution during Reconstruction could have led to different consequences. *Why were former slaves calling for "forty acres and a mule?" Would widespread landownership among freedmen have made Reconstruction more successful?*

| Grades 9-12 | **Examples of student achievement of Standard 3B include:** |

▶ Analyze how traditional beliefs and values inhibited the role and success of the Freedmen's Bureau. *How did the belief in limited government, the sanctity of private property, white supremacy, and self-help affect the Bureau's success? To what extent was the Freedmen's Bureau successful in securing employment, education, and support services for African Americans and white refugees? In what ways did the Freedmen's Bureau contribute to the economic and social transformation of the South during Reconstruction? In what ways did the Bureau contribute to racial stereotyping and paternalism? How did the labor contracts negotiated by the Freedmen's Bureau affect African Americans?*

▶ Analyze the struggle between former masters aiming to recreate a disciplined labor force and former slaves seeking to create the greatest degree of economic autonomy, and explain how such conflicts affected economics, politics, and race relations in the postwar South. *How did the southern Black Codes reflect attempts to limit the freed slaves' newfound freedom and force them back to work on the plantations? What effect did passage of such laws in the South have on northern Republicans? Why did sharecropping evolve as the eventual solution to the labor problem in the postwar cotton South, and why did the newly emancipated slave often choose it over wage labor?*

▶ Examine how black churches and schools formed the basis for self-help within the African American community. *To what extent were African American goals of education, economic development, and establishing and reaffirming community achieved? What examples illustrate the desire of African Americans to establish independence and gain control over their own lives and destinies? How effective were black churches in dealing with social, economic, and political issues of importance to the African American community? What is the role taken by African American churches today?*

▶ Research efforts of African Americans to achieve economic independence during Reconstruction by examining letters, government documents reflecting the appeals and demands of freedmen for landownership. *What did a South Carolina freedman mean when he said "If I can't own de land, I'll hire or lease land, but I won't contract"? How did the insistence on landownership provide a major impetus for change from contract labor to tenancy and sharecropping?*

Students Should Be Able to:

3C Demonstrate understanding of the successes and failures of Reconstruction in the South, North, and West by:

9-12 Evaluating to what extent northern capital and entrepreneurship stimulated economic development in the postwar South. [**Consider multiple perspectives**]

5-12 Examining the progress of "Black Reconstruction" and legislative reform programs promoted by reconstructed state governments. [**Marshal evidence of antecedent circumstances**]

7-12 Evaluating Reconstruction as a revolution. [**Evaluate major debates among historians**]

7-12 Assessing how the political and economic position of African Americans in the northern and western states changed during Reconstruction. [**Evidence historical perspectives**]

7-12 Analyzing how the Civil War and Reconstruction changed gender roles and status in the North and West. [**Analyze cause-and-effect relationships**]

5-12 Evaluating why corruption increased in the postwar period. [**Analyze multiple causation**]

Grades 5-6

Examples of student achievement of Standard 3C include:

▶ Make a chart comparing northern and southern economic conditions and family life before and after the Civil War. *How did conditions in each area change over the war years?*

▶ Examine the lives of African Americans such as Charlotte Forten, Robert Elliot, Hiram Revels, and Blanche Bruce, who served as teachers and political leaders during Reconstruction. *What significant contributions did African Americans make to further the aims of Reconstruction?*

▶ Construct a response in the form of an editorial, speech, or role-play activity to the passage of the 15th amendment from the perspective of Susan B. Anthony and Elizabeth Cady Stanton. *Why did Anthony and Stanton, who had supported the abolition of slavery, voice opposition to the 15th amendment?*

▶ Draw evidence from historical accounts, biographies, and political cartoons to provide examples of corruption in the period following the Civil War. Investigate the life of William Marcy Tweed. Explain what Tweed meant when he said: "I don't care so much what the papers write about me. My constituents can't read. But . . . they can see pictures." *How important were cartoonists in drawing attention to political corruption?*

▶ Use historical fiction such as *Two Tickets to Freedom* by Florence Freedman and *Words by Heart* by Ouida Sebestyen to investigate personal accounts of life during Reconstruction.

| Grades 7-8 | **Examples of student achievement of Standard 3C include:** |

▶ Draw upon evidence from biographies and other historical sources, including state legislation passed in southern states during Reconstruction to assess the contributions of African Americans who served in state and national offices, such as Hiram Revels, Blanche Bruce, and B.S. Pinchback.

▶ Draw upon different historical interpretations of Reconstruction and documentary evidence to construct a sound historical argument agreeing or disagreeing with the statement: *"Reconstruction failed because of a lack of commitment to carry out its basic goals and objectives."*

▶ Use historical fiction such as *Freedom Road* by Howard Fast and *Out from this Place* by Joyce Hensen to examine personal challenges to Freedmen during Reconstruction.

▶ Develop a historical narrative assessing the changes in the political and economic position of African Americans in the North in the post-Civil War era. *Did attitudes toward free blacks in the North change after the Civil War? To what extent were Jim Crow laws passed in the North? How did the social conditions of African Americans in the North compare with those in the South?*

▶ Drawing from historical evidence, construct sound arguments to support or refute the images of corruption reflected in the majority of political cartoons of the post-Civil War era. *Did political cartoonists accurately reflect the degree of corruption in the United States in the postwar era?*

| Grades 9-12 | **Examples of student achievement of Standard 3C include:** |

▶ Analyze the successes and achievements of "Black Reconstruction." *To what extent were African American goals of education, economic development, and establishing and reaffirming community achieved? What examples illustrate the desire of African Americans to establish independence and gain control over their own lives and destinies?*

▶ Assess the impact of the uses of fraud and violence on the end of Reconstruction in 1877 as a means of testing a recent historian's assertion that: *"The end of Reconstruction would come not because propertyless blacks succumbed to economic coercion, but because a politically tenacious black community, abandoned by the nation, fell victim to violence and fraud."*

▶ Compare the various viewpoints on the nature of Reconstruction by analyzing different interpretations of the era. *How have historians viewed the "Radical" Republicans, the former plantation owners, the freedmen, the carpetbaggers, and the scalawags? Was Reconstruction a "tragic era" or did it not go far enough? In what way did Reconstruction lay the groundwork for the Civil Rights movement of the 1960s?*

▶ Construct a sound argument, debate, or historical narrative on questions such as: *Was Reconstruction a half-way revolution? Could African Americans have attained full equality during Reconstruction? Why did some freedmen (i.e., Exodusters) choose to migrate West?*

◆ Analyze how economic expansion and development were affected by the Civil War and Reconstruction. *How did land grants, subsidies to railroads, and tariff and monetary policies affect U.S. growth and development? Was the government following a policy of laissez faire in economic development or actively engaging in aid?*

◆ Evaluate the extent to which gender roles and status were affected by the Civil War and Reconstruction. *Why did leaders like Elizabeth Cady Stanton, Susan B. Anthony, and others feel betrayed by Reconstruction? How did the National Woman Suffrage Association (NWSA) and the American Woman Suffrage Association (AWSA) differ? Which do you think had a better strategy? Why?*

◆ Evaluate the extent of corruption in state and national politics. *To what extent did crooked business deals, in securing contracts during the Civil War, encourage corruption in the government after the war? How was William Marcy Tweed able to come to power in New York? Why was the city called "Boss Tweed's New York"?*

Cartoon critical of a new form of slavery imposed by the White League and the Ku Klux Klan. Thomas Nast, Harper's Weekly, October 24, 1874

ERA 6

The Development of the Industrial United States (1870-1900)

From the era of Reconstruction to the end of the 19th century, the United States underwent an economic transformation that involved the maturing of the industrial economy, the rapid expansion of big business, the development of large-scale agriculture, and the rise of national labor unions and pronounced industrial conflict.

Students can begin to see a resemblance to possibilities and problems that our society faces today. The late 19th century marked an outburst of technological innovation, which fueled headlong economic growth and material benefits for many Americans. Yet, the advances in productive and extractive enterprises that technology permitted also had ecological effects that Americans were just beginning to confront. In the last third of the 19th century, the rise of the American corporation and the advent of big business brought about a concentration of the nation's productive capacities in many fewer hands. Mechanization brought farming into the realm of big business and turned the U.S. into the world's premier producer of food — a position it has never surrendered.

This period also witnessed unprecedented immigration and urbanization, both of which were indispensable to industrial expansion. American society became more diverse as immigrants arrived from southern and eastern Europe — and also from Asia, Mexico, and Central America, creating a new American mosaic. The old Protestant European Americans' sway over the diverse peoples of this nation would never be the same.

In studying the paradoxical legacies of this period students will find that what many at the time thought was progress was regarded by many others as retrogressive. First, the disruptive effects of agricultural modernization on family farms were manifold, and they led American farmers to organize protest movements as never before. Second, the dizzying rate of expansion was accomplished at the cost of the wars against the Plains Indians, which produced the "second great removal" of indigenous peoples from their ancient homelands and ushered in a new federal Indian policy that would last until the New Deal. Third, the social problems that accompanied the nation's industrial development fueled the rise of national labor unionism and unprecedented clashes in industrial and mining sites between capital and labor. Fourth, after the Civil War, women reformers suffered an era of retrenchment on issues concerning economic and political rights. Lastly, the wrenching economic dislocations of this period and the social problems that erupted in rural and urban settings captured the attention of reformers and politicians and gave rise to third-party movements and the Progressive movement.

Overview

Standard 1: How the rise of big business, heavy industry, and mechanized farming transformed the American peoples

Standard 2: Massive immigration after 1870 and how new social patterns, conflicts, and ideas of national unity developed amid growing cultural diversity

Standard 3: The rise of the American labor movement, and how political issues reflected social and economic changes

Standard 4: Federal Indian policy and United States foreign policy after the Civil War

"This, then, is held to be the duty of the man of wealth: To set an example of modest, unostentatious living, shunning display or extravagance; to provide moderately for the legitimate wants of those dependent upon him; and, after doing so, to consider all surplus revenues which come to him simply as trust funds, which he is called upon to administer, and strictly bound as a matter of duty to administer in the manner which, in his judgment, is best calculated to produce the most beneficial results for the community — the man of wealth thus becoming the mere trustee and agent for his poorer brethren, bringing to their service his superior wisdom, experience, and ability to administer, doing for them better than they would or could do for themselves."

— ANDREW CARNEGIE, *WEALTH*

New York workers demonstrating for an eight-hour day. Frank Leslie's Illustrated Newspaper, *June 29, 1872*

S T A N D A R D   1

Students Should Understand: *How the rise of big business, heavy industry, and mechanized farming transformed the American peoples.*

Students Should Be Able to:

1A Demonstrate understanding of the connections between industrialization, the rise of big business, and the advent of the modern corporation by:

5-12 Explaining how technological, transportation, communication, and marketing improvements and innovations transformed the American economy in the late 19th century. **[Examine the influence of ideas]**

7-12 Comparing the various types of business organizations. **[Compare and contrast differing institutions]**

5-12 Evaluating the careers of prominent industrial and financial leaders. **[Assess the importance of the individual in history]**

7-12 Explaining how business leaders sought to limit competition and maximize profits in the late 19th century. **[Examine the influence of ideas]**

7-12 Comparing the ascent of business entrepreneurs today with those of a century ago. **[Hypothesize the influence of the past]**

Grades 5-6

Examples of student achievement of Standard 1A include:

▶ Construct a timeline listing the significant improvements in transportation and communication and the important inventions of the post Civil War era. Draw upon data from the time line to develop a historical narrative explaining the rapid expanse of industry and commerce. *What contributed to the rapid economic growth of the United States? How did inventions change the way people lived and worked? Who were the great inventors of the period? How did trade, shipping, railroads, large business and new farming practices change during the period? What were the effects of technological change on the environment? To what extent would life be different today without the benefit of technological change and the inventions of the latter part of the 19th century?*

▶ Assemble the evidence and write a newspaper story (ca. 1900) reflecting the major technological, transportation, and communication changes occurring since 1870 and explain how they changed the lives and standard of living of a majority of citizens.

| Grades 7-8 | **Examples of student achievement of Standard 1A include:** |

▶ Draw evidence from popular literature, biographies and other historical sources to evaluate the influence of the Horatio Alger stories on the notion of the "American Dream." *How many of the great business leaders of the late 19th century fit the Horatio Alger model? What do the "rags to riches" stories tell about American values? To what extent is the "rags to riches" dream alive today? How does contemporary literature or television promote the dream of "rags to riches"?*

▶ Construct a historical narrative assessing the impact of modern technology, new inventions, and advances in transportation and communication on society. *To what extent did advances in transportation and communication promote the development of urban areas? How did the new technology change rural America?*

▶ Draw upon evidence from a variety of primary and secondary sources including letters, public addresses, and biographies to construct a character sketch of a prominent industrial leader. *What benefits did the individual's success bring to American society? How did these "captains of industry" build great fortunes? How did they use their wealth? What effects did the practices employed by these business leaders have on competition? What role did government take in promoting business? Were the prominent business leaders of the day "captains of industry" or "robber barons"?*

▶ Draw from historical sources and current events to compare prominent contemporary business leaders with the "industrial giants" of the late 19th century. *To what degree are the men and women in the forefront of American business today different from earlier entrepreneurs? What role has free competition played in the development of today's business leaders?*

| Grades 9-12 | **Examples of student achievement of Standard 1A include:** |

▶ Using a variety of historical, literary, graphic, and visual sources, create a narrative explaining the changing nature of business enterprise in the late 19th century. *What were the social origins of most business leaders of the period in terms of race, religion, ethnicity, class, education, and occupation? Which had a greater impact on economic expansion in the period 1870-1900, individual business leaders, such as Rockefeller and Carnegie, or market forces (e.g., supply and demand)? Did the judicial system help or hinder the economic transformation of the United States in the period?*

▶ Utilize a variety of historical sources, including primary documents, to complete a case study of how a business leader gained dominance in a particular industry in the late 19th century. *How did business leaders seek to maximize profits and limit competition? Did the business leader pursue horizontal or vertical integration? Why? To what extent did managerial organization, technological innovation, and individual decision making contribute to the success of the business?*

▶ Conduct a trial of John D. Rockefeller on the following charge: *"The plaintiff had knowingly and willfully participated in unethical and amoral business practices designed to undermine traditions of fair and open competition for personal and private aggrandizement in direct violation of the common welfare."*

Students Should Be Able to:

1B Demonstrate understanding of how rapid industrialization affected urban politics, living standards, and opportunity at different social levels by:

`5-12` Explaining how geographic factors and rapid industrialization created different kinds of cities in diverse regions of the country. [**Draw upon data in historical maps**]

`5-12` Tracing the migration of people from farm to city and their adjustment to urban life. [**Evidence historical perspectives**]

`7-12` Analyzing how industrialization and urbanization affected the division of wealth, living conditions, and economic opportunity. [**Interrogate historical data**]

`7-12` Analyzing how urban political machines gained power and how they were viewed by immigrants, middle-class reformers, and political bosses. [**Consider multiple perspectives**]

`9-12` Explaining how urban dwellers dealt with the problems of financing, governing, and policing the cities. [**Evaluate alternative courses of actions**]

Grades 5-6

Examples of student achievement of Standard 1B include:

▶ Identify places and regions where industries and transportation expanded during the late 19th century and explain the geographic reasons for building factories, commercial centers, and transportation hubs in these places.

▶ Compare the size of major cities then and now, using census data and historical pictures. *Which cities had the best ports? What made some cities grow and others stay the same size or get smaller?*

▶ Describe living conditions in the growing cities in the late 19th century. Draw upon historical accounts, stories, and pictures, to compare opportunities and problems of 19th-century families in large cities to those who live in urban American today. *What drew different groups of people to the big cities in the late 19th century? What draws people to the cities today?*

Grades 7-8

Examples of student achievement of Standard 1B include:

▶ Construct a data sheet listing diverse and common factors of five selected large cities in different regions of the country (e.g., Boston, Philadelphia, Atlanta, Chicago, San Francisco). *How did physical geography influence the location of the selected cities? What influence did new methods of transportation and communication have on the growth and development of cities? To what extent did economic development such as industrialization and commerce contribute to the growth of these urban centers?*

▶ Draw from a demographic map, graphs, and statistical data to trace the internal migration from farm to city in the latter part of the nineteenth century. *What geographic factors contributed to the growth of cities? What accounted for the movement to the cities? How did urban living conditions differ from those in rural areas? Do the same factors attract people to large cities today? Do cities today have the same advantages as they did in the late 19th century?*

▶ Draw evidence from a variety of historical documents including eyewitness accounts, art, and period literature, to construct a pictorial essay explaining how industrialization and urbanization affected living conditions in late 19th-century cities.

▶ Construct an oral report that examines how urban political machines gained power and how they addressed the challenges of governing large cities. *Who were the most notorious political bosses of the era? What tactics did they use to govern cities? In what ways did machine politics help the urban poor? Why were immigrants willing to cooperate with political bosses?*

▶ Draw upon political cartoonists and reform writers such as Thomas Nast and Lincoln Steffens to examine the negative impact of machine politics.

Grades 9-12

Examples of student achievement of Standard 1B include:

▶ Select a city for study and, drawing upon a variety of sources, review its demographic, economic, and spatial expansion in the late nineteenth century. *What were the factors influencing the city's growth in the late 19th century? How did the city's population, work force, and residential patterns change in the period 1870-1900?*

▶ Draw upon such sources as Jacob Riis's *How the Other Half Lives* (1890), Stephen Crane's *Maggie: A Girl of the Streets* and *George's Mother*, pictures and diagrams of the "dumbbell tenement," and other visual and graphic material, to determine how city residents dealt with such problems as developing adequate water supplies, sewer systems, public health measures, public safety, public and private education, paving or roads, transportation, and housing in the late 19th century.

▶ Utilizing a variety of sources, including eyewitness accounts, construct a historical narrative or a case study examining the methods urban bosses used to win support of immigrants. *How effective were urban bosses in supporting the interests of immigrants and the urban poor? Were they demigods or demagogues? Explain. To what extent was Lord James Bryce's characterization of city government in the United States as a "conspicuous failure" in his* The American Commonwealth *(1888) a correct appraisal?*

▶ Construct a case study of political bosses such as William Marcy Tweed and George Washington Plunkitt. *How did middle-class reforms and urban bosses view the role and responsibilities of city government? How democratic were the "goo-goos" (good government advocates)?*

Boss Tweed, Cartoon by Thomas Nast, Harper's Weekly, October 21, 1871

Students Should Be Able to:

1C Demonstrate understanding of how agriculture, mining, and ranching were transformed by:

`5-12` Explaining the major geographical and technological influences affecting farming, mining, and ranching. [**Draw upon data in historical maps**]

`5-12` Explaining the conflicts that arose during the settlement of the "last frontier" among farmers, ranchers, and miners. [**Consider multiple perspectives**]

`9-12` Analyzing the role of the federal government, the problem of aridity, and the cross-cultural encounters between diverse people in the development of the West. [**Formulate a position or course of action on an issue**]

`7-12` Explaining how commercial farming differed in the Northeast, South, Great Plains, and West in terms of crop production, farm labor, financing, and transportation. [**Formulate historical questions**]

`7-12` Evaluating the gender and ethnic diversity of farmers, miners, and ranchers in the West. [**Examine the influence of ideas**]

`7-12` Explaining the significance of farm organizations. [**Analyze multiple causation**]

Grades 5-6

Examples of student achievement of Standard 1C include:

▶ Draw from various resources including historical novels and physical maps, to examine how geography impacted the way people lived and worked in the West.

▶ Draw upon primary sources and literature including the Little House series by Laura Ingalls Wilder and *Prairie Songs* by Pam Conrad to explain the idea of the "frontier." *What kind of people were drawn to the West? Where did they come from and how well did they get along with one another? What was the role of women and children on farms, ranches, and in mining towns?*

▶ Compare life on the Great Plains with life in urban areas in the latter part of the 19th century. *What was the average work week like for farmers compared to urban workers in terms of hours worked, income, and leisure time and opportunities?*

Grades 7-8

Examples of student achievement of Standard 1C include:

▶ Draw upon topographical, climate, and land-use maps, period literature, diaries and journals, and visual evidence of the late 19th-century frontier to explain the influence of geography and technology on farming, ranching, and mining in the West.

▶ Construct a simulated journal, classroom newspaper, or skit which reflects the different perspectives of ranchers, farmers, and miners in the West. Draw evidence from historical sources and novels such as *A Lantern in Her Hand* by Bess Streeter Aldrich, *Prairie Songs* by Pamela Conrad, *The Obstinate Land* by Harold Keith, and *Shane* by Jack Schaefer. *What were the issues behind the conflicts? What disputes developed over water rights and open ranges?*

- Draw evidence from letters, diaries, contemporary art, photography, and literary works, to construct a simulated journal or short story reflecting the daily life of women on the western frontier. *How did life experiences in the Great Plains and West differ from those in the East and Midwest? What impact did these experiences have on the expansion of woman's rights?*

- Examine cross-cultural encounters and explain the conflicts that arose among different racial and ethnic groups in western mining regions, farming communities, and urban areas. *To what extent were the old Spanish and Mexican land grants recognized by local and state governments and new settlers? What experiences did Asian immigrants encounter? What discriminatory practices existed? What conflicts developed between Native Americans and white settlers in mining regions and farming communities in the West? What were the experiences of African Americans in the West? What was the role of the Buffalo Soldiers in the West?*

| Grades 9-12 | **Examples of student achievement of Standard 1C include:** |

- Contrast the romantic depiction of life in the West with the reality, and describe some of the hardships faced by settlers in the late 19th century. *What led to conflicts between cattle ranchers on the one hand and farmers and sheep herders on the other? How was ethnic conflict portrayed in the Murietta stories and the Cortina uprising? What was the role of vigilantes in the West?*

- Analyze the role of religion in stabilizing the new western communities.

- Review data from a variety of sources which reflect the extension of railroad lines, increased agricultural cultivation and productivity, and the effect of improved transportation facilities on commodity prices. *What was the average size of farms in the North, South, Great Plains, and West in 1870 and in 1900? What agricultural commodities were the principal source of farm income in these regions? How did the increased use of agricultural machinery affect productivity, indebtedness, farm ownership, and the average size of farms?*

- Draw from a variety of historical, literary, and statistical data, to analyze the racial, ethnic, and gender composition of farmers, miners, and ranchers in the West in the late 19th century. *How were gender and racial roles defined on the farming, mining, and ranching frontiers?*

- Utilize a variety of historical and graphic data, such as the social and political programs of the Patrons of Husbandry, Greenbackers, Northern, Southern, and Colored Farmers' Alliances to analyze the impact of the crop-lien system in the South, transportation and storage costs for farmers, and the price of farm staples such as wheat, corn, and cotton in the period 1870-1896. *What caused the decline in farm commodity prices? How did the government's monetary policy affect the price of farm commodities? What were the major grievances of the primary farm organizations in the West and South during the period? What major solutions did they offer?*

Students Should Be Able to:

1D Demonstrate understanding of how industrialism, urbanization, large-scale agriculture, and mining affected the ecosystem and initiated an environmental movement by:

5-12 Providing examples of pollution and the depletion of natural resources during the period 1870-1900 and analyzing their environmental costs. [**Utilize visual and mathematical data**]

7-12 Explaining how rapid industrialization, extractive mining techniques, and the "gridiron" pattern of urban growth affected the scenic beauty and health of city and countryside. [**Compare and contrast differing values and behaviors**]

7-12 Explaining the origins of environmentalism and the conservation movement in the late 19th century. [**Examine the influence of ideas**]

Grades 5-6

Examples of student achievement of Standard 1D include:

▶ Describe the efforts of late 19th-century reformers to control pollution, and compare their activities with current efforts.

▶ Examine photographs or art works which show the effects of mining and industrial development on health and scenic beauty. *What was the effect of strip mining on soil erosion?*

▶ Analyze the effect of men such as John Muir in promoting concern for the natural environment. *Why was the Sierra Club established? What were its goals?*

Grades 7-8

Examples of student achievement of Standard 1D include:

▶ Draw upon primary sources such as journals, letters, contemporary art, and photography to examine the environmental impact of industrialization and the depletion of natural resources. *What contrasts are presented in visual records of the period? What were the origins of the late 19th-century environmental movement? How successful were they? What role did local, state, and national government play in the attempt to preserve natural resources?*

▶ Draw from a variety of primary and secondary sources including period literature, to construct a well-reasoned argument, debate, or historical narrative on such questions as: *What measures could have been taken to provide for mining and industrial development and environmental protection? What are some current issues over the same question? What lessons regarding the conflict between economic expansion and environmental protection can be determined from the study of history?*

Grades 9-12

Examples of student achievement of Standard 1D include:

▶ Draw upon visual sources such as the paintings of the Hudson River School artists, Currier and Ives prints, the writings of John Muir, and Frederick Jackson Turner's celebration of the frontier to analyze how the emphasis on staple crop production, strip mining, lumbering, ranching, and the destruction of western buffalo herds led to massive environmental damage in the late 19th century. *Who were the leaders and primary supporters of the conservation movement in the late 19th century? What arguments did environmentalists and conservationists of the time employ? How did local, state, and national leaders respond to environmental and conservation concerns? How did ordinary people respond to environmental and conservation concerns?*

▶ Construct a historical narrative examining the impact of the rapid increase in population and industrial growth in urban areas in the late 19th century. Respond to H. L. Mencken's claim that Baltimore in the 1880s smelled "like a billion polecats" and the comment by Cleveland's mayor who, in 1881, called the Cuyahoga River "an open sewer through the center of the city." *Why did the "gridiron pattern" become the standard for urban growth in the late 19th century? What problems resulted? How did inefficient procedures for garbage collection and sewage disposal and treatment effect urban life? How did city leaders and residents cope with the major environmental problems facing cities?*

John Muir (1838-1914), naturalist, conservationist, writer. Courtesy Sierra Club, reproduced from the Dictionary of American Portraits, *Dover Publications, 1967*

STANDARD 2

Students Should Understand: *Massive immigration after 1870 and how new social patterns, conflicts, and ideas of national unity developed amid growing cultural diversity.*

Students Should Be Able to:

2A Demonstrate understanding of the sources and experiences of the new immigrants by:

7-12 Distinguishing between the "old" and "new" immigration in terms of its volume and the newcomers' ethnicity, religion, language, and place of origin. [**Analyze multiple causation**]

5-12 Tracing the patterns of immigrant settlements in different regions of the country. [**Reconstruct patterns of historical succession and duration**]

5-12 Analyzing the obstacles, opportunities, and contributions of different immigrant groups. [**Evidence historical perspectives**]

7-12 Evaluating how Catholic and Jewish newcomers responded to discrimination and internal divisions in their new surroundings. [**Obtain historical data**]

| Grades 5-6 | Examples of student achievement of Standard 2A include: |

▶ Explain how immigration changed after 1870. Use maps and pictorial resources to show where people came from and where they settled. *Which immigrant groups came to your community in the late 19th century? How were immigrants welcomed by the English, Scots, Irish, German, and other earlier settlers?*

▶ Describe the ways in which immigrants learned to live and work in a new country. Draw upon excerpts from first-hand accounts, stories, and poems which describe living and working conditions. *How did urban reformers like Jane Addams and Jacob Riis try to serve the needs of new immigrants? What role did public schools have in helping immigrants settle into their new communities?*

▶ Use old photographs, oral histories, and other sources to compile a history of the experiences of family members who immigrated to the United States.

▶ Use stories such as *Tales from the Gold Mountain* by Paul Yee and *Samurai of the Gold Hill* by Yoshiko Uchida to examine early Chinese and Japanese immigration to California.

▶ Examine the experiences of Jewish immigrants through children's stories such as *The Cat Who Escaped from Steerage* by Evelyn Wilde Meyerson.

Grades 7-8

Examples of student achievement of Standard 2A include:

▶ Compare and contrast immigration in the 1880s with that of the 1840s. *To what extent did the motives for immigration differ for the earlier and the later period? From what regions of the world did most immigrants come?*

▶ Draw evidence from a variety of historical sources to construct a chart showing different attitudes toward immigrants. *How did Americans react to the new immigration? Did the nativism of the 1840s differ from that of the 1880s? How did the languages and religious beliefs of the new immigrants affect the nativists? What factors contributed to changing attitudes toward immigrants? How did immigrants respond to hostility?*

▶ Draw upon evidence from biographies and other historical sources such as *The Life Stories of Undistinguished Americans*, edited by Hamilton Holt, to construct historical assessments of the contributions of immigrants in American society.

▶ Draw upon evidence from biographies and other historical sources to construct sound historical assessments of the contributions of immigrants in American society.

▶ Interpret documentary evidence from diaries, letters, and political cartoons such as those of Thomas Nast to assess the religious intolerance Catholic and Jewish immigrants faced.

Grades 9-12

Examples of student achievement of Standard 2A include:

▶ Draw upon such sources as copies of immigrants' letters written home and excerpts from ethnic newspapers to compare the experiences of the new immigrants in the period 1870-1900 with the message of Emma Lazarus's poem, "The New Colossus." *What were the expectations of the new immigrants? Were they able to attain their goals? How did parochial and other religious schools serve the interests of the newer immigrants? Why were the last four lines of "The New Colossus" placed on the Statue of Liberty? How do they compare with the rest of the poem? Do the terms "melting pot" or "salad bowl" best describe the acculturation experience of the newer immigrants? Are both terms inadequate?*

What kind of communal associations and institutions did immigrant groups organize to ease their transition in the United States and to preserve their cultural and ethnic identities? Why did many native-born citizens favor restricting immigration through the imposition of a literacy test rather than through a quota system?

▶ Construct a historical narrative drawing upon historical evidence to examine the reasons for hostility to the "new" immigrants in the 1880s and 1890s using examples such as the antiforeign hysteria in the aftermath of the Haymarket Affair, attacks on Jewish merchants and residents in Louisiana and Mississippi (1880s and 1890s), anti-Italian hysteria in New Orleans (1891), and attacks on Polish and Hungarian strikers in Pennsylvania (1887).

▶ Draw upon such immigration restriction measures as the Chinese Exclusion Act (1882), Gentleman's Agreement (1907), Literacy Test (1917), Emergency Quota Act (1921), Immigration Restriction Act (1924), and the McCarran-Walter Act (1952) to determine the trends, changes, reasons for changes, and the tensions between American ideals and reality.

Students Should Be Able to:

2B **Demonstrate understanding of Social Darwinism, race relations, and the struggle for equal rights and opportunities by:**

`7-12` Explaining the ideas of the Social Darwinists and their opponents. [**Examine the influence of ideas**]

`5-12` Analyzing political, social, and economic discrimination against African Americans, Asian Americans, and Hispanic Americans in different regions of the country. [**Identify issues and problems in the past**]

`9-12` Analyzing the arguments and methods by which various minority groups sought to acquire equal rights and opportunities. [**Evaluate the implementation of a decision**]

Grades 5-6

Examples of student achievement of Standard 2B include:

▶ Draw upon photographs and narratives to explain how diverse people fared across the country. *Did minority groups and immigrants find it easy to establish and practice their own religion and customs? What methods were used to stop emigration from Asia? How were minorities and immigrants treated in the workplace? What steps did they take to stop discrimination?*

▶ Give examples of Jim Crow laws and explain how African Americans worked to end these restrictions.

Grades 7-8

Examples of student achievement of Standard 2B include:

▶ Define Social Darwinism and illustrate through specific historical examples the application of the philosophy.

▶ Draw from a variety of sources including letters, journals, popular literature, political cartoons, and Supreme Court cases, to construct a historical narrative examining racial and ethnic discrimination in the United States. *What forms of discrimination did Asian Americans and Hispanic Americans face in the West and Southwest? How did they respond to discriminatory practices? To what extent did legislation limit the rights of Asian and Hispanic Americans?*

What were Jim Crow laws? To what extent were discriminatory practices against African Americans different in the North and South? What were the issues involved in the Plessy v. Ferguson *case? What impact did this decision have on race relations?*

▶ Construct a historical narrative examining the efforts of minority groups to attain equal rights in the latter part of the 19th century and appraise the leadership roles of individuals who were outspoken in opposition to discrimination and racial prejudice.

▶ Examine personal encounters with Jim Crow laws through literature using historical fiction such as *I Be Somebody* by Hadley Irwin.

Grades 9-12

Examples of student achievement of Standard 2B include:

▸ Drawing upon the arguments of advocates of Social Darwinism such as William Graham Sumner, John Fiske, and Andrew Carnegie, and opponents such as Lester Frank Ward, John Dewey, Richard T. Ely, and William James, analyze the impact of Social Darwinism on public policy in the late 19th century. *How did Social Darwinism justify the political, economic, and social dominance of white, Anglo-Saxon, Protestant males?*

▸ Use examples of literacy tests and selections from the Mississippi Constitution of 1890 and the South Carolina adoption of the Mississippi formula in 1896 to analyze the origin and purpose of the "Jim Crow" system. *How did poll taxes and residency requirements help to bolster the system? What were the goals and consequences of the Immigration Restriction League?*

▸ Utilizing selections from the anti-lynching appeals of Ida Wells Barnett, Booker T. Washington's "Atlanta Exposition Address," W. E. B. Du Bois's *The Souls of Black Folk*, and appeals of other African American leaders of the late 19th century, explain the various proposals advanced to combat political disenfranchisement, Jim Crow laws, and the widespread lynching of the 1890s.

▸ Analyze the meaning of the *Yick Wo* v. *Hopkins* (1886) and *Plessy* v. *Ferguson* (1896) Supreme Court cases. *What do the decisions indicate about racism and discrimination in America in the 1890s? What was the reasoning in the minority opinions? Were the implications of the decisions similar or different?*

▸ Use historical fiction such as *The Sport of Gods* by Paul Laurence Dunbar to explore the experiences of an African American family's migration from the South to New York City in the 1890s.

MR. BERGH TO THE RESCUE

The Defrauded Gorilla. *"That Man wants to claim my Pedigree. He says he is one of my Descendants."* Mr. Bergh. *"Now, Mr. Darwin, how could you insult him so?"*

Harper's Weekly, *August 19, 1871*

Students Should Be Able to:

2C Demonstrate understanding of how new cultural movements at different social levels affected American life by:

7-12 Describing how regional artists and writers portrayed American life in this period. [**Read historical narratives imaginatively**]

5-12 Investigating mass entertainment and leisure activities at different levels of American society. [**Draw upon visual sources**]

5-12 Listing the new forms of popular culture and explaining the reasons for their development. [**Examine the influence of ideas**]

9-12 Explaining Victorianism and its impact on manners and morals. [**Analyze cause-and-effect relationships**]

Grades 5-6

Examples of student achievement of Standard 2C include:

▶ Compare children's toys, games, and entertainment in the late 19th century with those of today. *Where did children go for entertainment in the late 19th century? How do those earlier entertainments compare with entertainment opportunities available today? What inventions and media changes make our choices different from those of children in the late 19th century?*

▶ Use stories, narratives, and photographs to compare the expected behavior for children then with those in our time.

Grades 7-8

Examples of student achievement of Standard 2C include:

▶ Draw upon the art of the late 19th century to develop a historical narrative or construct a project that examines the ways in which leading artists such as Mary Cassatt and Winslow Homer portrayed life. *How does art reflect attitudes and values of society? How did the work of leading artists differ?*

▶ Compose a list of the different sports, entertainment, and recreational activities popular in the latter part of the 19th century and explain the reasons for their popularity. *What recreational activities were associated with the wealthy? Which were popular with the middle and working classes? What recreational activities are commonly shown in the art of the period? How did increased leisure time affect spectator sports and entertainment?*

▶ Examine the changes in lifestyles of the late 19th century. *How did department stores and chain stores illustrate the change in the role of the family from producers to consumers? How did public education reflect the changes taking place in the country? How were changes in childhood reflected in new games played and the differing expectations of children? How did women's clothing and dress styles (e.g., the "Gibson Girl") change in the late 19th century?*

Grades 9-12

Examples of student achievement of Standard 2C include:

▶ Evaluate the portrayal of regional life in the writings of social realist authors such as George Washington Cable, Willa Cather, Edward Eggleston, Hamlin Garland, Joel Chandler Harris, Bret Harte, William Dean Howells, Charles W. Chesnutt, Mary Noailles Murfree, O. E. Rölvaag, Mark Twain, Edith Wharton, and Constance Fenimore Woolson. *How did different authors portray life in the late 19th century? Why are most of the famous authors of the period referred to as social realist writers? What were the regional themes found in their works?*

▶ Compare the various forms of leisure activities available to different classes, such as organized and spectator sports, theaters and symphonies, vaudeville, amusement parks, circuses, city parks, bicycling, croquet, and golf, tennis, polo, and horse racing.

▶ Draw upon evidence from a variety of sources including art and literature of the late 19th century to evaluate the effects of Victorianism on proper codes of conduct. *What do Thomas Eakins's paintings* Gross Clinic *and* Agnew Clinic *say about the meaning of Victorianism and the nature of gender roles? What do the architectural layouts and pictures of interior rooms tell about lifestyles, class differences, and gender roles during the Victorian era? How do the reform movements led by Frances Willard and Anthony Comstock reflect the enduring moral code of Victorianism?*

Cap Anson, c. 1880,
Bettmann Archives

STANDARD 3

Students Should Understand: *The rise of the American labor movement, and how political issues reflected social and economic changes.*

Students Should Be Able to:

3A Demonstrate how the "second industrial revolution" changed the nature and conditions of work by:

7–12 Assessing the effects of the rise of big business on labor and explaining the change from workshop to factory in different regions of the country. [**Analyze cause-and-effect relationships**]

9–12 Explaining how gender, race, ethnicity, and skill affected employment in different regions of the country. [**Formulate historical questions**]

7–12 Analyzing how working conditions changed and how the workers responded to deteriorating conditions. [**Explain historical continuity and change**]

5–12 Analyzing the causes and consequences of the employment of children in the industrial workplace. [**Evidence historical perspectives**]

Grades 5-6

Examples of student achievement of Standard 3A include:

▶ List the changes in the way businesses operated after the Civil War and explain how workers lives were affected by these changes.

▶ Describe working conditions in urban factories. *What kind of working conditions did men, women, and children experience? How are workers protected from such conditions now?*

▶ Develop a skit or role-play activity that explores the reasons for child labor and its consequences.

Grades 7-8

Examples of student achievement of Standard 3A include:

▶ Draw upon evidence from monographs and other historical sources to construct a sound historical assessment of the connection between ethnic diversity and occupational patterns. *What factors affected the allocation of skilled and high paying jobs? What types of jobs were these? Do these occupations exist today? Are the same types of people engaged in such work? Are those who now hold those jobs afforded the same status in society as their late 19th-century counterparts?*

▶ Construct a historical narrative examining the changes in the size and shape of the work force and in working conditions in the manufacturing sector. *What affect did the rise of big business have on the number of manufacturing workers needed in American industry? Which jobs — both skilled and unskilled — were most affected by change during the period? What were working conditions like at the time?*

Wages? Benefits? Safety precautions? What place did women and children play in this work force? To what degree did their experiences differ from those of the men?

◗ Examine typical working conditions, interpreting documentary evidence from the period, including photographs, newspaper articles, and biographies. *What do the sources reveal about the nature and condition of work during the late 19th century? What modern-day comparisons or observations might be made to evaluate the differences between the past and the present day?*

Grades 9-12

Examples of student achievement of Standard 3A include:

◗ Examine how the rise of big business and the increasingly impersonal nature of work in the burgeoning factories affected workers and their responses to the new order. *How did the workers respond to the rigid timetables of factory work? How did factory owners try to instill discipline? Why were tensions created in relationships between factory owners and employees?*

◗ Assess the inroads women made in traditional male-dominated professions and occupations. *Why did early labor unions refuse to admit women? Why did the Knights of Labor admit women as members while other unions did not? How did the employment of African American women differ from immigrant and native-born white women?*

◗ Draw evidence from primary sources to examine the legal status of women in the late 19th century. *What were the issues raised by Myra Bradwell? What was the legal reasoning in the* Bradwell *v.* Illinois *case (1873)? What occupations does the decision imply women are fit for? Why? To what extent did the Bradwell case typify the status of women in the professions throughout the latter part of the century?*

◗ Drawing on such sources as John Spargo's *The Bitter Cry of the Children* and a variety of other literary, historical, and visual sources, construct a narrative explaining the reasons for the increase in child labor, the type of work performed by children, the occupations in which they were employed, and the dangers they faced during the workday.

Women working in clerical jobs in the early 20th century.
Library of Congress

Students Should Be Able to:

3B Demonstrate understanding of the rise of national labor unions and the role of state and federal governments in labor conflicts by:

`9-12` Analyzing how "reform unions" and "trade unions" differed in terms of their agendas for reform and for organizing workers by race, skill, gender, and ethnicity. [**Compare and contrast differing values and behaviors**]

`7-12` Explaining the ways in which management in different regions and industries responded to efforts to organize workers. [**Formulate historical questions**]

`5-12` Analyzing the causes and effects of labor conflicts. [**Assess cause-and-effect relationships**]

`7-12` Explaining the response of management and government at different levels to labor strife in different regions of the country. [**Compare competing historical narratives**]

Grades 5-6

Examples of student achievement of Standard 3B include:

▶ Draw information from journals, letters, and historical accounts of labor strikes to determine the causes and results of labor conflicts in the post-Civil War period. *Where did major conflicts erupt? Who were the prominent labor leaders? How effective were the strikes? What were some of the methods used to break strikes?*

▶ Use historical fiction such as *Trouble at the Mines* by Doreen Rappaport to investigate the strikes in the coal mines and the organizing efforts of Mother Mary Jones.

Grades 7-8

Examples of student achievement of Standard 3B include:

▶ Draw upon historical sources to examine the development of trade unions in the United States. *In what ways did trade unions differ from earlier reform unions? What circumstances prompted workers to attempt to band together? How did management from different regions and different industries respond to union organization?*

▶ Consult primary and secondary sources to assess the causes and effects of various labor conflicts in the late 19th century. Develop a visual point/counterpoint exhibition detailing the rifts between workers and management in the Railroad Strike (1877), the Haymarket Affair (1886), the Homestead and Coeur d'Alene strikes (1892), and the Pullman Strike (1894). *What were the reasons underlying the workers decision to strike? What stance did management take in response to workers demands? How, why, and to what extent did government come to be involved in the crisis? What was the legacy of labor unrest in this period?*

▶ Draw upon historical novels such as *Breaker* by N.A. Perez and *The Tempering* by Gloria Skurzyuski to investigate labor organizing and the experiences of immigrants in the labor movement.

Grades 9-12

Examples of student achievement of Standard 3B include:

▶ Contrast the National Labor Union and Knights of Labor with the American Federation of Labor in terms of the types of workers organized; their view of immigrants, African Americans, Chinese, and women workers; and their position on strikes and reform agendas. *Why did most unions support a "lily white" policy in the late 19th century? How and why did the Knights of Labor differ? Why did the Knights of Labor display racial hostility to the Chinese in contrast to their policy toward African American and women workers? Why did the American Federation of Labor avoid involvement in broad-based reform and political movements, accept the social and political order under capitalism, and favor the "business unionism" of Samuel Gompers?*

▶ Drawing evidence from the writings of Terence Powderly, Samuel Gompers, and Eugene V. Debs, and historical accounts of the Haymarket Affair (1886), the Homestead and Coeur d'Alene strikes (1892), and the Pullman strike (1894), analyze the extent of radicalism in the labor movement. *Why did Henry Clay Frick feel that he was defending American Republicanism in the Homestead Affair? Why did the Amalgamated Association of Steel and Iron Workers believe their actions were in the true spirit of Republicanism? Which point of view would you support?*

▶ Analyze the labor conflicts of 1894 and their impact on the development of American democracy. *Why was Coxey's Army formed and what was its impact? What did Thorstein Veblen mean when he argued that the men of Coxey's Army changed the phrase of the Declaration of Independence from "life, liberty, and the pursuit of happiness" to "life, liberty, and the means of happiness"? Why did Attorney General Olney seek an injunction against the Pullman strikes? How did the Pullman strikers justify their actions? How did President Cleveland justify the use of the U.S. Army? Would you agree with the president's decision? Why was the Pullman strike called "Debs's Resolution?"*

Railroad strike of 1877 — Strikebreaking train operators dragged from their work by strikers, Library of Congress

Students Should Be Able to:

3C Demonstrate understanding of how Americans grappled with the social, economic, and political problems of the late 19th century by:

`7-12` Explaining how Democrats and Republicans responded to civil service reform, monetary policy, tariffs, and business regulation. [Consider multiple perspectives]

`9-12` Explaining the causes and effects of the depressions of 1873-79 and 1893-97 and the ways in which government, business, labor, and farmers responded. [Analyze cause-and-effect relationships]

`7-12` Explaining the political, social, and economic roots of Populism. [Examine the influence of ideas]

`9-12` Analyzing the Omaha Platform of 1892 as a statement of grievances and an agenda for reform. [Interrogate historical data]

`5-12` Analyzing the issues and results of the 1896 election and determining to what extent it was a turning point in American life. [Analyze cause-and-effect relationships]

`7-12` Evaluating the successes and failures of Populism. [Examine the influence of ideas]

Grades 5-6

Examples of student achievement of Standard 3C include:

▶ List the third parties that were formed in the post-Civil War period and explain why they were established.

▶ Examine Thomas Nast's political cartoons to explore the issues of importance in the period. Compare the Nast cartoons to present-day political cartoons. *What do the Nast cartoons tell about important political issues of the day? What symbols did Nast use to represent the Republican party? The Democratic party?*

▶ Research the lives of important individuals such as Grover Cleveland, Belva Lockwood, Samuel Gompers, Mary Elizabeth Lease, William Jennings Bryan, and George Washington Carver, and chart the significant events in their lives.

▶ Explain why people organized to improve working conditions, hours, and wages. Use a balance sheet to list the demands of labor and the response from management. *Why did tension grow in factories and mines during the late 19th century? How do workers and owners solve their problems today?*

Grades 7-8

Examples of student achievement of Standard 3C include:

▶ Define socialism. *What were the goals of the Socialist party? What group of people were most likely to support the socialists?*

▶ Construct a historical argument in the form of balance sheets, debates, or narratives to examine the position of the major political parties on the paramount issues of the day. *How did the Democratic and Republican parties differ on issues relating to business regulation?*

▸ Draw upon evidence from biographies and other historical sources to assess the importance of individuals such as Samuel Tilden, Grover Cleveland, and Thomas Nast in promoting political reforms. *How did the Democratic and Republican parties respond to demands for political reform? Who were the Mugwumps and what were their goals? How did the Pendleton Act address political patronage?*

▸ Explain the goals of the Populist Party and identify the leading Populists of the period. *What did the founders of the Populist Party see as the major problems in America? What policies did they advocate in order to address the roots of their concerns? How effective were Mary Elizabeth Lease and William Jennings Bryan in arousing western farmers?*

Grades 9-12

Examples of student achievement of Standard 3C include:

▸ Draw from a variety of sources to construct a historical narrative that assesses the appeal of the Democratic, Republican, and Greenback Labor parties to socioeconomic groups and different sections of the country. *Why was voter turnout and party loyalty so high in the period 1870-1896? Why did a large majority of urban workers in the North support the Democratic party? Why did African American voters tend to support the Republican party? What was the role of third parties like the Greenback-Labor and Socialist parties in the last third of the 19th century? What impact did third parties have on the two major parties?*

▸ Draw upon a variety of historical and graphic data to evaluate whether or not the contraction of the money supply was the chief cause of the decline in farm prices and income in the period 1873-1896.

▸ Evaluate to what extent the Democratic and Republican parties deserved the label "Tweedledee and Tweedledum." *Who were the "Mugwumps" and why did they support Cleveland in the election of 1884? Was the tariff a major issue in the 1880s and 1890s? How did the Cleveland and Harrison administrations deal with the tariff?*

▸ Using data such as the "Ocala Demands" and the writings of Tom Watson, analyze the reaction of western and southern farmers to the cycle of falling prices, scarce money, and debt. *What were the goals and achievements of the National Farmers Alliance and Industrial Union? What was its relationship to the National Colored Farmers' Alliance? To the Northwestern Alliance? Why did Jerry Simpson and Mary Elizabeth Lease become alliance leaders?*

▸ Use the Omaha Platform of 1892 as the focus of historical inquiry to uncover the problems that prompted the establishment of the Populist Party. *To what extent, if any, were provisions of the Omaha Platform incorporated into the platforms of the two major parties over the following generation? What influence did the Populists have on the later Progressive movement? In what ways was the Populist movement a democratic political movement or a regressive, nostalgic right-wing movement?*

▸ Construct a historical argument, debate, or narrative to present evidence on issues such as the following: *Farmers are to blame for their own inability to adjust to the changing industrial scene.*

♦ Assess the overall successes and failures of the Populist movement in meeting the needs of American society. *What were the issues raised by the Populists? To what extent did Populism differ in different sections of the country? What position did Populists take on immigration and woman suffrage? What leadership role did women play in the populist party? How did Populism contribute to the movement to disfranchise African Americans in the southern states?*

♦ Analyze William Jennings Bryan's "Cross of Gold" speech at the 1896 Democratic convention. *To what extent may it be argued that the "Cross of Gold" speech won Bryan the Democratic nomination but lost him the election?*

♦ Examine the election of 1896. *Why did Populists decide to endorse the Democratic nominee for President? What effect did that endorsement have on the future of the Populist party? Why were Populists and Democrats unable to gain substantial support from urban women in 1896? What were the principal arguments and strategies used by William McKinley and Mark Hanna to ensure a Republican victory? What were the major components of the "full dinner pail"? How did American farmers fare in the decade after 1896?*

William Jennings Bryan (1860-1925),
Library of Congress

"You shall not press down upon the brow of labor this crown of thorns, you shall not crucify mankind upon a cross of gold."

— CHICAGO DEMOCRATIC CONVENTION, 1896

STANDARD 4

Students Should Understand: *Federal Indian policy and United States foreign policy after the Civil War.*

Students Should Be Able to:

4A Demonstrate understanding of various perspectives on federal Indian policy, westward expansion, and the resulting struggles by:

7-12 Identifying and comparing the attitudes and policies toward Native Americans by government officials, the U.S. Army, missionaries, and settlers. [Interrogate historical data]

5-12 Comparing survival strategies of different Native American societies in this era. [Evidence historical perspectives]

7-12 Evaluating the legacy of 19th-century federal Indian policy. [Hypothesize the influence of the past]

Grades 5-6

Examples of student achievement of Standard 4A include:

▶ Chart the movement of Native Americans to reservations in western states from the end of the Civil War to 1900. *Why did Native Americans sign treaties to accept life on reservations in faraway areas? How did they resist enforced migrations?*

▶ Explain the effect of government policies on Native American nations and compare Indian landholdings after the Civil War with their holdings at the end of the century.

Grades 7-8

Examples of student achievement of Standard 4A include:

▶ Draw from a variety of primary sources such as speeches, letters, and oral histories to construct a historical narrative explaining different attitudes toward Native Americans in the latter half of the 19th century. *To what extent had governmental policies towards Native Americans changed? What was the public's reaction to the Indian wars of the post-Civil War era? How did prevailing attitudes of easterners differ from westerners? What was the impact of Helen Hunt Jackson's* A Century of Dishonor?

What attempts were made to assimilate Native Americans? What role did missionaries play in promoting the assimilation of Native Americans? What was the impact of the government's reservation policy? What was the intent of the Dawes Severalty Act of 1887? To what extent did it achieve its goals? How did Native Americans respond to the Dawes Act?

▶ Draw upon speeches and appeals by Indian leaders, military records, biographies, and other historical data to construct a historical narrative explaining the various strategies Native American societies employed in response to the increase in white settlement, mining activities, and railroad construction in the West. Assess the effectiveness of these survival strategies.

▶ Use historical fiction such as *Ramona* by Helen Hunt Jackson and *Creek Mary's Blood* by Dee Brown to explain the American Indian's fight for survival.

Grades 9-12

Examples of student achievement of Standard 4A include:

▶ Construct a historical narrative or debate which critiques the Dawes Severalty Act of 1887. *Why in the mid-1880s did support for dismantling the reservation system and "assimilating" Native Americans into the dominant culture gain ascendancy? How did the effort to assimilate Native Americans affect the expropriation of Indian lands in the late 19th century? How did the admission of new western states affect relations between the United States and Native American societies?*

▶ Draw upon a variety of visual sources, including the paintings of such artists as George Catlin, Frederic Remington, and Charles M. Russell to explain the depiction of whites and Native Americans and examine how cultures were portrayed.

▶ Marshal historical evidence to construct a sound argument or narrative reacting to the following statement: *"Over the long term, the completion of the transcontinental railroad and trunk lines and the willful and premeditated slaughter of the buffalo herds, did more to defeat the Plains Indians and their way of life, than all the military campaigns of the period 1870-1895."*

▶ Examine the life of a notable Native American leader such as Red Cloud, Chief Joseph, Crazy Horse, Black Elk, Geronimo, or Wovoka, and construct a character sketch evaluating his leadership, values, and determination to serve his people. *What were his leadership characteristics? What respect did he garner from his people? How did government officials portray Native American leaders? What was the reaction of the general public to Indian leaders? How were they represented in the eastern and western press?*

Lakota camp in South Dakota, 1891, Library of Congress

Students Should Be Able to:

4B **Demonstrate understanding of the roots and development of American expansionism and the causes and outcomes of the Spanish-American War by:**

`5-12` Tracing the acquisition of new territories. [**Reconstruct patterns of historical succession and duration**]

`9-12` Describing how geopolitics, economic interests, racial ideology, missionary zeal, nationalism, and domestic tensions combined to create an expansionist foreign policy. [**Analyze cause-and-effect relationships**]

`5-12` Evaluating the causes, character, and objectives of the Spanish-American War. [**Interrogate historical data**]

`7-12` Explaining the causes and consequences of the Filipino insurrection. [**Analyze cause-and-effect relationships**]

Grades 5-6

Examples of student achievement of Standard 4B include:

▶ Locate on a world map areas which the United States annexed in the post-Civil War era and explain the primary reason or reasons for interest in each of these areas.

▶ Explain the conditions which led the United States to war with Spain in 1898. Why was the *U.S.S. Maine* sent to Havana harbor? Should the United States have declared war because of the sinking of the *Maine*?

▶ Develop biographical sketches of leading personalities of the Spanish-American War including Valeriano "Butcher" Weyler, William McKinley, Theodore Roosevelt, and Emilio Aguinaldo.

Grades 7-8

Examples of student achievement of Standard 4B include:

▶ Interpret documentary evidence from speeches, letters, and journals to construct historical arguments, debates, or narratives on reasons for U.S. expansionism in the late 19th century. *What were the geographic factors that motivated the United States to expand beyond the continental limits? What economic factors led the United States to pursue an imperialist policy in the late 19th century? How was the theory of Social Darwinism used to justify expansion? What were the arguments advanced by individuals who opposed expansion?*

▶ Analyze Rudyard Kipling's poem, "The White Man's Burden: The United States and the Philippine Islands" as to the reasons used to justify U.S. expansion. *Why did Theodore Roosevelt call the poem "rather bad poetry but good sense from the expansionist point of view"? How did Mark Twain satirize American expansionism when he wrote, "our usual flag, with the white stripes painted black and the stars and stripes replaced by a skull and crossbones"?*

▶ Draw evidence from a variety of historical sources that provide different perspectives to debate the issue, *"Was the United States justified in going to war against Spain in 1898?"*

◗ Interpret documentary evidence from a variety of primary sources to construct sound historical arguments, debates, or narratives on the consequences of the Spanish-American War. *What role did the U.S. take in Cuba following the Spanish-American War? How did the war affect U.S. involvement in international relations? What were the constitutional issues raised by the acquisition of new territories?*

◗ Use a variety of primary sources including cartoons, newspaper headlines, and editorials to explain the distortions and sensationalism of the press and its impact on public opinion.

◗ Construct a historical argument assessing the consequences of the annexation of the Philippines. *What were the basic arguments politicians used to justify annexation of the Philippines? What was the Filipino response to U.S. incursions? What were the human costs of the war compared with those of the Spanish-American War? What were the long-term consequences of U.S. annexation of the Philippines?*

Grades 9-12	**Examples of student achievement of Standard 4B include:**

◗ Utilize such sources as Senator Albert Beveridge's "March of the Flag" speech, Alfred Thayer Mahan's *The Influence of Sea Power upon History*, and the program of the anti-imperialist league, to compare the positions and arguments of imperialists and anti-imperialists. *To what extent was "sea power" a factor in U.S. expansionism? What special interests did the United States have in acquiring Hawaii and Samoa?*

◗ Using selections from Josiah Strong's *Our Country*, analyze the Protestant missionary zeal for expansionism. *Why does Strong call it America's divine mission? To what extent did workingmen, business leaders, and farmers support expansion?*

◗ Weigh the relative importance of ideological, economic, and religious factors which contributed to late 19th-century imperialism.

◗ Construct a historical argument about or debate the following assertion: *President McKinley allowed himself to be stampeded into war with Spain by the "jingoes" in his own party and by public opinion at large after Spanish officials had agreed to the terms specified in his ultimatum. What was President McKinley's reasoning for taking control of the Philippines? Was the U.S. justified in annexing the Philippines? In the long run, would the United States have been better off keeping Cuba and relinquishing the Philippines?*

◗ Evaluate changing U.S. attitudes toward Emilio Aguinaldo from Senator George Hoar's remark in 1898 that Aguinaldo was the "George Washington of the Philippines" to the issue of warrants for his arrest after the Treaty of Paris. *Why did Aguinaldo oppose U. S. annexation of the Philippines? What were his basic goals? How effective was Aguinaldo's leadership during the Filipino insurrection?*

ERA 7

The Emergence of Modern America (1890-1930)

The study of the emergence of modern America begins with the Progressive Era, which deserves careful study because it included the nation's most vibrant set of reform ideas and campaigns since the 1830s-40s. Progressives were a diverse lot with various agendas that were sometimes contradictory, but all reformers focused on a set of corrosive problems arising from rapid industrialization, urbanization, waves of immigration, and business and political corruption. Students need to appreciate how central these were to Progressivism. A distinctively female reform culture powerfully shaped the movement.

Two of the problems confronted by Progressives are still central today. First, the Progressives faced the dilemma of how to maintain the material benefits flowing from the industrial revolution while bringing the powerful forces creating those benefits under democratic control and enlarging economic opportunity. Second, Progressives faced the knotted issue of how to maintain democracy and national identity amid an increasingly diverse influx of immigrants and amid widespread political corruption and the concentration of political power.

Students cannot fully understand the Progressive movement without considering its limitations, particularly its antagonism to radical labor movements and indifference to the plight of African Americans and other minorities. As in so many aspects of American history, it behooves students to understand different perspectives — in this case on the reform impulse of the early 20th century. Progressivism brought fusion in some areas of reform, but it also created fissures. Among those was the ongoing, heated controversy about female equality, particularly in the area of economic protectionism.

All issues of American foreign policy in the 20th century have their origins in the emergence of the U.S. as a major world power in the Spanish-American War at the end of the 19th century and in the involvement of the U.S. in World War I. The American intervention in World War I then cast the die for the United States as a world power for the remainder of the century.

In the postwar period the prosperity of the 1920s and the domination of big business and Republican politics are worthy of study, but the most compelling stories that will capture students' attention reside in the cultural and social realms. First, students should be fascinated with the women's struggle for equality, which had political, economic, and cultural dimensions. Second, students should understand how radical labor movements and radical ideologies provoked widespread fear and even hysteria. Third, they need to study the recurring racial tension that led to black nationalism and the Harlem Renaissance and the first great northward migration of African Americans on the one hand and the resurgence of the KKK on the other hand. Fourth, they need to understand the powerful movement to Americanize a generation of immigrants and the momentous closing of the nation's gates through severe retrenchment of the open-door immigration policies. Lastly, they should examine the continuing tension among Protestants, Catholics, and Jews, most dramatically exemplified in the resurgence of Protestant fundamentalism.

Overview

Standard 1: How Progressives and others addressed problems of industrial capitalism, urbanization, and political corruption

Standard 2: The changing role of the United States in world affairs through World War I

Standard 3: How the United States changed from the end of World War I to the eve of the Great Depression

John McCutcheon, The Tribune, *Chicago, 1918*

S T A N D A R D   1

Students Should Understand: *How Progressives and others addressed problems of industrial capitalism, urbanization, and political corruption.*

Students Should Be Able to:

1A Demonstrate understanding of the origin of the Progressives and the coalitions they formed to deal with issues at the local and state levels by:

⬛ 9-12 Examining the social origins of the Progressives. [**Interrogate historical data**]

⬛ 7-12 Explaining how intellectuals and religious leaders laid the groundwork and publicists spread the word of defects in urban industrial society and suggested remedies. [**Assess the importance of the individual**]

⬛ 7-12 Evaluating Progressive attempts to restore democracy at the local and state levels. [**Examine the influence of ideas**]

⬛ 9-12 Evaluating Progressive attempts to regulate big business, curb labor militancy, and protect the rights of workers and consumers. [**Evaluate alternative courses of action**]

⬛ 5-12 Evaluating Progressive attempts at social and moral reform. [**Marshal evidence of antecedent circumstances**]

⬛ 7-12 Analyzing Progressive programs for assimilating the influx of immigrants before World War I. [**Formulate a position or course of action on an issue**]

| Grades 5-6 | Examples of student achievement of Standard 1A include: |

▶ Use photographs of child labor, urban tenements, schools, and slums, along with first-hand accounts and stories, to describe the conditions that led Progressives to propose far-reaching reforms. *How did migrants from rural areas and immigrants from other lands experience life in growing urban centers?*

▶ Generate a chart listing issues important to Progressives. Use newspapers and media reports to list and compare current social issues. *How do problems today compare to those tackled by the Progressives? How have social problems changed in our time?*

▶ Use census records, personal accounts, and pictorial sources to explain immigration to the United States. *Where did most immigrants settle? How did schools, religious groups, settlement houses, and philanthropists help immigrants cope with crowded urban living conditions?*

| Grades 7-8 | Examples of student achievement of Standard 1A include: |

▶ Draw upon evidence from the work of muckrakers such as Upton Sinclair, Jacob Riis, Lincoln Steffens, Lewis Hine, and Ida Tarbell to reveal chronic problems of urban industrial society. *Why were individuals who attempted to instigate reforms called muckrakers? Who might be considered muckrakers in contemporary American society, and how do they go about bringing attention to their causes?*

▶ Chart Progressive social reforms of such areas as education, conservation, temperance, and the "Americanization" of immigrants. Identify the people who were instrumental in promoting these reforms, and evaluate the relative success of their efforts.

▶ Draw upon biographies to examine the contributions to Progressivism by such governors as Hiram Johnson, Robert La Follette, and Charles Evans Hughes.

Grades 9-12

Examples of student achievement of Standard 1A include:

▶ Draw upon such sources as the *Dictionary of American Biography*, a variety of literary sources, historical narratives, newspaper accounts, and political commentaries by Progressives to analyze the personal background of Progressives, their critique of urban-industrial America, their goals and political strategies for effecting change, and their successes as well as failures. *What were the social backgrounds of Progressive reformers (social class, age, education, occupation, gender, race, and religion)? How did their social backgrounds contribute to their critiques, goals, political strategies, and successes? What were the major structural changes they proposed for government at the local and state levels? What was the impact of the social gospel movement on the reform agenda? What were their proposals in education, conservation, the consumption of alcohol, and the assimilation of immigrants? What were the Progressive proposals for the regulation of big business, the protection of consumers, and the improvement of working conditions?*

▶ Read selections from *The Autobiography of Lincoln Steffens*, Ida Tarbell's *The History of Standard Oil*, Upton Sinclair's *The Jungle*, Henry Demarest Lloyd's *Wealth against Commonwealth*, Jacob Riis's *How the Other Half Lives*, and *McClure's Magazine* to evaluate the evidence and arguments offered by the social critics of urban-industrial society in the late 19th and early 20th centuries. *What were the targets of Progressive criticism? What were the primary arguments and evidence used in their brief against urban-industrial society?*

▶ Compare and contrast reforms pertaining to government and business at the local and state level of government to ascertain which changes had lasting impact. *What were the major reforms implemented at the local level? Which cities and mayors deserve recognition for outstanding leadership of the reform movement at the local level? What were the major reforms implemented at the state level during the Progressive Era? What states and governors deserve recognition for outstanding leadership of the reform movement at the state level?*

▶ Explain how racial and ethnic conflicts contributed to delayed statehood for New Mexico and Arizona.

▶ Read selections from the writings of major leaders such as Florence Kelley, Charlotte Perkins Gilman, Margaret Sanger, Carrie Nation, Jacob Riis, Emma Goldman, Washington Gladden, Walter Rauchenbush, and John Dewey, who were involved in social and moral reform, and analyze why some proposals endured, while others failed.

▶ Draw data from the Dillingham Commission, Madison Grant's *Passing of the Great Race* (1916), and other historical and sociological sources to appraise the impact of the "new nativism." *How did such works affect the movement to "Americanize" the newer immigrants? To what extent did they lead to the movement to restrict immigration? How did such views affect the status of African Americans, Native Americans, Asian Americans, and Hispanic Americans?*

Students Should Be Able to:

1B Demonstrate understanding of Progressivism at the national level by:

5-12 Evaluating the presidential leadership of Theodore Roosevelt, William Howard Taft, and Woodrow Wilson in terms of their effectiveness as spokespersons for Progressivism and passage of reform measures. [**Assess the importance of the individual**]

7-12 Explaining why the election of 1912 was a pivotal campaign for the Progressive movement at the national level. [**Interrogate historical data**]

7-12 Comparing the New Nationalism, New Freedom, and Socialist agendas for change. [**Compare and contrast differing sets of ideas**]

5-12 Describing how the 16th, 17th, 18th, and 19th amendments reflected the ideals and goals of Progressivism. [**Evaluate the implementation of a decision**]

9-12 Explaining how the decisions of the Supreme Court affected Progressivism. [**Interrogate historical data**]

Grades 5-6

Examples of student achievement of Standard 1B include:

▶ Use biographies as references to compare Presidents Roosevelt, Taft, and Wilson and their ideas for reform. *How did each of these national leaders hope to solve human problems in urban centers and the work place. How well did they succeed in reaching their goals during their lifetimes?*

▶ Explain the 16th, 17th and 18th amendments. Using role-playing, an art project, or writing assignments, have students respond to such questions as: *How did these amendments reflect the ideas of the Progressives? Why, as senator from your state, would you have voted for or against each of these amendments? How would each of these amendments affect your life if you were one of the following people: (a) a store owner; (b) a homemaker; (c) a farmer; (d) a student or, (e) a mayor of a city?*

▶ Examine the movement for woman suffrage through historical fiction using stories such as *Never Jam Today* by Carol Bolton and *Does Anyone Care About Lou Emma Miller?* by Alberta Wilson Constant.

Grades 7-8

Examples of student achievement of Standard 1B include:

▶ List the major reforms initiated by the Roosevelt, Taft, and Wilson administrations and construct a historical argument evaluating the commitment of each to Progressive ideals.

▶ Utilize such visual sources as photographs, newsreel images, cartoons, and caricatures of Roosevelt, Taft, and Wilson to interpret how they were popularly portrayed as leaders of reform.

▶ Use maps and statistical data to investigate the results of the presidential election of 1912. *What factors contributed to Wilson's victory? In what way was the election of 1912 a high watermark for Progressivism?*

▶ Identify the Progressive amendments to the Constitution and analyze the movements that culminated in each amendment. *How did the alliance of the Anti-Saloon League and the Women's Christian Temperance Union produce the 18th Amendment? What did the proponents think it would solve? Why was the Income Tax Amendment considered progressive? Why was there a movement for direct elections of senators? Was this a change for the better?*

Grades 9-12

Examples of student achievement of Standard 1B include:

▶ Draw upon a variety of historical narratives, biographical and newspaper accounts, personal letters, and memoirs to compare Presidents Roosevelt, Taft, and Wilson as leaders of the Progressive movement. *What was the substance of Progressive reforms during the presidency of Theodore Roosevelt? What were his major contributions to Progressivism? How did Taft's background and training influence his view of the presidency and his style of leadership? What kind of progressive qualifications did Wilson bring to the presidency?*

Was Theodore Roosevelt a "trust buster" in the progressive sense or was he resorting to political rhetoric? What was the progressive Republicans' case against Taft? Was it justifiable? How are the weaknesses and strengths of Progressivism illustrated in the Wilson administration? How did Wilson respond to the requests of African Americans, women, and labor?

▶ Analyze the Hetch Hetchy controversy by explaining the motives of the central participants and the impact of the battle. *How did Pinchot defend his position? Do you agree?*

▶ Assess the platforms of the Democratic, Republican, Progressive, and Socialist parties in the 1912 presidential elections; analyze their similarities and differences; and explain why the 1912 campaign was the high tide of Progressivism. *What were the political and issue-oriented factors affecting the rift within the Republican party after 1909? In what ways did the Square Deal, New Nationalism, and New Freedom differ? In what ways were they similar? What factors influenced the outcome of the election? To what extent was Wilson's reform program from 1913 to 1916 a simple updating of the Omaha Platform of 1892?*

▶ Analyze the methods that Carrie Chapman Catt used in her leadership of the National Woman Suffrage Association to get the 19th Amendment passed and ratified. *Why did Wilson change his mind about the amendment? Which of Catt's tactics were most successful? Why?*

▶ Evaluate whether the Supreme Court aided or retarded Progressivism by analyzing key decisions and reasoning in such cases as: (a) *U.S. v. E.C. Knight Company* (1895); (b) *Northern Securities Company v. U.S.* (1904); (c) *Lochner v. New York* (1905); (d) *Muller v. Oregon* (1908); (e) *Standard Oil of N.J. v. U.S.* (1911); and (f) *Hammer v. Dagenhart* (1918).

Students Should Be Able to:

1C Demonstrate understanding of the limitations of Progressivism and the alternatives offered by various groups by:

[5-12] Examining the perspectives of African Americans on Progressivism and their alternative programs. **[Consider multiple perspectives]**

[7-12] Evaluating the critique of the Progressive movement by various labor organizations and the examining programs they offered. **[Consider multiple perspectives]**

[9-12] Examining issues raised by women but ignored by mainstream Progressives. **[Formulate a position or course of action on an issue]**

[9-12] Evaluating the changing attitude toward Native American assimilation under Progressivism and the consequences of the change. **[Explain historical continuity and change]**

Grades 5-6

Examples of student achievement of Standard 1C include:

▶ Use stories, narratives, and biographies to identify issues that were important to African Americans, Native Americans, women, and organized workers.

▶ Read biographical sketches of such persons as Ida Wells-Barnett, Booker T. Washington, and W. E. B. Du Bois, and create a collage illustrating these African Americans during the Progressive period.

Grades 7-8

Examples of student achievement of Standard 1C include:

▶ Compare the goals and strategies for change advocated by Booker T. Washington and W. E. B. Du Bois. *How did African Americans use Progressive tactics to attempt change? How successful were they in securing the passage of legislation such as anti-lynching laws? What was the legacy of* Plessy v. Ferguson?

▶ Use primary documents such as speeches, posters, songs, and poems to explain the message of the Industrial Workers of the World (IWW). *Who were the leaders of the radical labor movement and what strategies did they advocate to achieve their goals? How did the goals of the IWW differ from those of the Progressives?*

▶ Develop character sketches of individual women and examine the issues they raised during the Progressive era. *Why did mainstream Progressives abandon women's issues? How did women respond?*

Grades 9-12

Examples of student achievement of Standard 1C include:

▶ Use selections from *The Souls of Black Folk* to show how W. E. B. Du Bois criticized Booker T. Washington. *Why did Du Bois believe that the substitute of "man training for materialism fostering intelligence and knowledge of the world" is progressive for African Americans? What was Du Bois's role in founding the NAACP? Why was it established? To what extent were the efforts of Washington and Du Bois complementary?*

▶ Use selections from Mary Church Terrell's *Autobiography* to explain her quest for social justice. *To what extent did the Progressives' emphasis on decentralization and localism work to the disadvantage of African Americans? How were Charlotte Hawkins Brown, Ida Wells-Barnett, and Mary Church Terrell activists? What were their major contributions?*

▶ Draw from a variety of historical sources including pictures and newspaper articles to explain how the International Ladies Garment Workers Union (ILGWU) and the "1909 uprising of the 20,000" exemplified an alternative to mainstream Progressivism.

▶ Use selections from Margaret Sanger's "Woman Rebel" and Charlotte Perkins Gilman's *Herland* to explain how the "New Woman" ideas and activities were an alternative to Progressivism and its effects on women.

▶ Analyze the debate among leading women on the suffrage movement. *How did Susan B. Anthony use the traditional ideas of domesticity to support her reasoning? How did Gilman's reasoning differ? Who was threatened by Gilman's ideas and why? How did the activities of Margaret Sanger, Louise Bryant, and Emma Goldman add to Progressive fears about disorder? How did Alice Paul's Congressional Union and the National American Woman Suffrage Association (NAWSA) differ in their approach to suffrage?*

▶ Compare earlier white views of desirable Native American assimilation at the time of the Dawes Act of 1887 with the changing perception in the first two decades of the 20th century. *Why did Native Americans come to be perceived increasingly as peripheral members of society? Why did so many whites increasingly view the assimilation of Native Americans as no longer including full citizenship and equality? How did the case of* Lone Wolf v. Hitchcock (1903) *and the Burke Act of 1906 affect Native Americans and the disposition of tribal lands? What was the impact of western politicians and their constituents on the decisions to decrease federal restriction on the sale and taxation of Indian allotments? What were the effects on ownership of tribal lands?*

▶ Evaluate the success of the Progressive movement. *How democratic was the Progressive movement? How did Progressives' views of the immigrant strengthen the position of urban bosses? What was the outcome of reforms such as the initiative and the direct primary? How did voter registration laws affect the participation of voters? How did the disenfranchisement of African Americans in the South, occurring at the same time as Progressivism, display the paradox of Progressive reform?*

Tuskegee Institute, Library of Congress

STANDARD 2

Students Should Understand: *The changing role of the United States in world affairs through World War I.*

Students Should Be Able to:

2A Demonstrate understanding of how the American role in the world changed in the early 20th century by:

5-12 Analyzing the reasons for the Open Door Policy. [**Formulate a position or course of action on an issue**]

7-12 Evaluating Theodore Roosevelt's Big Stick diplomacy in the Caribbean and comparing it to his mediation of the Russo-Japanese War. [**Compare and contrast differing sets of ideas**]

7-12 Explaining United States relations with Japan and the evolution and significance of the "Gentlemen's Agreement." [**Consider multiple perspectives**]

7-12 Evaluating how Taft's Dollar Diplomacy differed from Roosevelt's Big Stick diplomacy. [**Compare and contrast differing sets of ideas**]

7-12 Evaluating Wilson's moral diplomacy, especially in relation to the Mexican Revolution. [**Examine the influence of ideas**]

Grades 5-6

Examples of student achievement of Standard 2A include:

▶ Explain the Open Door Policy. Locate China on a map and show areas that were dominated by European countries and Japan. *Why was the United States interested in having an "open door" in China? What products did the U.S. want from China? Why was trade with China important to the U.S.?*

▶ Locate on a map places that the United States claimed, occupied, or protected in the Caribbean after the Spanish-American War. *What did President Roosevelt mean when he said, "I have always been fond of the West African proverb, 'Speak softly and carry a big stick; you will go far'"?*

▶ Construct a journal or classroom newspaper examining the importance of an interoceanic canal.

Grades 7-8

Examples of student achievement of Standard 2A include:

▶ Explain American diplomatic initiatives in East Asia. *To what extent did the Open Door Policy differ from previous U.S. policy? How were goals of both the United States and Japan met by the Gentlemen's Agreement of 1907?*

◆ Define Roosevelt's Big Stick policy and explain how it was applied to Latin America. *Why did Theodore Roosevelt believe that the United States had the right to intervene in the affairs of Latin American nations? How did the construction and control of the Panama Canal underscore the perceived role of the United States in the region? How did contemporary political cartoonists depict Roosevelt's foreign policy?*

◆ Develop a historical argument assessing differences in the foreign policy approaches of Roosevelt's Big Stick, Taft's Dollar Diplomacy, and Wilson's Moral Diplomacy. Conduct historical research to develop a case study of one such episode (e.g., Panama, Nicaragua, or Mexico). *What were the foreign policy goals of each administration? What was the reaction of Latin Americans to U.S. intervention in the Caribbean, Central America, and Mexico? What is the legacy of such policies in the present-day relationships between the United States and Latin America?*

Grades 9-12

Examples of student achievement of Standard 2A include:

◆ Use the Open Door Notes to explain the commercial basis of American foreign policy in East Asia. *To what extent were the Open Door Notes part of a quest for "informal empire" rather than open imperialism in East Asia? How did the Open Door Notes lay the basis for America's future protection of China's territorial integrity?*

◆ Use the texts of the Monroe Doctrine and the Roosevelt Corollary to determine to what extent there is a connection. *Is the Roosevelt Corollary a legitimate use of the Monroe Doctrine or a distortion of it? Under the Roosevelt Corollary, were nations entitled to complete sovereignty?*

◆ Use cartoons and newspaper articles to explain the U.S. role in the Panama Revolution of 1903. *Was the construction of the Panama Canal in the U.S. national interest? Were Roosevelt's responses to the Panamanian Revolution justifiable? What were the long-range effects of his actions? Was Theodore Roosevelt abusing his powers as president to act on the Canal without congressional approval?*

◆ Use primary sources illustrating the West Coast hostility to Japanese immigrants to explain the connection between the 1906 segregation of San Francisco schools and the Gentlemen's Agreement. *What was the Japanese perspective on the segregation issue? How did the issue affect Japanese-U.S. relations? Why did Roosevelt feel it was necessary to send the Great White Fleet to Japan in 1908? How did it affect diplomatic relationships with Japan?*

◆ Draw from a variety of sources including Taft State Department documents to explain Dollar Diplomacy. *What reasons did Taft give for his administration's policy of Dollar Diplomacy in China and the Caribbean? To what extent was Dollar Diplomacy the implementation of the Roosevelt Corollary?*

◆ Use Wilson's "Mobile Declaration" to explain his "missionary diplomacy." *Did Wilson contradict his foreign policy goals when he sent General Pershing into Mexico and employed a large military force along the Mexican-U.S. border? How did Wilson's policy in Mexico underscore the significance of Porfirio Diaz's lamentation: "Poor Mexico. So far from God and close to the United States"?*

Students Should Be Able to:

2B **Demonstrate understanding of the causes of World War I and why the United States intervened by:**

5-12 Explaining the causes of World War I in 1914 and the reasons for the declaration of United States neutrality. [**Identify issues and problems in the past**]

7-12 Describing the course of World War I and its impact on the world prior to U.S. entry. [**Analyze cause-and-effect relationships**]

7-12 Analyzing the impact of United States public opinion on the Wilson administration's evolving foreign policy, 1914-1917. [**Examine the influence of ideas**]

7-12 Evaluating Wilson's leadership during the period of neutrality and his reasons for intervention. [**Assess the importance of the individual**]

Grades 5-6

Examples of student achievement of Standard 2B include:

▶ Describe the German and Allied use of new weapons and technology. Using pictures, maps, and news accounts, answer such questions as: *How did new weapons used in World War I, such as the "Big Bertha" cannon, poison gas, and steel tanks, change warfare? How did the use of submarines and blockades push the United States toward a declaration of war?*

▶ Use a map to locate the Allied and Central Powers and examine the extent of World War I in Europe.

Grades 7-8

Examples of student achievement of Standard 2B include:

▶ Examine the reasons why many Americans initially saw no reason to join in the war in Europe and construct a response to each of the following quotations: *The United States should "set an example for peace for the world"* (Secretary of State William Jennings Bryan), and *"Our whole duty for the present, at any rate, is summed up by the motto: 'America First: Let us think of America before we think of Europe'"* (President Woodrow Wilson).

▶ Examine the system of alliances through which nations in Europe sought to protect their interests, and explain how nationalism and militarism contributed to the outbreak of war. *What measures might have been taken to avert the war? How did the war expand beyond European boundaries to become a world war? Why did the United States declare neutrality at the beginning of the war?*

▶ Analyze maps and photographs of battle scenes in order to explain the nature of the war in Europe. Investigate how technological developments employed in the "Great War" contributed to the brutality of modern war. *How did the American public respond to the images of total war? What impact did Allied propaganda have on public opinion in the United States? How did ethnic American groups figure in the debate about the course of the war?*

▶ Debate the proposition, *"The United States should have maintained its neutrality during the course of World War I."* Prepare evidence considering such factors as British interference with U.S. shipping, the sinking of the *Lusitania*, Wilson's election pledge to keep the United States out of the war, unrestricted submarine warfare, and the Zimmermann Telegram.

Grades 9-12

Examples of student achievement of Standard 2B include:

▶ Draw upon a variety of historical narratives, literary sources, newspaper accounts, and magazine descriptions to analyze the motivations of the leading world powers, their relative success in mobilizing their populations, the relative success of their propaganda campaigns to influence neutral nations, and the events and policies leading to their success or failure prior to entry by the United States. *Once hostilities began, what were the motivations of the various belligerents for fighting the war? To what extent were countries successful in mobilizing their people and resources for fighting the war? How successful were the propaganda campaigns the belligerents aimed at neutral nations? Prior to the entry of the United States, how successful were the military strategies pursued by belligerents?*

▶ Draw on a variety of historical, visual, and literary sources including Erich Maria Remarque's *All Quiet on the Western Front* and Dalton Trumbo's *Johnny Got His Gun* to provide examples of how World War I contributed to a general spirit of disillusionment.

▶ Draw upon biographies, historical narratives, newspaper accounts, and magazine descriptions to analyze Wilson's leadership during the period of neutrality. *Was Secretary of State William Jennings Bryan right in calling for a ban on loans and the sale of munitions to the belligerents? Was there any inconsistency between Wilson's warning American citizens to get out of Mexico and his refusal to warn them to stay out of the European war zone? How did Wilson respond to the Zimmermann Note? Do you agree with his response?*

▶ Draw upon biographies, historical narratives, newspaper accounts, and magazine descriptions to write an essay on Wilson's second term as president. *During the presidential election of 1916, was Wilson honest and forthright with the American people about our prospects as a participant? How did the Wilson administration respond to the propaganda campaigns conducted by Germany and Britain in the United States? How would you evaluate the response? Was Wilson following a policy of neutrality during the first three years of the war? Did Wilson's declaration of war focus primarily on U.S. national interest? Explain.*

Students Should Be Able to:

2C Demonstrate understanding of the impact at home and abroad of United States involvement in World War I by:

`7-12` Explaining U.S. military and economic mobilization for war and the role of labor, women, and African Americans in the war effort. [**Identify issues and problems in the past**]

`9-12` Analyzing the impact of public opinion and government policies on constitutional interpretation and civil liberties. [**Evaluate the implementation of a decision**]

`5-12` Explaining how the American Expeditionary Force contributed to the Allied victory. [**Interrogate historical data**]

`7-12` Evaluating the significance of the Russian Revolution, its impact on the war, and on the foreign policies of the United States and Allied powers. [**Marshal evidence of antecedent circumstances**]

`5-12` Evaluating Wilson's Fourteen Points, negotiation of the Versailles Treaty, and the national debate over treaty ratification and the League of Nations. [**Evaluate the implementation of a decision**]

Grades 5-6

Examples of student achievement of Standard 2C include:

▶ Explain how the United States rapidly prepared for war in 1917 by examining memorabilia such as recruitment posters, war bond appeal flyers, pictures of women at work, and appeals urging African Americans to move north to fill jobs to support the war effort.

▶ Assess the peace process by reading Wilson's call for a League of Nations to preserve peace. *How did the Congress, the press, and the people respond to this idea? Did the United States become part of the League? When did our country join an international peacekeeping organization? Where has the United Nations tried to promote peace in the world?*

Grades 7-8

Examples of student achievement of Standard 2C include:

▶ Compare government actions to mobilize support and suppress opposition for the war effort. *What type of propaganda measures were utilized by the government to win popular support for such measures as military conscription and the sale of liberty bonds? During wartime, should the government have the right to limit civil liberties?*

▶ Research the role of women in wartime industry using primary source materials such as journals, periodical literature, and photographs to write fictional diaries, letters, and narratives reflecting the impact of the war on women.

▶ Examine a map of World War I military engagements and indicate the campaigns in which the American Expeditionary Force participated. Investigate the importance of U.S. forces in the victory over the Central Powers. Analyze such things as photographs, poetry, literature, art, and music to appraise the impact of war on American troops.

◆ Explain Wilson's goals in recommending the establishment of a League of Nations. *Why did domestic opposition to the League of Nations arise? What were the basic arguments against it? How does the League of Nations envisioned by Wilson compare to the present United Nations?*

Grades 9-12

Examples of student achievement of Standard 2C include:

◆ Draw upon sources such as historical narratives, newspaper articles, and personal memoirs to analyze the reasons for passage of the Selective Service Act in May 1917, and explain what areas of the country most legislative opponents of the measure represented. *What reasons did opponents of the Selective Service Act offer against passage of the measure? Did the Selective Service Act reflect the ideals and objectives of Progressivism?*

◆ Analyze President Wilson's declaration in 1917 that: "It is not an army that we must shape and train for war, it is a nation." Compare how U.S. mobilization in World War I differed from previous wars considering the role of the following in the mobilization effort: (a) War Industries Board; (b) Railroad Administration; (c) Food Administration; (d) Fuel Administration; (e) U.S. Shipping Board; and (f) Committee on Public Information (Creel Committee).

◆ Evaluate why so many Americans at the local, state, and national levels who had supported the war for the purpose of "making the world safe for democracy" denied it to many of their fellow citizens at home, actively prosecuted dissenters, and violated the civil liberties of nonconformists and opponents of the war. *In what respects were measures such as the Espionage and Sedition Acts violations of basic constitutional rights? On what grounds did Wilson support passage of such measures as the Espionage and Sedition Acts? To what extent did the Wilson administration contribute to the wartime hysteria? How did Justice Oliver Wendell Holmes's opinion in* Schenck v. U.S. (1919) *affect free speech? Do you agree with his reasoning? How did his opinion in* Abrams v. the U.S., *given eight months later, differ?*

◆ Explain the wartime contributions of labor and analyze how the war transformed the role and labor of women. *How did the role of Samuel Gompers and the American Federation of Labor differ from that of "Big Bill" Haywood and Eugene Debs in terms of support for the war?*

◆ Draw upon newspaper reports, editorials, advertisements, cartoons, historical narratives, and literary sources such as Richard Wright's *Native Son* to explain the "Great Migration" of African Americans to northern cities. *What opportunities were open to African Americans in northern urban centers? How difficult was it for African Americans from the rural south to adapt to life in urban areas? What did African American migrants contribute to the culture of northern cities? What were the major causes and consequences of racial tensions and conflict in the North (e.g., East St. Louis, Illinois, 1917) and South (e.g., Houston, 1917) during the war?*

◆ Examine point six of the Fourteen Points, which dealt specifically with Russia. *Did Wilson's subsequent actions in regard to Russia violate the principles set forth in his Fourteen Points? What was the nature and purpose of the U.S. Siberian expedition? What were the long-term consequences of Allied and American military intervention in Russia?*

▶ Draw upon the Fourteen Points and supplementary declarations negotiated by U.S. and Allied leaders to evaluate the efficacy of the Treaty of Versailles. *Were the terms that Germany agreed to in the armistice realized in the Versailles Peace Treaty? How did the Allied secret treaties, negotiated during the war, complicate Wilson's task at Paris in 1919? What major conflicts over self-determination arose at Paris and embittered the settlement?*

▶ Construct a sound argument about or debate such questions as: *Did Wilson miscalculate early popular support for the League of Nations and therefore refuse to compromise with his opponents? Was Henry Cabot Lodge really an "irreconcilable" disguising himself as a "revisionist" in order to defeat "Wilson's treaty?" How did Wilson's medical problems and subsequent incapacitation affect the Versailles Treaty and League of Nations ratification struggle in 1919-1920?*

Argonne Forest, National Archives

STANDARD 3

Students Should Understand: *How the United States changed from the end of World War I to the eve of the Great Depression.*

Students Should Be Able to:

3A Demonstrate understanding of the cultural clashes and their consequences in the postwar era by:

7-12 Examining the "red scare" and Palmer raids as a reaction to Bolshevism. [**Marshal evidence of antecedent circumstances**]

5-12 Analyzing the factors that lead to immigration restriction and the closing of the "Golden Door." [**Interrogate historical data**]

7-12 Examining race relations, including increased racial conflict, the resurgence of the Ku Klux Klan, and the emergence of Garveyism. [**Analyze cause-and-effect relationships**]

7-12 Examining the clash between traditional moral values and changing ideas as exemplified in the Scopes Trial and Prohibition. [**Examine the influence of ideas**]

9-12 Analyzing the emergence of the "New Woman" and challenges to Victorian values. [**Examine the influence of ideas**]

Grades 5-6

Examples of student achievement of Standard 3A include:

▶ Examine the effects of "nativism" and anti-immigrant attitudes. Looking at census charts, compare rates of immigration before and after the passage of restrictive laws in 1921 and 1924. *Why did nativists feel that immigration was harmful and had to be restricted in the early 1920s? Who did they think should live in this country? Why did Congress pass laws to sharply limit immigration from southern and eastern Europe? Did these laws further restrict the immigration of Asian peoples?*

▶ Assess the spread of the Ku Klux Klan's influence in different sections of the country in the 1920s. Analyze photographs showing cross burning, the march in Washington, D.C., and violence against African Americans and immigrants. *How did the Ku Klux Klan regard African Americans, Asians, southern and eastern European immigrants, and Jewish and Catholic Americans?*

▶ Draw historical evidence from narratives, stories, diaries, and photographs to describe how women's lives changed after World War I. *How did women contribute to improvement in schools, hospitals, settlement houses, and social agencies? How did the spread of electrification and growing use of household appliances like the refrigerator, washing machine, and vacuum cleaner improve the life of homemakers?*

▶ Use historical fiction such as *Shadrach's Crossing* by Avi to examine smuggling during Prohibition.

| Grades 7-8 | **Examples of student achievement of Standard 3A include:** |

‣ Debate the proposition: In order to defend American society from the threat of communists it may become necessary to restrict civil liberties.

‣ Construct a sound historical argument, or conduct a Socratic seminar on the topic: "Immigration restrictions of the 1920s rendered the Statue of Liberty obsolete." *Did the quota system discriminate against particular groups of immigrants? How did the restriction of European immigration affect Mexican American immigration?*

‣ Assess the degree to which the rebirth of the Ku Klux Klan exemplified hostility toward people of color, religious minorities, and immigrants in many parts of American society. *What accounts for the development of large Klan organizations in northern states?*

‣ Construct a historical narrative comparing attitudes toward women with changing values and new ideas regarding such things as employment opportunities, appearance standards, leisure activities, and political participation.

| Grades 9-12 | **Examples of student achievement of Standard 3A include:** |

‣ Analyze the major causes of the Red Scare and explain the role of J. Edgar Hoover and Attorney General A. Mitchell Palmer in contributing to the hysteria. Draw historical evidence from speeches, political cartoons, news reports, editorials, and journal articles to analyze how words and images were used to stir fears of Bolshevism and foreigners. *To what extent was Bolshevism a real or imagined threat to the United States? How effective was propaganda in winning public support for the Palmer raids?*

‣ Draw evidence from the Sacco and Vanzetti trial proceedings and commentary by journalists to analyze the issues raised by the celebrated case. *How did the Sacco and Vanzetti case relate to the Palmer raids? Did Sacco and Vanzetti get a fair trial?*

‣ Use statistical charts and the immigration laws of 1917, 1921, and 1924 to explain the changes in the ethnic composition of immigrants and the fears it represented. *What factors contributed to the passage of restrictive immigration laws in the twenties? How was "American" being defined?*

‣ Draw historical evidence from biographies, newspapers, and works of authors reflecting different attitudes on race, such as Madison Grant, Thomas Dixon, James Weldon Johnson, W. E. B. Du Bois, and Claude McKay, to construct a historical narrative assessing the impact and consequences of racism in the postwar era. *What were the underlying causes of the northern race riots of the postwar era? What were the origins and goals of the Garvey movement? How successful was Marcus Garvey?*

‣ Gather evidence from a variety of sources including the Ku Klux Klan's book of rules (The Khloran) and descriptions of Klan ceremonies to examine the purposes and goals of the "New Klan." *To what extent did the "New Klan" differ from the earlier Klan? How did the ritual and ceremonies of the Klan appeal to a need for community? To what extent were the immigration laws related to the revival of the Klan? What was the role of women in the "New Klan"?*

◆ Use selections from the Scopes trial or excerpts from *Inherit the Wind*, to explain how the views of William Jennings Bryan differed from those of Clarence Darrow. *How did William Jennings Bryan attack evolutionary thought? How does his attack relate to fundamentalist thinking? What techniques did Clarence Darrow use to counter Bryan's arguments? How did Darrow represent modernist, urban thinking?*

◆ Use newspaper and magazine articles to determine whether the dry crusade was a symbolic expression of ethnocultural differences and urban-rural tension. *Which groups supported the 18th Amendment? Why? Why did reformers consider a "noble experiment" in the 1920s? Why did it ultimately prove unsuccessful?*

◆ Use pictures, journal articles, and the writings of H. L. Mencken and Charlotte Perkins Gilman to explain how the image of the "flapper" symbolized the "New Woman." *Why were clothes called "The Great Liberator of the Decade"? How did the media image of women conform to reality? How did the images and goals of the "New Woman" affect middle-class behavior and family relationships? What fears did the "New Woman" image arouse?*

Ku Klux Klan parade, Washington D.C., 1925, Library of Congress

Students Should Be Able to:

3B Demonstrate understanding of how a modern capitalist economy emerged in the 1920s by:

5-12 Explaining how inventions, technological innovations, and principles of scientific management transformed production and work. [**Examine the influence of ideas**]

7-12 Examining the changes in the modern corporation, including labor policies and the advent of mass advertising and sales techniques. [**Analyze cause-and-effect relationships**]

9-12 Analyzing the new downtowns and suburbs and how they changed urban life. [**Explain historical continuity and change**]

Grades 5-6

Examples of student achievement of Standard 3B include:

▶ Assess the changes in your community and urban/suburban settings by looking at historical pictures, visiting museums, and interviewing and reading accounts by those who lived in the 1920s. *How did earlier improvements in steel construction and elevators allow for great change in cities in the 1920s? Why did people prize home ownership? Why did so many people leave the cities for the suburbs? What made travel to work easier for people in cities and suburbs?*

Grades 7-8

Examples of student achievement of Standard 3B include:

▶ List new inventions and technological advances which affected the lives of Americans in the 1920s, and describe how management techniques changed the methods of production. *Why was Henry Ford the symbol of the new industrial order in the twenties? In what respects was automobile manufacturing the characteristic industry of 1920s America? How did the automobile change American life in the 1920s?*

▶ Analyze the impact of advertising on the desire for new products. Compare advertising media from the 1920s with contemporary media, using the Sears Roebuck Catalogue or automobile, cigarette, and appliance advertisements from newspapers and magazines.

Grades 9-12

Examples of student achievement of Standard 3B include:

▶ Examine such companies as General Electric, the Endicott-Johnson Shoe Company, or International Business Machines (IBM) to explain how new inventions, technological advances, and improvements in scientific management revolutionized productivity and the nature of work in the twenties. *How did the expanded "rule of reason" decision in the 1920 U.S. Steel case favor the growth and development of modern corporations? How did Frederick W. Taylor's evaluation of shop organization, task analysis, industrial engineering, and worker motivation contribute to increased efficiency and productivity in the 1920s? How did Taylor's innovations affect public education and the schooling of children?*

◗ Explain how the "new paternalism" of the modern corporation, as illustrated in the rise of "welfare capitalism" and the rapid growth of personnel departments seeking to create a cooperative, highly motivated, and productive work force, contributed to the improvements in industrial efficiency and production in the postwar period.

◗ Construct a historical narrative explaining how new forms of advertising, installment buying, and sales techniques contributed toward the creation of a new consumer culture in the twenties. *How was a deodorant advertising slogan, "Make your arm pits, charm pits," reflective of new methods of advertising? How did national advertising and sales campaigns impact the American economy?*

◗ Analyze the reasons for development of skyscrapers and their impact on the concept of community and individualism. *How did the architecture of Frank Lloyd Wright develop the urban "civic center"? How did he try to bridge individualism, equality, and urban congestion in his architecture? How did his architecture portray middle class culture in suburbia?*

Magazine Advertisement, Library of Congress

Students Should Be Able to:

3C Demonstrate understanding of the development of mass culture and how it changed American society by:

`5–12` Analyzing how radio, movies, and popular magazines and newspapers created mass culture. [**Examine the influence of ideas**]

`7–12` Explaining the emergence of distinctively American art and literature including the contributions of the Harlem Renaissance and the "Lost Generation." [**Formulate historical questions**]

`5–12` Examining how increased leisure time promoted the growth of professional sports, amusement parks, and national parks. [**Analyze cause-and-effect relationships**]

Grades 5-6

Examples of student achievement of Standard 3C include:

▶ Construct projects such as wall charts, murals, short stories, poems, skits, or songs to compare media and recreation available in the 1920s. Compare the print media, radio, and movies produced in the '20s to information sources available today. *What did families do at home to get information and entertain themselves? Where did they go outside their homes for recreation? Which inventions and technologies have changed the ways in which we get information and entertainment since the 1920s?*

▶ Investigate the work of an individual who contributed to the Harlem Renaissance to define the movement. Draw from the music, art, and literature of major figures in the Harlem Renaissance such as Langston Hughes, James Weldon Johnson, Zora Neale Hurston, Bessie Smith, Duke Ellington, and Archibald Motley. *What issues and ideas did they portray in their work?*

▶ Draw evidence from a variety of sources, such as maps, historical narratives, and photographs, to examine the growth of professional sports facilities, fair grounds, amusement parks, and recreational areas in your region. *When were these places developed in your community, county, or state? How did people reach these places? How did these recreational areas change the local environment?*

▶ Draw evidence from photographs, movies, and family albums to examine the changes that contribute to the reason why people call this era the "Roaring Twenties." *How did clothing and fashion change in the 1920s? What was the dance rage of the period? What would it have been like to live in the 1920s?*

Grades 7-8

Examples of student achievement of Standard 3C include:

▶ Define mass culture and describe examples of the means by which cultural norms and fads are disseminated today. Compare these findings with the society of the 1920s. *How were such things as fashion and hair styles, slogans or phrases, and popular dances introduced into mainstream society? How have movies, radio, and print media influenced change in American culture?*

▶ Examine how literature and art in the 1920s questioned traditional values and culture. *What did the writers of the Lost Generation think about American society? Who were the prominent writers and what were the themes of their works? To what extent did the Harlem Renaissance capture the diversity of African American culture? Who were the leading writers and artists of the Harlem Renaissance? What was the impact of their works?*

▶ Investigate how Americans used the luxury of increased leisure time. Answer such questions as: *What accounted for the increase of leisure time in the 1920s? How did the automobile promote the use of national parks? Why have the 1920s been called the "Golden Age of Bat, Club, Glove, and Ball?" Who were the popular sports figures of the era?*

Grades 9-12

Examples of student achievement of Standard 3C include:

▶ Assemble evidence regarding the national impact of radio, high circulation print media, and movies, and construct a valid historical argument on such questions as: *To what extent was a national popular culture created by syndicated presses or national press associations? In the 1920s, was the radio a more powerful form of media for the shaping of a national popular culture than television is today? How constructive were the movies in shaping national popular culture?*

▶ Draw upon a variety of historical narratives and literary sources to analyze the emergence of a distinctive American art and literature. *How did the writers of the Lost Generation capture the changes taking place in the United States? How did the creative work of the Harlem Renaissance reflect the experience of African Americans? How did the poetry of Langston Hughes illustrate the themes of the Harlem Renaissance? To what extent did authors such as Claude McKay, Zora Neale Hurston, and Countee Cullen employ similar themes in their works?*

▶ Construct a historical narrative or visual display which explains how the work of such artists as Georgia O'Keefe, Robert Henri, William Glackens, George Luks, Everett Shinn, John Sloan, George Bellows, and Edward Hooper reflected the urban landscape of the early 20th century. *In what respects was the Armory Show of 1913 revolutionary? Why did its display of modern art shock so many people? How did the themes of cynicism and disillusionment influence the work of artists in the postwar period?*

▶ Describe the origin of the blues and explain how it reflected the jazz experience of African Americans. *Why did the blues and jazz become a part of the national culture? What messages did the music contain?*

▶ Drawing upon a variety of historical narratives, literary sources, newspaper accounts, and magazine descriptions, analyze how the increased leisure time achieved in the 1920s promoted the growth of professional sports, amusement parks, and national parks. *How did the desire for the emerging leisure time comport with the Protestant work ethic dominant in the 19th century? How did the creation of national parks affect Native American culture, Indian reservations, and white images of Indians?*

Students Should Be Able to:

3D Demonstrate understanding of politics and international affairs in the 1920s by:

`7-12` Evaluating the waning of Progressivism and the "return to normalcy." [**Explain historical continuity and change**]

`5-12` Analyzing the effects of woman suffrage on American society. [**Evaluate the implementation of a decision**]

`7-12` Describing the goals and evaluating the effects of Republican foreign policy in the 1920s. [**Analyze cause-and-effect relationships**]

Grades 5-6

Examples of student achievement of Standard 3D include:

▶ Construct a time line of the woman suffrage movement from the Seneca Falls Convention of 1848 to the ratification of the 19th Amendment. *Why did women want to be able to vote? How did the 19th Amendment change political life in America? How have voting rules changed for African Americans, young people, Native Americans, and immigrants since the ratification of the 19th Amendment?*

Grades 7-8

Examples of student achievement of Standard 3D include:

▶ Investigate the changes in Progressivism during the Harding and Coolidge administrations. *Were the 1920s an extension of the Progressive era or a retreat from Progressive ideals? How would a Progressive respond to Coolidge's statement: "The man who builds a factory builds a temple. The man who works there, worships there"?*

▶ Examine the impact of woman suffrage on American society in the decade following the passage of the 19th Amendment. *Did the right to vote guarantee equality for women? Why did women such as Alice Paul call for the passage of an Equal Rights Amendment as a means to end gender discrimination? Did a majority of women actively support the ERA?*

▶ Locate on a world map United States territories and spheres of influence in the 1920s and investigate the foreign policy of Republican administrations. *What was the role of the U.S. in disarmament conferences? Was the United States willing to enter into associations or make treaties with major European powers? Did U.S. policy in Latin America differ from that of previous administrations? To what extent did Presidents Harding, Coolidge, and Hoover carry out the Big Stick policy of Theodore Roosevelt?*

Grades 9-12

Examples of student achievement of Standard 3D include:

▶ Gather evidence from a variety of historical sources to assess the Harding and Coolidge administrations and analyze the effects of World War I on the vitality of Progressivism. *In what respects did the "return to normalcy" reflect a rejection of Wilsonianism and Progressivism? How did Harding's support of federal anti-lynching legislation, rights for African Americans, and his record in civil liberties contrast with his predecessor? What was the impact of the Coolidge-Mellon economic program? To what degree was it a break with the economic policies of Progressives?*

▶ Examine the effect of woman suffrage on women and society in the 1920s. *Why was Alice Paul's sponsorship of the Equal Rights Amendment so little supported by women in the 1920s? What issues concerning protective labor for women and children arose in the 1920s? How unified were women on these issues?*

▶ Describe Republican efforts to ensure a peaceful and stable world order in the 1920s and evaluate whether or not they were successful. *Were there discernible differences in U.S. foreign policy toward Asia, Europe, and Latin America in the 1920s? How realistic were the agreements reached at the Washington Naval Conference of 1921-22 in protecting the long-term interests and security of the United States? In what respects were Republican foreign policies in the 1920s different from Progressive policies? How did the Clark Memorandum (1928) and the Hoover administration reorient U.S. foreign policy toward Latin America?*

Suffragists, Bain Collection, Library of Congress

ERA 8

The Great Depression and World War II (1929-1945)

The Great Depression and the New Deal deserve careful attention for four reasons. First, Americans in the 1930s endured the greatest economic crisis in American history. Second, the depression wrought deep changes in people's attitudes toward government's responsibilities. Third, organized labor acquired new rights. Fourth, the New Deal set in place legislation that reshaped modern American capitalism.

The effect of the Great Depression on people's lives was one of the great shaping experiences of American history, ranking with the American Revolution, the Civil War, and the industrial revolution. More than Progressivism, the Great Depression brought about changes in the regulatory power of the federal government and in the government's role in superimposing relief measures on the capitalist system, bringing the U.S. into a mild form of welfare state capitalism, such as had appeared earlier in all of the industrial European nations. This era provides students with ample opportunities to test their analytic skills as they assay Franklin Roosevelt's leadership, the many alternative formulas for ending the Great Depression, and the ways in which the New Deal affected women, racial minorities, children, and other groups.

World War II deserves careful attention as well. Although it was not the bloodiest in American history, it solidified the nation's role as a global power and ushered in social changes that established reform agendas that would occupy the United States for the remainder of the 20th century. The role of the United States in World War II was epochal for its defense of democracy in the face of totalitarian aggression. Yet students should learn about the denial of the civil liberties of interned Japanese Americans and the irony of racial minorities fighting for democratic principles overseas that they were still denied at home. Students will need to assess carefully the course of the war, the collapse of the Grand Alliance, and its unsettling effects on the postwar period. Also, they should evaluate the social effects of war on the homefront, internal migration to war production centers, the massive influx of women into previously male job roles, and the attempts of African Americans and others to obtain desegregation of the armed forces and end discriminatory hiring.

Overview

Standard 1: The causes of the Great Depression and how it affected American society

Standard 2: How the New Deal addressed the Great Depression, transformed American federalism, and initiated the welfare state

Standard 3: The origins and course of World War II, the character of the war at home and abroad, and its reshaping of the U.S. role in world affairs

S T A N D A R D   1

Students Should Understand: *The causes of the Great Depression and how it affected American society.*

Students Should Be Able to:

1A Demonstrate understanding of the causes of the crash of 1929 and the Great Depression by:

7-12 Explaining the "trickle down" economic policies of the Coolidge-Mellon years and their economic impact on wealth distribution, investment, and taxes in the period 1925-1929. [**Analyze multiple causation**]

5-12 Analyzing the causes and consequences of the stock market crash of 1929. [**Compare competing historical narratives**]

7-12 Evaluating Hoover's response to the Great Depression and explaining the reasons for the deepening crisis in the period 1929-1933. [**Assess the importance of the individual in history**]

5-12 Evaluating the major causes of the Great Depression. [**Analyze multiple causation**]

9-12 Explaining the global context of the depression and the reasons for the worldwide economic collapse. [**Evaluate major debates among historians**]

| Grades 5-6 | **Examples of student achievement of Standard 1A include:** |

▶ List the factors that contributed to the causes of the Great Depression. Through a role-playing activity, skit, or reader's theater, examine the effects of the depression on farmers, city workers, and military veterans. *Why were farm products destroyed while people were hungry in the towns and cities? Why were workers unable to find jobs? How did mechanization displace workers? What did World War I veterans do to demand bonuses and jobs?*

▶ Contrast pictures of life in the "Roaring Twenties" with those showing depression conditions of the 1930s. Draw evidence from graphs and charts, documentary photographs, and oral history interviews to explain the changes in American life after the stock market crash of 1929.

| Grades 7-8 | **Examples of student achievement of Standard 1A include:** |

▶ Define "trickle down" economics and construct a chart illustrating the effects of the economic decisions of the Coolidge administration on large businesses, urban labor, and agriculture. *How was the Coolidge economic program supposed to work to promote economic growth? What were the arguments used by those who supported and those who opposed the policy? According to Coolidge, what role was government to play in the system? To what extent did "trickle down" economics benefit owners of large businesses, laborers, and farmers?*

▶ Explain the factors that contribute to the fluctuation of the stock market and construct a historical narrative to examine the causes and consequences of the market crash of 1929.

▶ Chart the measures the Hoover administration took to stem the tide of the Great Depression and construct a historical argument, debate, or narrative evaluating the effectiveness of these measures. *To what extent did President Hoover's philosophy of "rugged individualism" influence his recommendations for measures to stop the depression? What factors contributed to the continuing economic crisis? What impact did the closing of banks have on the economy? How did the worldwide depression impact the United States economy?*

▶ Draw upon evidence from a variety of primary and secondary sources, including data from graphs and charts, to assess the central political and economic causes of the Great Depression. *How did the distribution of income and wealth affect the U.S. economy in the 1920s? To what extent did the agricultural problems of the post-World War I era contribute to the depression?*

| Grades 9-12 | **Examples of student achievement of Standard 1A include:** |

▶ Draw upon the historical, literary, and graphic evidence to answer such questions as: *How was the "trickle down" theory supposed to ensure economic prosperity and growth? How did it work in reality? What factors contributed to the increasing consolidation of business in the 1920s? What major scientific and technological changes contributed to the increased productivity of business in the 1920s? How did Sinclair Lewis's character Babbitt reflect the business creed of the 1920s? How and why did the depression tarnish the popular image of American businessmen? Why did union membership decline so significantly in the 1920s? What major changes affected the lives and prosperity of workers in the 1920s? How did American tariff policy and international economic developments affect the Great Depression?*

▶ Consider the following statement: "From the top of prosperity in 1929 to the bottom of depression in 1933," writes one historian, "GNP dropped by a total of 29 percent, consumption expenditures by 18 percent, construction by 78 percent, and investment by an incredible 98 percent. Unemployment rose from 3.2 to 24.9 percent. By almost any standard the United States was in the worst crisis since the Civil War." *How did the Hoover administration attempt to stem the tide of depression and bring about recovery? Why did Hoover place such strong emphasis on maintaining the gold standard and supporting a balanced budget? How did such emphases affect recovery? Why did Hoover's efforts fail? How did the collapse of the banking system affect the economy?*

▶ Some critics of Herbert Hoover argue that while he provided relief for banks, he refused it to people, and while he helped feed foreigners, he let his own people starve. Draw upon the available evidence to assess the validity of such a view.

Students Should Be Able to:

1B Demonstrate understanding of how American life changed during the depression years by:

5-12 Explaining the effects of the Great Depression and Dust Bowl on American farmers, tenants, and share-croppers. **[Analyze multiple causation]**

7-12 Analyzing the impact of the Great Depression on industry and workers and explaining the response of local and state officials in combating the resulting economic and social crises. **[Analyze multiple causation]**

7-12 Analyzing the impact of the Great Depression on the American family and gender roles. **[Consider multiple perspectives]**

7-12 Explaining the impact of the Great Depression on African Americans, Mexican Americans, and Native Americans. **[Consider multiple perspectives]**

9-12 Explaining the cultural life of the depression years in art, literature, and music and evaluating the government's role in promoting artistic expression. **[Draw upon visual, literary, and musical sources]**

Grades 5-6

Examples of student achievement of Standard 1B include:

◗ Draw evidence from diaries, journals, oral histories, literature, documentary films, and photography to develop a skit or role play activity which examines life in the Midwest during the depression and the experiences of farmers who migrated to California in search of work.

◗ Use children's trade books such as *Nelda* by Pat Edwards and *Elderberry Thicket* by Joan Zeier to illustrate the effects of the depression on families.

◗ Explore the effects of the Great Depression on the local community by interviewing family members, long-time community residents, and library and local historical society resources. Compare photographs of homes and businesses then and now. *What happened to local families, businesses, farms, and banks during the depression? Did people in the local community lose their homes and farms? How did this compare to what was happening in the rest of the country at that time? Where did people turn for help in their community?*

◗ Describe how the drought of 1932 changed farming conditions in the Midwest. Draw upon documentary photographs, literature, and personal accounts to demonstrate how farm owners, tenant farmers, and sharecroppers were affected. Develop skits or stories depicting their problems.

◗ Draw upon evidence from diaries, journals, oral histories, documentary films, and photographs to develop picture boards, role-play activities, or stories examining the lives of diverse groups during the depression. *How did farm families fare when they moved westward to California? Where did unemployed city workers turn for help? How did people manage when homes were foreclosed?*

◗ Examine folk songs, pictures, and public art to learn about problems during the depression. Develop a classroom musical program or art show comparing issues faced during the depression with problems in our communities now. *How did aid for families during the depression compare with efforts to help the homeless today?*

| Grades 7-8 | **Examples of student achievement of Standard 1B include:** |

▶ Use historical fiction such as *I Remember Valentine* by Liz Hamilton, *No Promises in the Wind* by Irene Hunt, *Lackawanna* by Chester Aaron, and *Tracks* by Clayton Bess to explore the impact of the depression on young adults.

▶ Draw upon documentary photographs, ballads, demographic data, and unemployment trends to evaluate the effects of the Great Depression on the American people. *What was the response of Dust Bowl farmers to the crisis? What was the nature of their migration — where did they go and how did they get there? How did factory workers and other urban dwellers respond to rising unemployment, bank failures, and the like? What programs were developed by local officials to aid the affected?*

▶ Gather evidence from oral histories, letters, journals, and documentary photographs to examine the effects of the depression on American families and gender roles. *How did unemployment affect the self-esteem of heads of households? What pressures did it place on families? What effect did the depression have on women who were employed outside the home? What employment opportunities were open to women during the depression?*

▶ Chart the effects of the Great Depression on African Americans and Hispanics and construct a historical argument, debate, or narrative comparing their experiences with those of other Americans. *How did African Americans and Hispanics react to the events of the depression? Which of the various New Deal measures — such as the CCC and the WPA — most profoundly influenced their lives?*

▶ Draw evidence from *Roll of Thunder Hear My Cry* by Mildred Taylor to investigate the victimization of African American and white sharecroppers during the depression and Taylor's sequel, *Let the Circle Be Unbroken*, to examine a family's determination to resist prejudice.

| Grades 9-12 | **Examples of student achievement of Standard 1B include:** |

▶ Draw upon such historical, literary, and visual sources as Carey McWilliams's *Ill Fares the Land*, John Steinbeck's *The Grapes of Wrath*, James Agee and Walker Evans's *You have Seen their Faces*, Pare Lorentz's documentaries for the Farm Security Administration — *The River* and *The Plow That Broke the Plains* — and the photographs of Dorothea Lange and others to analyze the reasons for and effects of the Dust Bowl on farmers and their families in the Great Plains.

▶ Draw upon the historical evidence to answer such questions as: *How do you account for the poverty amidst plenty during the depression? What was the purpose and success of the Southern Tenant Farmers' Organization? Did farmers have legitimate complaints concerning exploitation by a variety of middlemen as the chief source of their problems, or did their economic hardship result primarily from overproduction and the vagaries of a market economy?*

▶ Draw on a variety of personal reminiscences and periodicals of the period to write a sound historical account of the impact of the Great Depression on local, state, and charitable resources in the period 1930-1938.

▶ Draw upon a variety of historical, literary, and visual sources to explain the impact of the Great Depression on the lives of workers and their families. *What effect did the Great Depression have on traditional gender roles? Why did the number of working women increase in the 1930s? Did women take jobs from men? What effect did the Great Depression have on marriages, divorces, and the number of children born in the 1930s? How did the Great Depression affect the lives of children and teenagers? What effect did prolonged unemployment have on male heads of families and how did the Great Depression affect traditional authority relationships within the family?*

▶ Examine the evidence and develop a sound historical argument explaining the impact of the Great Depression on African Americans in the North and South and how blacks responded to the crisis. Draw on historical accounts of the cases of Angelo Herndon and the Scottsboro Boys and the Supreme Court's rulings in *Powell* v. *Alabama* (1932) and *Norris* v. *Alabama* (1935) to explain how racism affected the conditions and position of African Americans in the 1930s.

▶ Drawing on a variety of historical data, explain the hardships faced by Mexican-Americans during the depression and evaluate the role of state and immigration officials in protecting the rights of Mexican Americans.

▶ Draw evidence from oral histories to research the repatriation of Mexican-Americans between 1931 and 1934. *Were Mexican-Americans forced to return to Mexico or was their request for repatriation an expression of their desire to return home?*

▶ Draw on the tradition of documentary expression in the 1930s by such practitioners as Erskine Caldwell, Dorothea Lange, Arthur Rotherstein, Ben Shahn, Roy Stryker, James Agee, Walker Evans, John Grierson, Pare Lorentz, and Dwight Macdonald to explain how their work reflected American conditions in the 1930s, and evaluate their impact on the New Deal. *How did the Works Progress Administration promote art in the period 1935-41?*

▶ Assess the impact of mass media on the American culture in the 1930s. *What factors contributed to the nationalization of culture? What kinds of movies and radio shows were most popular and why? How did popular culture divide along class lines? How did popular sports and athletic heroes and heroines reflect the ideals and interests of people? How did regionalist artists such as Thomas Hart Benton and Grant Wood portray American life?*

Depression family, photograph by Dorothea Lange, Library of Congress

STANDARD 2

Students Should Understand: *How the New Deal addressed the Great Depression, transformed American federalism, and initiated the welfare state.*

Students Should Be Able to:

2A Demonstrate understanding of the presidency of Franklin D. Roosevelt and the New Deal by:

`5-12` Contrasting the background and leadership abilities of Franklin D. Roosevelt with those of Herbert Hoover. **[Assess the importance of the individual in history]**

`7-12` Analyzing the link between the early New Deal and Progressivism. **[Compare and contrast differing sets of ideas]**

`9-12` Contrasting the "first" and "second" New Deals and evaluating the success of the relief, recovery, and reform measures associated with each. **[Compare and contrast differing sets of ideas]**

`9-12` Analyzing the factors contributing to the forging of the Roosevelt coalition in 1936 and explaining its electoral significance in subsequent years. **[Examine the influence of ideas]**

`7-12` Analyzing the impact of the New Deal on African Americans, Mexican Americans, Native Americans, and women. **[Identify issues and problems in the past]**

`7-12` Evaluating the role and contributions of Eleanor Roosevelt to the New Deal. **[Assess the importance of the individual in history]**

Grades 5-6 — Examples of student achievement of Standard 2A include:

▶ Drawing upon library resources, compare the leadership styles that Herbert Hoover and Franklin D. Roosevelt brought to the presidency. *How did the public respond to both presidents? Was public reaction to these two presidents fair?*

▶ Gather evidence from interviews and community libraries and historical societies to investigate ways in which New Deal legislation touched the lives of local families and people in your state or region. *How did women in your local community try to improve life for children and families? What roles did they play in organizing day-care centers, medical clinics, and food pantries?*

▶ Drawing upon biographies, find out how women like Eleanor Roosevelt, Frances Perkins, and Mary McLeod Bethune contributed to New Deal programs.

Grades 7-8 — Examples of student achievement of Standard 2A include:

▶ Compare Herbert Hoover and Franklin Roosevelt with regard to their personal and political responses to the Great Depression. *To what degree were the personal backgrounds of these leaders alike? To what extent were they different? How might one account for the different mind-set with which each leader responded to the Great Depression?*

▶ Interrogate historical data from a variety of sources to explain the link between Progressivism and the early New Deal.

▶ Chart the relief, recovery, and reform measures associated with the "first" and "second" New Deal and construct a historical argument, debate, or narrative evaluating the relative success of each program. *What were the social, economic, and political ramifications of these two New Deal plans? How did they differ?*

▶ Evaluate the commitment of Eleanor Roosevelt to improving conditions in the United States during the New Deal. *What specific efforts did the First Lady make in response to the crisis? How successful was she in fulfilling her agenda? Why might she be considered to be among the nation's most exceptional and accomplished presidential spouses?*

Grades 9-12

Examples of student achievement of Standard 2A include:

▶ Assemble the evidence to answer such questions as: *How did philosophical and political approaches of Hoover and Roosevelt in dealing with the depression differ? To what extent did Hoover pave the way for Roosevelt and the New Deal? What was new about the New Deal? Which groups benefited most from the early New Deal? In what ways did the New Deal complete the work of the Populists and Progressives or venture into new fields?*

▶ Drawing upon the historical evidence, evaluate FDR's commitment to advancing the civil and political rights of African Americans. *Why did African American voters increasingly change political allegiance from the Republican to the Democratic party after 1934? How did increased African American support for the Democrats affect Democratic policies? How did southern Democrats respond to the New Deal and efforts to improve the life and conditions of African Americans?*

▶ Drawing on a variety of historical sources, assess how African Americans planted the seeds of a civil rights revolution during the 1930s. *How did Charles Houston and his law students at Howard University lay the groundwork for the legal assault on segregation in the 1930s? How did African American leaders like Mary McLeod Bethune, Robert Weaver, William Hastie, Booker T. McGraw, and Robert J. Vann influence the New Deal?*

▶ Investigate the Indian Reorganization Act of 1934 and explain how it affected Native Americans. *What role did John Collier play in securing a "new deal" for Native Americans?*

Students Should Be Able to:

2B Demonstrate understanding of the impact of the New Deal on workers and the labor movement by:

5-12 Explaining the impact of the New Deal on American workers and the labor movement. **[Analyze cause-and-effect relationships]**

7-12 Explaining the emergence of labor militancy and the struggle between craft and industrial unions. **[Compare and contrast differing sets of ideas]**

7-12 Evaluating the commitment of labor unions to organizing African Americans, Mexican Americans, and women. **[Consider multiple perspectives]**

9-12 Explaining the impact of the New Deal on nonunion workers in the period 1933-40. **[Formulate a position or course of action on an issue]**

Grades 5-6

Examples of student achievement of Standard 2B include:

▶ Research the American labor movement during the Great Depression and New Deal. Use lyrics of songs such as "Brother, Can You Spare a Dime?" "Union Maid," and "Which Side Are You On?" to examine the effects of the depression and New Deal on the American labor movement. *What do the songs tell you about the condition of working men and women in the United States in the 1930s?*

Grades 7-8

Examples of student achievement of Standard 2B include:

▶ Interrogate historical data from a variety of sources including personal narratives, newspapers and periodicals, historical photographs, and documentary films to determine the impact of the first and second phases of the New Deal on the labor movement. *How valuable was Section 7a of the NIRA in promoting unionism? How successful were New Deal measures in reducing the number and frequency of strikes? How militant were these unions? To what extent did the New Deal support unions over management?*

▶ Evaluate the commitment of labor unions to organizing African Americans, Mexican Americans, and women and securing equitable conditions and pay for minorities.

▶ Write a character sketch of one labor leader or advocate for labor during the New Deal. Describe the stated objectives of the individual and how he or she responded to the crises of layoffs, anti-union tactics, and unemployment. Select from individuals such as: A. Phillip Randolph, John L. Lewis, Upton Sinclair, and Frances Perkins.

▶ Drawing data from art and photographs depicting the depression era labor movements and lyrics of labor songs, examine the emotional appeal to support unions.

▶ Analyze how the WPA projects affected local areas. Survey the local community for buildings, bridges, murals or other public works projects sponsored by New Deal agencies. *How did the Federal Theatre Project drama companies influence small town America? How did artists working for the Federal Arts Project transform post offices, schools, and other public buildings?*

Grades 9-12

Examples of student achievement of Standard 2B include:

▶ Drawing upon a variety of historical sources, explain the factors contributing to the success of CIO leadership in organizing the rubber, auto, and steel workers in the period 1937-1941. *Why did the American Federation of Labor prove reluctant to organize workers in the mass production industries? What role did Communist party organizers play in organizing workers in the 1930s? How did Roosevelt and the New Deal advance the interests of working class Americans? What workers benefited most from New Deal reforms? How did the general public respond to the "sit-down strikes" of 1937-38 and what effect did public perception have on support for the New Deal? What workers were least affected by unions? How did the New Deal affect nonunion workers?*

▶ Draw upon methods of historical research including oral history to formulate questions in assessing labor's commitment to organizing African Americans, Mexican Americans, and women workers during the 1930s. *To what degree did the American Federation of Labor (AFL) encourage women and minorities to join unions? What role did Asa Phillip Randolph play in promoting unionization of African American workers? How did the Congress of Industrial Organizations (CIO) differ from the AFL in promoting interracial industrial unions? How committed were unions in organizing migrant farm workers? What unions did Mexican American workers establish to protect their interests? What impact did the Great Depression have on women in the work place? How did the AFL respond to women in the work force? What was the impact on women workers of the AFL's program to restore "family life"?*

▶ Construct a historical investigation assessing the causes, strategies, and leadership of major strikes during the New Deal. Evaluate strikers' success in attaining their stated goals. Select from the rash of strikes in 1936 and 1937, including the celebrated General Motors sit-down strike.

▶ Explain the effects of New Deal agricultural programs on farm laborers by examining the Agricultural Adjustment Administration (AAA) and the Southern Tenant Farmers' Union (STFU). *Why was the STFU outraged with the application of the AAA? What methods did they use to change the system? What conclusions may be drawn from the fact that white and African American tenant farmers in the South worked together in the STFU?*

Women bound for the picket line, San Joaquin Valley, California, Library of Congress

Students Should Be Able to:

2C Demonstrate understanding of opposition to the New Deal, the alternative programs of its detractors, and the legacy of the "Roosevelt Revolution" by:

7-12 Explaining the reasoning of the Supreme Court decisions on the early New Deal. [**Compare and contrast differing sets of ideas**]

7-12 Evaluating Roosevelt's response to the Court's invalidation of the early New Deal. [**Examine the influence of ideas**]

7-12 Analyzing the opposition to the New Deal. [**Compare and contrast differing sets of ideas and values**]

5-12 Evaluating the significance and legacy of the New Deal. [**Evaluate the implementation of a decision**]

Grades 5-6

Examples of student achievement of Standard 2C include:

▸ Construct a balance sheet listing major New Deal programs which are still in effect today. Explain how these New Deal programs affect our life today.

▸ Explain a variety of political cartoons which support and oppose Roosevelt's "court packing" proposal. *What do these cartoons tell about the struggle over the Roosevelt plan? Why did Roosevelt abandon his proposal?*

Grades 7-8

Examples of student achievement of Standard 2C include:

▸ Draw upon evidence from a variety of primary and secondary sources including presidential pronouncements, speeches, and political cartoons to explain the controversy between Roosevelt and the Supreme Court. *What were the decisions reached by the judicial branch as a result of legal challenges to early New Deal measures? What constitutional arguments did the Supreme Court use to strike down various executive branch initiatives? What was Roosevelt's plan in response to the decisions of the Supreme Court? How successful was he in carrying out his plan?*

▸ Draw upon evidence from differing perspectives to assess the roots of the opposition to Roosevelt's policies. *What prompted attacks on the New Deal from the political right and left? What was it that prompted attacks from the political left? To what degree did this opposition coincide? What were the effects of such opposition on New Deal initiatives?*

▸ Construct a sound historical argument, debate, or narrative evaluating the significance and legacy of the New Deal and the extent to which the New Deal influenced the public's belief in the responsibility of government to deliver public services.

▸ Examine film documentaries and speeches of Dr. Francis Townsend and Senator Huey Long to explore the ideas of the Townsend Plan and the "Share the Wealth" program. *To whom did they appeal? Why did they attract public attention? What threats did they present to the New Deal?*

Grades 9-12

Examples of student achievement of Standard 2C include:

▶ Examine the Supreme Court's reasoning in *Schechter* v. *U.S.* (1935), *U.S.* v. *Butler* (1936), *West Coast Hotel Company* v. *Parish* (1937), and *National Labor Relations Board* v. *Jones and Laughlin* (1937) Investigate Roosevelt's response to the rulings and debate such questions as: *Was Roosevelt's "court packing" scheme appropriate? Was his proposal constitutional? Were the rulings by the Supreme Court the death knell of the New Deal? Would the acceptance of the Roosevelt plan have destroyed the constitutional system of checks and balances? How does "a switch in time save nine"?*

▶ Construct a sound argument, debate, or historical narrative examining the opposition to the New Deal from the perspective of the conservative Liberty League, the radical Communist party, or the protest movement of Coughlin and Long. *How did the proposals of the "Share the Wealth" movement differ from those of the Communist party? How did they differ from the Liberty League's agenda? What was the effect of such programs on the New Deal? Was the criticism of Roosevelt and the New Deal justified? To what extent did the opposition of these groups solidify popular support for the New Deal?*

▶ Examine the proposals of Upton Sinclair's EPIC campaign in California. *What groups opposed it? Why did it fail? What were the reasons for the growth of the American Communist party during the 1930s? To whom did the party have the greatest appeal?*

▶ Utilizing a variety of historical and statistical sources, analyze the class basis for support and opposition to the New Deal in the Northeast, South, Midwest, and Far West.

▶ Drawing upon a variety of examples from the New Deal era, explain how this reflects the ideology and significance of FDR and the New Deal. *Was the New Deal able to solve the riddle of depression? Who did the New Deal help the most? the least? What groups and regions most supported the New Deal? Did the New Deal go far enough? Would American voters in the 1930s have supported more radical changes? How did the New Deal change the relationship between state and federal government?*

▶ Evaluate Roosevelt from different perspectives. *How do current historians evaluate Roosevelt's domestic programs?*

A cartoon illustrating the public outcry to Roosevelt's court-packing plan, Library of Congress

S T A N D A R D   3

Students Should Understand: *The origins and course of World War II, the character of the war at home and abroad, and its reshaping of the U.S. role in world affairs.*

Students Should Be Able to:

3A Demonstrate understanding of the international background of World War II by:

7-12 Analyzing the factors contributing to the rise of Fascism, National Socialism, and Communism in the in the war period. [**Analyze multiple causation**]

7-12 Explaining the breakdown of the Versailles settlement and League of Nations in the 1930s. [**Challenge the arguments of historical inevitability**]

9-12 Explaining President Roosevelt's emphasis on hemispheric solidarity as exemplified in the Good Neighbor Policy. [**Draw upon data in historical maps**]

7-12 Analyzing the reasons for American isolationist sentiment in the interwar period and its effects on international relations and diplomacy. [**Analyze cause-and-effect relationships**]

5-12 Evaluating the Roosevelt administration's response to aggression in Europe, Africa, and Asia from 1935 to 1941. [**Formulate a position or course of action on an issue**]

7-12 Analyzing the growing tensions with Japan in East Asia. [**Marshal evidence of antecedent circumstances**]

| Grades 5-6 | **Examples of student achievement of Standard 3A include:** |

▶ Use political and physical maps to examine the global involvement of nations and people before World War II. Identify the geographic features that affected the U.S. policy of isolationism before World War II. Locate countries in the Western Hemisphere affected by Roosevelt's Good Neighbor Policy. Locate countries that were affected by prewar events such as the Japanese invasion of Manchuria, Italian invasion of Ethiopia, foreign involvement in the Spanish Civil War, the Munich conference over Czechoslovakia, and German demands for the Polish Corridor. Locate countries that formed the Allied and Axis powers at the beginning of World War II.

▶ Locate Pearl Harbor and describe the events that brought the United States into World War II in 1941.

| Grades 7-8 | **Examples of student achievement of Standard 3A include:** |

▶ Draw upon historical sources to construct a historical narrative explaining the rise of Italian Fascism, German Nazism, and Soviet Communism between the First and Second World Wars. *What economic factors contributed to the rise of dictatorships in Europe? How did political instability contribute to the rise of Mussolini and Hitler? To what extent was nationalism a factor contributing to the rise of dictatorial regimes in Europe?*

▶ Construct a sound historical argument or debate examining statements such as: *"The failure to enforce the Treaty of Versailles led to World War II;" or "the lack of support for the League of Nations encouraged aggressive policies by dictatorial regimes."*

▶ Construct a historical narrative comparing the Roosevelt administration's response to Italian aggression in Ethiopia, the Japanese invasion of China, German militarism and European appeasement, and fascist support for Spain during the Civil War. *What were American interests in Europe and Asia? To what extent did the Neutrality Acts limit Roosevelt's options in dealing with international aggression? Would public opinion have supported U.S. intervention in Africa, Asia, and Europe in the 1930s?*

▶ Construct a time line from 1900 to 1941 listing the events which caused tensions between the United States and Japan. Draw from a variety of sources such as newspaper stories and editorials, treaties, international agreements, propaganda graphics, and documentary photographs to explain the reasons for rising tensions.

Grades 9-12

Examples of student achievement of Standard 3A include:

▶ Draw on examples of Roosevelt's foreign policy toward Latin America and explain the reasons for the Good Neighbor Policy in Latin American. Compare the Good Neighbor Policy to Theodore Roosevelt's Big Stick Policy, Taft's Dollar Diplomacy, and Wilson's Watchful Waiting. Develop a chart on the goals, methods, and results of each of the policies.

▶ Use speeches and laws to decide whether the U.S. was already at war in the Atlantic when the Japanese attacked Pearl Harbor. *Why did FDR use the metaphor of a "quarantine" in his speech of October 5, 1937? Did this speech contradict American neutrality? Was the arming of American merchant ships an offensive or defensive act? Did FDR make the right decisions in calling for "cash and carry," "destroyers for bases," "lend lease," and the arming of merchant ships? What were his alternatives? What were the consequences of each action?*

▶ Analyze diplomatic correspondence, legislative actions, and political speeches to determine the reasons for the Japanese attack on Pearl Harbor on December 7, 1941. *Why did Japan set up the East Asian Co-Prosperity Sphere? How did the United States respond? When and why did the United States cut off oil to Japan? Was this an act of war? Should the United States have accepted the November 10 proposal from Japan? Were the differences between the United States and Japan in the 1930s negotiable or irreconcilable? How did Japan justify its attack on Pearl Harbor? Why did FDR call it a "day that will live in infamy"?*

▶ Analyze the effect of the Nazi-Soviet Non-Aggression Pact of 1939 on the U.S. Communist party. *How did the U.S. Communist party react to the Soviet pact with Nazi Germany? To what extent did the Non-Aggression Pact weaken the antiwar movement in the U.S.?*

Students Should Be Able to:

3B Demonstrate understanding of World War II and how the Allies prevailed by:

[5-12] Explaining Axis and Allied military strategy and contrasting military campaigns in the European and Pacific theaters in the period 1939-1945. [Draw upon the data in historical maps]

[7-12] Analyzing the dimensions of Hitler's "Final Solution" and the Allies' response to the Holocaust. [Interrogate historical data]

[9-12] Analyzing the Roosevelt administration's wartime diplomacy. [Hypothesize the influence of the past]

[7-12] Analyzing President Truman's decision to employ nuclear weapons against Japan and evaluating the moral and political implications of that decision. [Formulate a position or course of action on an issue]

[5-12] Explaining the costs of the war for the Allies and the Axis powers. [Utilize visual and mathematical data]

[7-12] Explaining the organization and functions of the United Nations. [Utilize visual and mathematical data]

Grades 5-6

Examples of student achievement of Standard 3B include:

◗ Locate the major theaters of war in North Africa, Europe, and the Pacific on a world map.

◗ Draw upon children's trade books such as *Alan and Naomi* by Myron Levoy to examine the personal stories of the Holocaust.

◗ Construct a picture board, sketchbook, or report showing the diverse contributions of men and women during the war.

◗ Draw evidence from diaries, interviews, and documentary films and photographs to explain the human tragedy of the war on civilians.

Grades 7-8

Examples of student achievement of Standard 3B include:

◗ Use children's trade books such as *The Last Mission* by Harry Mazer to trace the war through the participation of young adults.

◗ Draw upon historical data and evidence from maps of Axis and Allied movements in Europe, Africa, and Asia to explain military strategy during World War II. *Why did Germany and the USSR sign a nonaggression pact in 1939? What military strategy did Germany use in its conquest of France in 1940? What was the importance of the "Battle for Britain"? What was the Japanese strategy in East Asia and the Pacific? What was Roosevelt's logic in fighting an aggressive war against the Axis powers in Europe and a defensive war in Asia? Why did the Allies launch an invasion of North Africa in 1942, Sicily in 1943, and Normandy in 1944? How did Roosevelt respond when he learned of the Nazi death camps?*

◗ Explain what was meant by the "Final Solution" and draw from primary sources such as eyewitness accounts, oral history, testimony of Nazi officials, and documentary photographs and films to examine the human costs of Nazi genocide.

▶ Using letters, laws, and newspaper articles, identify Roosevelt's immigration policy toward Jewish refugees from Hitler's Germany. *How did Americans respond to news of the Holocaust?*

▶ Examine the story of Anne Frank and explain how a U.S. citizen might have reacted had her diary been published during the war.

▶ Draw evidence from simulations or role-playing activities regarding the decision to use atomic weapons during World War II and debate the decision to bomb Hiroshima and Nagasaki.

▶ Draw upon visual data including documentary photographs, graphs, and charts indicating casualties to appraise the human costs of World War II.

▶ Construct historical narratives, oral reports, diagrams, or displays which explain the structure of the United Nations and compare its goals and objectives with those of the League of Nations. *How did the United Nations differ from the League of Nations? To what extent was the United Nations Security Council a fair representation of the "New World Order"? To what extent has the United Nations achieved its stated goals?*

Grades 9-12

Examples of student achievement of Standard 3B include:

▶ Using maps, newspaper and magazine accounts, letters, and speeches, analyze why there was a delay in creating a second front, the Soviet Union's role in helping to defeat the Axis Powers, and the reasons for the success of "D-Day."

▶ Construct a historical argument or debate to examine Allied response to the Holocaust. *When did the Allies discover the scope of Nazi persecution of European Jewry, as well as the persecution of Jehovah's Witnesses, gypsies, homosexuals, and other groups? What actions did European nations and the United States take to support Jewish immigration? Why did the Allies fail to organize rescue attempts and resist appeals to bomb rail lines leading to Auschwitz and other camps?*

▶ Compare Norman Rockwell's illustration of FDR's Four Freedoms speech in January 1941 with the ideas presented in the speech. *What images of America do they both convey? Is Rockwell's portrayal accurate? To what extent is FDR's speech idealistic? Rockwell's paintings?*

▶ Draw evidence reflecting different perspectives to analyze within its historical context the decision to use the atomic bomb on Japan. Construct a sound argument, debate, or position paper on the appropriateness of Truman's decision considering various factors such as: the Allied military position in the Pacific in 1945; estimated military and civilian casualties in a prolonged war; long-term consequences as understood in 1945; Japanese surrender overtures; and, the probability of Soviet entry into the war.

Students Should Be Able to:

3C Demonstrate understanding of the effects of World War II at home by:

5-12 Explaining economic and military mobilization during World War II. [**Utilize visual and mathematical data**]

7-12 Contrasting the contributions of United States minorities to the war effort with the racism and discrimination they faced. [**Marshal evidence of antecedent circumstances**]

5-12 Evaluating the internment of Japanese Americans during the war. [**Evaluate the implementation of a decision**]

7-12 Analyzing the effects of World War II on gender roles and the American family. [**Compare and contrast differing sets of ideas, values, and behaviors**]

7-12 Evaluating the war's impact on United States culture and technology. [**Draw upon visual and literary sources**]

Grades 5-6

Examples of student achievement of Standard 3C include:

▶ Locate the places where large numbers of Japanese Americans were living on the West Coast and the centers to which they were removed during the war. Construct an album of photographs and sketches which trace a Japanese American family from their home on the West Coast through their internment in a relocation center. Use personal stories such as *The Bracelet* by Yoshiko Uchida to examine childhood experiences in internment camps. Write journal entries, poems, or draw illustrations to express the feelings of the forced movement of Japanese Americans.

▶ Draw upon historical records, photographs, and stories such as *A Time Too Swift* by Margaret Poynter to examine the war effort at home. Interview people who remember wartime experiences and create albums, stories, or plays to show ways in which people's lives were affected by the war. *How were men and women mobilized to take part in the war effort? How did shortages and rationing affect people's lives?*

▶ Create a time line or wall chart showing major developments in aviation, weaponry, communication, and medicine during the war years. Explain how these inventions and discoveries changed our lives.

▶ Draw evidence from books, movies, and cartoons that show how entertainment changed during the war years.

Grades 7-8

Examples of student achievement of Standard 3C include:

▶ Analyze images of women workers, such as "Rosie the Riveter," and answer the following questions: *Why was she portrayed that way? Was this a complimentary image?*

▶ Explain the factors that led to the internment of Japanese Americans. Use oral histories and stories such as *Kim/Kimi* by Hadley Irwin, *Nisei Daughter* by Monica Itoi Sone, and *Journey to Topaz* by Yoshiko Uchida to compile case studies of the experiences of Japanese Americans during the war. *Was Roosevelt justified in ordering internment? How did Japanese Americans cope with their internment?*

▶ Plot on a U.S. map the great migrations during World War II, locating the cities to which most migrated. Analyze the tensions that resulted from the rapid increase in population. *What drew people to these cities? How did local residents show their resentment to the migrants? What were the factors behind the Detroit race riot of 1943? The Los Angeles "Zoot-suit" riot of 1943?*

▶ Examine the effects of rapid technological change during the war years. *What new employment opportunities were available? How was the wartime technology transferred to a peacetime economy?*

▶ Draw upon evidence from a variety of primary and secondary sources to examine the role of Hollywood movies, radio programs, and musical recordings on American culture during the war years.

Grades 9-12

Examples of student achievement of Standard 3C include:

▶ Interrogate historical data from a variety of sources including industry and military draft records, economic and employment statistics, and historical narratives to explain United States mobilization during World War II. *How did the industrial sector adapt to meet the necessities of war production? What types of jobs — both within and outside the factories — developed as a result of domestic mobilization? What role did women play in the workforce? To what extent were their experiences similar to or different from those of women during World War I?*

▶ Analyze how African Americans, Mexican Americans, and Native Americans contributed to the war effort, and examine the contradiction between their treatment at home and the goals that they were fighting for in Europe.

▶ Using novels, reports from government hearings, and pictures, analyze the effects of the relocation centers on Japanese American families and civil liberties. After reading selections from *Return to Manzanar, Citizen 13660,* or other memoirs of life in the camps, discuss questions such as: *How was family life affected by the camps? How did the contributions of the Nisei Battalion contrast with the treatment of Japanese Americans at home?*

▶ Assemble historical evidence to explore such questions such as: *On what grounds did government officials justify the internment of Japanese Americans? Was this an example of racism? What were the Supreme Court's decisions in U.S. v. Hirabayashi (1943); U.S. v. Korematsu (1944); U.S. v. Ex parte Endo (1944)? What constitutional issues were involved in the cases? Was the restriction of civil liberties during wartime justified? Why did Congress issue a public apology and vote to compensate surviving Japanese American internees in 1988?*

ERA 9

Postwar United States (1945 to early 1970s)

Although the study of the era following World War II can easily be dominated by a preoccupation with the Cold War, our understanding of present-day American society will be deficient without grappling with the remarkable changes in American society and culture in the 1950s and 1960s.

Students will need to understand how the postwar economic boom produced mighty changes in American education, in consumer culture, in suburbanization, in the return to domesticity for many women, in the character of corporate life, in technological explosion, and in sexual and cultural mores (both of which involved startling changes in dress, speech, music, film and television, family structure, uses of leisure time, and more). All of this can take on deeper meaning when connected to the advent of the civil rights and feminist movements that would become an essential part of the third great reform impulse in American history, from the 1950s forward. The reinvigoration of New Deal liberalism and its gradual exhaustion in the 1970s is worth probing as a case study of government's responsibilities, entitlements, and the continuing quest for social and economic equality that still preoccupies the American people.

The swordplay of the Soviet Union and the United States rightfully claims attention because it led to the Korean and Vietnam wars as well as the Berlin airlift, Cuban missile crisis, American interventions in many parts of the world, a huge investment in scientific research, and environmental damage that will take generations to rectify. The Vietnam War is especially noteworthy. It demonstrated the power of American public opinion in reversing foreign policy, it tested the democratic system to its limits, and it left scars on American society that have not yet been erased.

Overview

Standard 1: The economic boom and social transformation of postwar America

Standard 2: The postwar extension of the New Deal

Standard 3: The Cold War and the Korean and Vietnam conflicts in domestic and international politics

Standard 4: The struggle for racial and gender equality and for the extension of civil liberties

STANDARD 1

Students Should Understand: *The economic boom and social transformation of postwar America.*

Students Should Be Able to:

1A Demonstrate understanding of the extent and impact of economic changes in the postwar period by:

7-12 Analyzing the debate over demobilization and reconversion and its effects on the economy [**Marshal evidence of antecedent circumstances**]

5-12 Explaining the reasons for the sustained growth of the postwar consumer economy. [**Analyze cause-and-effect relationships**]

7-12 Explaining the growth of the service, white collar, and professional sectors of the economy. [**Analyze cause-and-effect relationships**]

9-12 Analyzing the impact of the Cold War on the economy. [**Identify issues and problems in the past**]

9-12 Analyzing the gap between the "affluent society" and "the other America." [**Consider multiple perspectives**]

| Grades 5-6 | **Examples of student achievement of Standard 1A include:** |

▶ Develop journals, albums, videos, or presentations answering questions concerning local life in the postwar decades. *What economic opportunities did members of the armed forces find when they came home after World War II? How did people find housing and work after the war? How did the landscape of America change after the war? How did transportation change?*

▶ Give examples of service sector jobs and explain why more service jobs were available after World War II.

▶ Construct a collage to show the difference in standards of living of the urban poor and suburban middle class.

| Grades 7-8 | **Examples of student achievement of Standard 1A include:** |

▶ Interrogate historical data from a variety of sources to evaluate the economic and political ramifications of demobilization after World War II. *What were the effects of demobilization and reconversion on American industry? How was the working life of women and minorities altered in the aftermath of the war? What was the economic effect of suburbanization and the return of women home from the factories?*

▶ Assess the economic impact of opportunities in the service sector and develop questions to guide historical research in appraising the expansion of service jobs in government and the private sector. *What factors contributed to the development of new government jobs? How did the expansion of hospitality and recreation industries offer service sector jobs?*

▶ Construct a sound argument, debate, or historical narrative examining the effects of postwar industrial development on the environment.

Examples of student achievement of Standard 1A include:

▶ Drawing upon a variety of memoirs, newspapers, and periodicals, examine the contrary proposals advanced for promoting postwar prosperity. *Why did so many economic advisers fear a postwar depression?*

▶ Construct a historical narrative explaining how increased defense spending and the unique position of the U.S. economy in the postwar era vis-à-vis European and Asian economies, led to unprecedented economic growth. *What opportunities were open to corporate employees? How did the growth of large corporations affect the lives of their employees? In what ways did corporations affect individuality? To what extent were women and minorities represented in the corporate structure?*

▶ Draw evidence from works such as Michael Harrington's *The Other America* and James Baldwin's *Notes of a Native Son* to examine the extent of poverty in the midst of affluence in postwar America. *Who were the "invisible poor"? What were the social and political factors that made the poor "invisible"? What groups made up the urban poor? To what extent did new technology contribute to poverty in Appalachia? How did geography contribute to poverty in areas like Appalachia?*

Bellglade, Florida, 1945
Rural poverty despite the postwar
economic boom, Library of Congress

Students Should Be Able to:

1B **Demonstrate understanding of how the social changes of the postwar period affected various Americans by:**

`7-12` Evaluating the effect of the GI Bill on American society. [**Hypothesize the influence of the past on the present**]

`9-12` Examining causes and results of new governmental spending on educational programs in the 1950s. [**Analyze cause-and-effect relationships**]

`9-12` Explaining the expansion of suburbanization and analyzing the impact of the "crabgrass frontier." [**Examine the influence of ideas**]

`7-12` Explaining the reasons for the "return to domesticity" and its effect on gender roles and family life. [**Consider multiple perspectives**]

`9-12` Examining the place of religion in postwar American life. [**Examine the influence of ideas**]

`5-12` Examining the influence of popular culture. [**Draw upon visual sources**]

`7-12` Analyzing the role of the mass media in homogenizing American culture and assessing its validity for the "other America." [**Analyze cause-and-effect relationships**]

Grades 5-6

Examples of student achievement of Standard 1B include:

▸ Create a scrapbook, play, or song showing how family life changed in local communities in the decades following World War II. Drawing upon stories, pictures, and media clips, contrast local experiences with those in other regions. *What happened when Americans moved from cities to suburban areas? Did most women work outside the home? How did movies, television, and advertisements influence ideas about family life? What did the "ideal family" look like in the media then? What do families look like in the media and advertisements now?*

Grades 7-8

Examples of student achievement of Standard 1B include:

▸ Use a variety of historical sources including oral histories, magazine advertisements, and catalogues to examine social changes in the postwar era. *What factors contributed to changing attitudes and values? What was the impact of the GI Bill? To what extent did the GI Bill improve the standard of living? What were the social effects of the return of women home from the factories in the postwar period? How did suburbanization promote social change?*

▸ Draw evidence from television, movies, photographs, and lyrics of popular songs to assess the homogenizing tendencies of popular culture and mass media in the 1950s. *How did clothing and hair styles portrayed in situation comedies such as* Father Knows Best, Leave it to Beaver, *and* I Love Lucy *or Dick Clark's* American Bandstand *set a pattern for accepted dress for adults, teenagers, and children? To what degree were the Hollywood portrayals of Americans and their lives representative of the people of the United States?*

▶ Draw evidence from oral histories, documentary photographs, films, music, and dress to construct a historical narrative, audiovisual presentation, or classroom newspaper illustrating the influence of popular culture in the postwar periods.

Grades 9-12

Examples of student achievement of Standard 1B include:

▶ Research the social and economic effects of the GI Bill. *What impact did the GI Bill have on higher education? What opportunities did it open? What effect did it have on new home construction? How did it foster a trend toward mass production? What impact did it have on the development of small businesses?*

▶ Draw evidence from documentary films, editorials, and periodical literature to evaluate how Soviet advances in space impacted the American educational system. Analyze political responses such as Senator Fulbright's incrimination, "The real challenge we face involves the very roots of our society. It involves our educational system, the source of our knowledge and cultural values. And here the administration's program for a renaissance of learning is disturbingly small-minded." *Why did the federal government appropriate increasing funds for educational programs? What was the effect of public spending on educational institutions? What new opportunities were opened to individuals?*

▶ Use advertisements, newspaper commentaries, and statistics to explain the meaning of the term "crabgrass frontier." *Why was the "house and the yard" considered an ideal? To what extent was the ideal real?* Explain the symbols involved in the term "Levittown." *What did people look for in suburbia? What did they find? What changes in social and economic patterns were brought about by the Interstate Highway System? What was the impact of suburbia on race relations? On the central cities?*

▶ Using pictures from women's magazines, the plots of TV programs, and selections from Betty Friedan's *The Feminine Mystique*, explain the impact of the Cold War on the lives and roles of women. *What was the impact of the "Baby Doll" look, the movies of Doris Day and Debbie Reynolds, the TV shows* Leave It To Beaver *and* I Love Lucy, *and* McCall's *definition of "togetherness" on women? What was the "Problem That Has No Name" that Betty Friedan was talking about?*

▶ Construct a historical narrative examining the development of ecumenicalism and the growing vitality of religious fundamentalism in postwar society. *To what extent did the ecumenism movement lead to a decline in overt anti-Catholic and anti-Semitic feelings?*

▶ Using the paintings of Edward Hopper and Jasper Johns and articles about the "Organization Man," analyze the effect of alienation on the individual and the society. *What does Edward Hopper's* The Lighthouse *or* The Sheridan Theater *tell you about loneliness? How does the artist use "empty spaces"? What are people's faces like? How does Jasper Johns show the American flag? What is he saying?*

STANDARD 2

Students Should Understand: *The postwar extension of the New Deal.*

Students Should Be Able to:

2A Demonstrate understanding of the political debate over continuation of the New Deal by:

`9-12` Explaining the postwar reaction to the labor movement and the responses of the Truman and Eisenhower administrations to labor's agenda. [**Consider multiple perspectives**]

`5-12` Analyzing Truman's support for civil rights and the effect on the Democratic party. [**Assess the importance of the individual in history**]

`7-12` Contrasting Truman's Fair Deal with Eisenhower's "Modern Republicanism." [**Compare and contrast differing sets of ideas**]

Grades 5-6

Examples of student achievement of Standard 2A include:

▶ Draw evidence from historical research to develop stories, skits, and readers' theater activities on the civil rights movement during the Truman presidency. *What rights did African Americans gain during the Truman presidency? Who opposed desegregation of the armed forces?*

Grades 7-8

Examples of student achievement of Standard 2A include:

▶ Chart the measures of the Truman Administration in the area of civil rights and construct a historical argument, debate, or narrative evaluating the effectiveness of his efforts as well as how it split the Democratic Party. *What steps did Truman take in the area of race relations? How successful was he in achieving his goals?*

▶ Analyze the success of Truman's Fair Deal program for securing fair employment practices and desegregation. *What impact did his efforts at desegregation have on the Democratic party? What were the goals of the States Rights ("Dixiecrat") and Progressive Democratic parties?*

▶ Examine Eisenhower's middle-of-the-road course. *What did Eisenhower mean when he referred to his beliefs as "dynamic conservatism" and "Modern Republicanism"?*

Grades 9-12

Examples of student achievement of Standard 2A include:

▶ Use charts, laws, and speeches to determine how the Fair Deal compared to the New Deal. *In which ways did the Fair Deal's goals and achievements build on Roosevelt's New Deal? In which ways did the goals and achievements go beyond those of the New Deal?*

▶ Analyze Truman's message vetoing the Taft-Hartley Bill for what it says about America's commitment to organized labor. *Why did Truman veto the bill?*

▶ Analyze writings of Eleanor Roosevelt, the publications of the NAACP, and "To Secure These Rights" in order to explain the civil rights program of the Truman administration. *Why did southern Democrats object to the civil rights proposals of the Truman administration? How did the Cold War influence the struggle for civil rights? Why was Truman able to win the 1948 election, even though newspapers projected his loss?*

▶ Drawing on the 1952 election campaign, analyze Republican opposition to the New Deal and the Fair Deal. *What image did Eisenhower project in the campaign? To what degree were Eisenhower's domestic and foreign policy priorities and objectives similar to and different from his predecessors? How have recent historians and political scientists re-evaluated the Eisenhower legacy?*

▶ Analyze Eisenhower's farewell address of January 17, 1961. *What was his warning regarding the military-industrial complex? What were the goals Eisenhower set for the nation in this farewell address?*

Dwight David Eisenhower,
President of the United States,
1953-1961, Library of Congress

Students Should Be Able to:

2B Demonstrate understanding of the New Frontier and Great Society and analyze their domestic accomplishments by:

`9-12` Analyzing Kennedy's commitment to liberalism and the reasons for his election in the 1960. **[Examine the influence of ideas]**

`5-12` Evaluating the domestic accomplishments of the New Frontier. **[Hold interpretations of history as tentative]**

`5-12` Analyzing Johnson's presidential leadership and evaluating the reforms of the Great Society. **[Evaluate the implementation of a decision]**

`7-12` Assessing the legacy of the New Frontier and Great Society. **[Evaluate major debates among historians]**

Grades 5-6

Examples of student achievement of Standard 2B include:

▶ Construct a chart or mural on the Kennedy and Johnson administrations. Drawing upon biographies, stories, and pictorial sources, chart major issues in each administration. List steps taken to try to meet problems. Made a collage or bulletin board contrasting those issues with current problems. *What programs did Presidents Kennedy and Johnson present to Congress to improve conditions for poor rural and urban families? Are any of these programs in place now?*

▶ Use pictures, quotations, biographies, and music to explain how Jacqueline Kennedy developed the images of Camelot to depict her husband's presidency.

Grades 7-8

Examples of student achievement of Standard 2B include:

▶ Compile a list of the major issues in the 1960 presidential campaign and assess Kennedy's stance on each. *What were the central domestic issues that divided candidates Kennedy and Nixon? To what extent was religion an issue in the campaign? How did Kennedy respond to issues relating to Cold War foreign policy?*

▶ Select several political cartoons on different issues in the 1960 campaign and explain the issue and the visual impact of the cartoon.

▶ Construct arguments in the form of balance sheets, debates, or narratives to marshal historical evidence to assess the impact of New Frontier and Great Society domestic programs. *How did the New Frontier differ from the Great Society? What impact did the Kennedy assassination have on the passage of reform legislation during the Johnson administration? How did Johnson's leadership style differ from that of Kennedy? What factors contributed to greater popular support for Great Society legislation? What New Frontier and Great Society legislation has had a lasting impact on American society?*

Grades 9-12

Examples of student achievement of Standard 2B include:

♦ Use video selections of the TV debates, campaign speeches of Nixon and Kennedy, and newspaper and periodical articles covering the campaign to analyze the "New Politics" introduced in the election of 1960. *How did the television debates shape the outcome of the election? How did charisma and image play a role in the campaign? Did they overshadow the issues? Why did Kennedy win the election? Was the election a mandate for liberalism?*

♦ Analyze Kennedy's inaugural address for what it says about citizenship, rights, and responsibilities. Richard Reeves has referred to it as "Kennedy's Music." *What does that mean? Did the inaugural address intensify the Cold War or was it a response to it? Was it a momentary, pragmatic political speech or one that embodies a long-lasting American passage?*

♦ Use Kennedy's acceptance speech at the 1960 nominating convention and historical accounts of the Kennedy administration to define and explain the meaning and impact of the "New Frontier." *Was there a "New Frontier" in domestic legislation?*

♦ Use legislation and programs such as the Civil Rights Act of 1964, the Voting Rights Act of 1965, the Elementary and Secondary Education Act of 1965, the Medicare Plan, the Economic Opportunity Act of 1964, Head Start, the Job Corps, the Appalachian Regional Development Act, the Metropolitan Redevelopment Act, and the Demonstration Cities Act to explain the meaning and impact of the Great Society. *How did Great Society proposals compare with the New Deal? Were the Great Society programs a success or a failure?*

♦ Explain Lyndon Johnson's statement: "They say Jack Kennedy's got style, but I'm the one who's got the bills passed." *How did the assassination of John Kennedy affect the implementation of the Great Society? Was Johnson trying to implement Kennedy's program or break experimental ground? Explain. What was the "Johnson treatment"? Was the "treatment" appropriate for a president?*

President John F. Kennedy with his wife Jacqueline and daughter Caroline, National Archives

STANDARD 3

Students Should Understand: *The Cold War and the Korean and Vietnam conflicts in domestic and international politics.*

Students Should Be Able to:

3A Demonstrate understanding of the origins and domestic consequences of the Cold War by:

5-12 Evaluating the "flawed peace" resulting from World War II and the effectiveness of the United Nations in reducing international tensions and conflicts. **[Draw upon the data in historical maps]**

9-12 Explaining the origins of the Cold War and the advent of nuclear politics. **[Hold interpretations of history as tentative]**

9-12 Explaining the relationship between the Cold War and the emergence of the internal security and loyalty programs under Truman and Eisenhower. **[Analyze the cause-and-effect relationships]**

7-12 Explaining the factors that led to the Korean conflict and analyzing the effects of the police action on U.S. foreign and domestic policy. **[Identify relevant historical antecedents]**

7-12 Explaining the major Soviet Union-United States clashes and analyzing the implementation of the containment policy during the Truman and Eisenhower administrations. **[Consider multiple perspectives]**

7-12 Explaining the rise of McCarthyism and evaluating its effects on civil liberties **[Analyze the cause-and-effect relationships]**

5-12 Analyzing the reasons for the demise of McCarthyism and explaining its overall significance and legacy. **[Examine the influence of ideas]**

Grades 5-6

Examples of student achievement of Standard 3A include:

▶ Locate and define the area in Europe that fell behind the "iron curtain." *What did Churchill mean when he used the "iron curtain" metaphor?*

▶ Explain basic terms relating to the postwar period such as Cold War, superpowers, arms buildup, nuclear threat, the space race, and human rights.

▶ Define McCarthyism. Through activities such as role play, skits, or readers' theater, show the effects of McCarthyism and explain how it changed the lives of individuals who were accused of supporting communism. *Why did McCarthy's popularity decline?*

Examples of student achievement of Standard 3A include:

▶ Explain what was meant by the terms "containment" and "massive retaliation." *What were the circumstances that led to Truman's development of containment as a strategy for U.S. foreign policy? What events led Eisenhower to expand the policy? What were the international confrontations that fueled the Cold War? What influence did atomic weapons have in sustaining the Cold War?*

▶ Describe the circumstances that led to the Marshall Plan and assess its accomplishments. *Why was the program offered to eastern as well as western Europe? To what extent was the Marshall Plan an instrument of the Cold War?*

▶ Construct a historical argument or debate on such questions as: *Did the Hiss and Rosenberg cases contribute to the rise of McCarthyism? Did the Korean War and conflicts in Europe and the Middle East stimulate "red-baiting" in the United States?*

▶ Compare McCarthyism to the post-World War I "red scare." *How serious was the communist threat in the 1920s and the 1950s? How did the two "red scares" play upon the fears of the American people? What methods did Attorney General Palmer and Senator McCarthy use in their attempts to halt internal subversion? Were they sincere in their efforts to "weed out" communists?*

▶ Draw upon primary and secondary sources, including personal narratives, biographies, and periodical literature, to examine the impact of McCarthyism on civil liberties. *What were the accusations brought against people in the film industry, ministers, government employees, and members of the military? How did McCarthyism affect individual lives? To what extent did McCarthyism repress civil liberties? What factors contributed to McCarthy's loss of influence? To what extent did McCarthy's anticommunist legacy continue after his fall from power?*

Examples of student achievement of Standard 3A include:

▶ Draw upon a variety of contemporary accounts, including newspapers and periodicals, government documents, and personal memoirs, to analyze the historical origins of the Cold War and evaluate the mutual suspicions and divisions fragmenting the Grand Alliance at the end of World War II. *Was the Cold War inevitable? If not, how could it have been avoided? How did U.S. support for "self-determination" conflict with the USSR's desire for security in Eastern Europe at the end of the war? Did the U.S. pursue "atomic diplomacy" in the postwar period? Explain.*

▶ Compare the "red scare" in the post-World War I period with the "second red scare" that emerged after World War II in terms of causes and consequences. *What role did J. Edgar Hoover play in the two "red scares"? How did Truman's support of the Federal Employee Loyalty Program contribute to the growing "red scare" in the postwar period? What was the basis for McCarthy's attack on Eisenhower? How did Eisenhower respond? Why did he not openly confront McCarthy?*

▶ Draw on such examples as the *Amerasia, Hiss, Hollywood Ten,* and *Rosenberg* cases to explain the emergence of McCarthyism and its impact on civil liberties. *What political, economic, and social groups most supported McCarthy? Least supported? Why? What was the impact of the McCarran Internal Security Act and the* Dennis *v. U.S. case (1951) on the anticommunist crusade? Did the Army-McCarthy hearings of 1954 significantly undermine McCarthyism?*

Students Should Be Able to:

3B Demonstrate understanding of U.S. foreign policy in Africa, Europe, the Middle East, and Latin America by:

5-12 Contrasting and evaluating the responses of the Truman and Eisenhower administrations to nationalism in Africa, Asia, Latin America, and the Middle East [**Compare and contrast differing sets of ideas**]

7-12 Evaluating and comparing the Kennedy and Johnson administrations' Latin American policy. [**Compare and contrast differing sets of ideas**]

7-12 Analyzing the Kennedy-Johnson policies toward the Soviet Union and the evolution from confrontation to coexistence. [**Examine the influence of ideas**]

9-12 Assessing the Kennedy-Johnson response to anticolonial movements in Africa. [**Examine the influence of ideas**]

Grades 5-6

Examples of student achievement of Standard 3B include:

▶ Work with maps to show the development of nation states in Africa, Asia, and the Middle East after World War II. Draw from biographies and stories to explain the establishment of independent nations. *Why did African countries change their names from those used by European colonizers? What countries in Asia became independent nations after World War II?*

▶ Locate the modern state of Israel on a map and explain how it became an independent country after World War II.

Grades 7-8

Examples of student achievement of Standard 3B include:

▶ Explain the Truman and Eisenhower doctrines in the context of the international tensions that prompted each.

▶ Draw evidence from a variety of sources including public speeches, memoirs, biographies, editorials, and documentary films to construct a sound argument, debate, or historical narrative appraising the Kennedy administration's Cuban policy. *Should President Kennedy have carried out the Eisenhower administration's plan to overthrow Fidel Castro? Should Kennedy have committed the U.S. military in the Bay of Pigs affair? How did the Cuban missile crisis differ from the Bay of Pigs? How was the Cuban missile crisis resolved?*

▶ Compare Kennedy's Latin America policy to Johnson's.

▶ Trace changes in U.S. foreign policy toward the Soviet Union during the Kennedy and Johnson administrations and explain reasons for these changes. *How did U.S. policy toward the Soviet Union change during the Kennedy and Johnson years? What was the significance of the Nuclear Test Ban Treaty of 1963? How did escalation of the war in Vietnam influence U.S.-Soviet relations?*

Grades 9-12

Examples of student achievement of Standard 3B include:

▶ Explain U.S. policy regarding the British mandate over Palestine and the establishment of the state of Israel. *Why did the U.S. State Department oppose recognition of the new state of Israel in 1948 and why was the U.S. the first country to extend recognition?*

▶ Draw upon such documents as George F. Kennan's "Mr. X" article, "The Sources of Soviet Conduct," in *Foreign Affairs* (1947), and Walter Lippman's *The Cold War* (1947) to analyze the major arguments supporting and opposing the "containment" policy. *How and why did the Truman administration implement the containment policy in Europe? Were they successful?*

▶ Analyze NSC-68 [National Security Council Paper #68], explain how it reoriented U.S. foreign policy in 1950, and evaluate its long-range effects on domestic policies and institutions. *How did the Korean War affect the basic premises of NSC-68? What was the fundamental disagreement between Truman and MacArthur during the Korean War? Which individual supported the better strategy? Why? How did the Eisenhower-Dulles emphasis on "massive retaliation," and "pactomania" seek to modify the containment policy?*

▶ Examine documents relating to the Bay of Pigs and the Cuban missile crisis, including the recently declassified documents to assess the wisdom of Kennedy's response to the crisis. *How would you account for the idealism of Kennedy's Alliance for Progress with the overt and covert interventionism of his Cuban policy? How did Kennedy's Cuban policy threaten the goals of the Alliance for Progress? What was "Operation Mongoose" and what were some of its major consequences? Did Lyndon Johnson follow Kennedy's policy in Latin America or did he change it? Explain. How did Latin American countries and the Organization of American States respond to the Kennedy-Johnson policies in the Americas? What were the "lessons" of the Cuban missile crisis? Did it contribute toward detente or accelerate the arms race?*

▶ Evaluate the response of the United States to "wars of national liberation" in Africa and Asia in the 1960s.

"Let all our neighbors know that we shall join with them to oppose aggression or subversion anywhere in the Americas. And let every other power know that this hemisphere intends to remain the master of its own house."

JOHN F. KENNEDY

Students Should Be Able to:

3C Demonstrate understanding of the foreign and domestic consequences of U.S. involvement in Vietnam by:

`7-12` Analyzing the Kennedy, Johnson, and Nixon administrations' Vietnam policy and the consequences of escalation of the war. [**Compare and contrast differing sets of ideas**]

`7-12` Analyzing growing disillusionment with the war. [**Analyze multiple causation**]

`9-12` Assessing the impact of class and race on wartime mobilization. [**Interrogate historical data**]

`5-12` Evaluating the effect of the war on Vietnamese and Americans in Vietnam. [**Evidence historical perspectives**]

`9-12` Explaining the provisions of the Paris Peace Accord of 1973 and evaluating Nixon's accomplishment. [**Differentiate between historical facts and historical interpretations**]

`9-12` Analyzing the constitutional issues involved in the war and the legacy of Vietnam. [**Formulate a position or course of action on an issue**]

Grades 5-6

Examples of student achievement of Standard 3C include:

▶ Locate Southeast Asia on a Pacific Rim map and identify countries in the region. Construct a time line illustrating the escalation of the Vietnam War during the 1960s.

▶ Draw upon a variety of primary sources including letters, diaries, songs, documentary films, and photographs to explain the personal impact of the war on Vietnamese civilians and U.S. and Vietnamese combatants in Southeast Asia.

▶ Use children's trade books such as *Charlie Pippin* by Candy Dawson Boyd to examine a young adult's perspective on the Vietnam war.

Grades 7-8

Examples of student achievement of Standard 3C include:

▶ Research the early involvement of the United States in Vietnam following World War II and compare the policies of the Truman and Eisenhower administrations. *Why did Eisenhower send military advisers to Vietnam? What was the "domino theory"? How did it later influence U.S. policy in Vietnam?*

▶ Construct a sound argument, debate, or narrative which marshals historical evidence on such questions as: *Was it necessary to escalate U.S. involvement in Vietnam to stop the spread of communism in Southeast Asia? Was the Kennedy administration's policy toward the Diem regime appropriate?*

▶ Interrogate historical data from a variety of sources to evaluate the impact of the Vietnam War on American society. *What factors contributed to the advent of opposition to American involvement in Vietnam? What were the moral and ethical issues involved in the protest movement?*

▶ Explain Nixon's Vietnamization policy and construct a historical argument assessing its effectiveness in bringing an end to the conflict.

- Draw evidence from speeches, contemporary literature, documentary films, and photographs to measure the impact of saturation bombing on North Vietnam and the effect of the invasion of Cambodia on the antiwar movement in the United States. *What factors led to the growth of student radicalism? What was the impact of the Kent State and Jackson State killings on public opinion? To what extent did television coverage of the war advance the antiwar movement?*

- Examine the controversy over the Vietnam War using novels such as *And One for All* by Theresa Nelson and *After the Dancing Days* by Margaret Rostkowski.

Grades 9-12

Examples of student achievement of Standard 3C include:

- Assemble the evidence and develop a sound historical argument on such questions as: *How did the "fall of China" syndrome affect the response of Democratic presidents to events in Vietnam? How did the overthrow of Diem in 1963 contribute to political instability in South Vietnam? What were the long-term consequences for the U.S.? How did the Tonkin Resolution expand presidential war powers? Was Johnson's policy of massive bombing of North Vietnam justified in light of Hanoi's military involvement in South Vietnam? Why was the Tet offensive a military victory but a political disaster for the United States? Did Johnson's withdrawal speech of March 31, 1968, represent a significant change in U.S. policy in Vietnam or an alteration in tactics in order to offset criticism of a policy increasingly under public attack?*

- Drawing on contemporary newspapers and periodicals and available secondary sources, analyze the diverse groups and major arguments advanced against the war. Analyze why the war contributed to a generational conflict and concomitant lack of respect for traditional authority figures. *How did the "counterculture" affect the student protest movement, music, art, and literature?*

- Use historical sources, including statistical information, to assess the validity of the class basis of combat service in Vietnam.

- Drawing on the historical evidence, assess the success and impact of Vietnamization and evaluate Nixon's expansion of the war and bombing in Southeast Asia. *What were the terms of the Paris Peace Accords? What are the legacies and lessons of the Vietnam War?*

- Debate the proposition that national security during the Vietnam War necessitated restriction of individual civil liberties and the press. *To what extent did voicing public dissent hinder the American war effort? Does the public's right to know take precedence over national security? What were the paramount constitutional issues raised during the Vietnam War? How were they settled?*

STANDARD 4

Students Should Understand: *The struggle for racial and gender equality and for the extension of civil liberties.*

Students Should Be Able to:

4A Demonstrate understanding of the "Second Reconstruction" and analyze its advancement of civil rights by:

`7–12` Explaining the postwar origins of the modern civil rights movement and the role of the NAACP in the legal assault on segregation. **[Analyze multiple causation]**

`5–12` Evaluating the Warren Court's reasoning in *Brown* vs. *Board of Education* and its significance in advancing civil rights. **[Analyze cause-and-effect relationships]**

`5–12` Explaining the resistance to civil rights in the South between 1954 and 1965. **[Identify issues and problems in the past]**

`7–12` Analyzing the roles and ideologies of Martin Luther King Jr. and Malcolm X in the civil rights movement and evaluating their legacies. **[Assess the importance of the individual in history]**

`7–12` Assessing the role of the legislative and executive branches in advancing the civil rights movement. **[Evaluate the implementation of a decision]**

`9–12` Explaining the change from the focus on *de jure* segregation to the nationwide assault on *de facto* segregation. **[Interrogate historical data]**

| Grades 5-6 | **Examples of student achievement of Standard 4A include:** |

▶ Define terms such as "freedom ride," "civil disobedience," and "nonviolent resistance" and explain how they were important in the civil rights movement.

▶ Present a dramatic reading of Martin Luther King Jr.'s "I have a Dream" speech and construct a collage, mural, or bulletin board display using excerpts from his speech to explain pictures of events in the civil rights movement.

▶ Construct a skit, role-playing activity, or readers' theater to explain issues brought before the U.S. Supreme Court in the *Brown* v. *Board of Education* case in 1954.

▶ Explain the lyrics of civil rights songs such as "We Shall Overcome," "Blowin' In the Wind," "If I Had a Hammer," and "O Freedom."

▶ Use children's trade books such as *Freedom's Children: Young Civil Rights Activists Tell Their Own Stories* by Ellen Levine and *The March on Washington* by James Haskins to examine the goals and accomplishments of individuals and groups in the civil rights movement.

Grades 7-8

Examples of student achievement of Standard 4A include:

▶ Construct a historical argument, debate, or narrative assessing the origins of the modern civil rights movement.

▶ Construct a time line illustrating important milestones in the civil rights movement between 1954 and 1965 and critically evaluate the effects of white resistance in the South. *What developments prompted African Americans as well as other American citizens to challenge entrenched economic, political, and social power ? What direction did these resistance measures take? To what extent did leaders in the civil rights movement agree on the means to reach their goals? How did the work of Martin Luther King Jr. and Malcolm X differ? What is the legacy of each in contemporary society, and how does each fare in the nation's historical memory?*

▶ Draw evidence from a variety of sources including court cases, laws enacted by Congress, and executive orders to assess the effects of constitutional steps taken in the judicial, legislative, and executive branches of the government as part of the civil rights movement.

▶ Draw evidence from Eisenhower's address to the nation to explain the president's reasons for dispatching federal troops to Little Rock in 1957.

Grades 9-12

Examples of student achievement of Standard 4A include:

▶ After reading the decisions in *Plessy* v. *Ferguson* (1896) and *Brown* v. *Board of Education* (1954), analyze the social and constitutional issues involved. *Are separate schools inherently unequal? How does the historical context explain the reversal of* Plessy v. Ferguson? *Why is the Brown decision called "sociological jurisprudence"? Was Eisenhower justified in sending troops to Little Rock, Arkansas?*

▶ Use "Letter From a Birmingham Jail," "I Have a Dream," and other writings of Martin Luther King Jr. to analyze his leadership of the civil rights movement. *How did Malcolm X feel about the March on Washington in 1963 and the philosophy of nonviolence? In what ways were King and Malcolm X similar and different in their goals and ideas? How did the Freedom Riders affect the civil rights movement? How did foreign affairs influence Kennedy's response to the Freedom Riders? Why did the civil rights movement undergo a change from an emphasis on "Black Rights" to "Black Power" after passage of the Voting Rights Act in 1965?*

▶ Examine the role of women such as Jo Ann Robinson, Rosa Parks, Ella Baker, and Fannie Lou Hamer in the civil rights movement and explain their influence in shaping and affecting the struggle for civil rights. *What was the significance of the change?*

▶ Analyze the connection between legislative acts, Supreme Court decisions, and the civil rights movement. *How did the Supreme Court's decision in* Heart of Atlanta *v.* United States *(1964) use the commerce clause of the Constitution to expand the scope of the Civil Rights Act? What was the impact of the decision?*

Students Should Be Able to:

4B Demonstrate understanding of how Asian Americans, Mexican Americans and Native Americans advanced the movement for civil rights and equal rights by:

5-12 Evaluating the grievances, goals, and accomplishments of the various Asian American groups in advancing the movement for civil and equal rights. [**Consider multiple perspectives**]

5-12 Evaluating the strategies of various Mexican American leaders and groups in advancing the movement for civil and equal rights. [**Assess the importance of the individual in history**]

5-12 Evaluating the grievances, goals, and accomplishments of the American Indian Movement. [**Evidence historical perspectives**]

9-12 Analyzing the reasons for the escalation from civil disobedience to "Brown Power" and "Red Power." [**Marshal evidence of antecedent circumstances**]

Grades 5-6

Examples of student achievement of Standard 4B include:

▶ Describe efforts to attain equality and civil rights for Native Americans, Asian Americans, and Mexican Americans in the postwar years. Drawing on biographies, stories, poetry, music, and pictorial resources, trace the demands made by diverse groups.

▶ Interview local people and investigate historical resources in the community to learn about issues important to groups in the region.

▶ List major grievances of national groups that made demands during the postwar period. Compare their goals, accomplishments, and failures. *Who were the major leaders in the struggle for equal rights? How did these men and women advance their ideas? What was the constitutional basis for their demands? What methods did they use to achieve their goals? Did their efforts make a difference in the way we think about equality and civil rights and the way we live now?*

Grades 7-8

Examples of student achievement of Standard 4B include:

▶ Trace the development of movements for equal rights by Asian Americans, Hispanic Americans, and Native Americans.

▶ Examine personal narratives to define the principal grievances of Asian Americans, Hispanic Americans, and Native Americans in the post-World War II period.

▶ Draw upon a variety of historical evidence including literature, poetry, art, and music to investigate the efforts of various organizations and individuals to improve the status of minority groups in contemporary American society.

▶ Examine personal accounts of migrant farmworkers using children's tradebooks such as *Voices from the Fields: Children of Migrant Farmworkers Tell Their Stories* by S. Beth Atkin.

▶ Use stories such as *Jimmy Yellow Hawk* by Virginia Driving Hawk Sneve, *And Now Miguel* by Joseph Krumhold, and *Sea Glass and Child of the Owl* by Laurence Yep to investigate personal narratives of young Native Americans, Hispanics, and Asians in searching for their own identity in American society.

▶ Construct a historical narrative assessing the means by which Asian Americans, Hispanic Americans, and Native Americans worked to improve civil and equal rights. *Who were the leaders in the struggle for civil and equal rights? What methods were used to achieve their goals? How did the struggle differ among groups? To what extent was civil disobedience used to attain their goals?*

Grades 9-12

Examples of student achievement of Standard 4B include:

▶ Explain the issues that led to the development of the Asian Civil Rights Movement.

▶ Interrogate historical data, contemporary poetry, literature, and political biographies of César Chavez, "Corky" Gonzalez, and Delores Huerta to analyze the issues and goals of the farm labor movement and La Raza Unida. *How does César Chavez describe the life of the migrant workers? How is this connected to Hispanic American rights? How do poems like Inez Hernandez's "Para Teresa" describe the emotions of Mexican Americans? How does it compare to the writings of Martin Luther King Jr. and Malcolm X?*

▶ Use newspaper and magazine reports of the seizure of Alcatraz (1969) and Second Wounded Knee (1973), and books such as Vine Deloria's *Custer Died for Your Sins* to explain the reasons for the Native American Civil Rights Movement. *How has "Red Power" been defined? Why did the American Indian Movement (AIM) seize Alcatraz Island in San Francisco Bay? How did the occupation end? What were the issues that led to Second Wounded Knee? Did AIM achieve its goals? Why or why not?*

Mural, Centro Cultural de La Raza, San Diego, CA

Students Should Be Able to:

4C **Demonstrate understanding of how women advanced the movement for civil rights and equal rights by:**

[7–12] Analyzing the factors contributing to modern feminism and the emergence of the National Organization for Women (NOW). [**Marshal evidence of antecedent circumstances**]

[5–12] Identifying the major issues affecting women and explaining the conflicts these issues engendered. [**Formulate a position or course of action on an issue**]

[9–12] Evaluating the conflicting perspectives over the ERA, Title VII, and *Roe v. Wade*. [**Consider multiple perspectives**]

| Grades 5-6 | Examples of student achievement of Standard 4C include: |

▶ Explain why the National Organization for Women was established. *What are the issues women raised in the postwar period? Were these issues resolved or are they still present today?*

▶ Draw evidence from documentary photographs, films, and newspaper and magazine advertisements to explain attitudes regarding women in the postwar period. Contrast the image of women today with that of the 1950s and 1960s.

| Grades 7-8 | Examples of student achievement of Standard 4C include: |

▶ Use a time line to trace the evolution of the movement for women's rights in the 20th century and construct a historical narrative examining the accomplishments and setbacks in the development of the modern feminist movement. *What factors contributed to the development of the modern feminist movement? What factors led to the development of the National Organization for Women (NOW)? To what extent were the gains women made in the work force during World War II continued in the postwar period? How did individuals such as Eleanor Roosevelt and Betty Friedan spur the development of the modern women's movement? How did the modern feminist movement reshape American society?*

▶ Draw upon evidence from different perspectives to construct a historical argument, debate, or personal narrative explaining the conflicts originating from within and without the women's movement in the 1970s.

▶ Construct a sound argument, debate, or historical narrative presenting historical evidence on such questions as: *Was the Equal Rights Amendment (ERA) a necessary step in securing and maintaining women's rights? What is the appropriate role of government in promoting equal employment opportunities for women? Are women's affirmative action programs necessary?*

Grades 9-12

Examples of student achievement of Standard 4C include:

▶ Use articles from *Ms.* magazine or selections from such books as *Sisterhood is Powerful,* edited by Robin Morgan, or *The Rebirth of Feminism* by Judith Hole and Ellen Levine and explain how feminism was compelling in its analysis of women's problems and the solutions offered. Explain how Jacqueline Kennedy epitomized the transition from the fifties to the sixties woman. *How were women from ethnic minorities affected by feminism? Was feminism previously a middle-class movement?*

▶ Using Supreme Court decisions, Title VII of the Civil Rights Act of 1974, Title IX of the Educational Amendment Act of 1972, and the Equal Credit Opportunity Act of 1974, explain the impact of modern feminism. *What does the slogan "the personal is political" mean? Why did the ERA fail to get ratified? Is it still needed? Why or why not? How are the civil rights movement and the women's rights movement connected?*

▶ Draw upon evidence reflecting different perspectives to examine the controversies over the Supreme Court decision in *Roe v. Wade. How did the reasoning in Griswold v.* Connecticut *lead to the right to privacy in* Roe v. Wade? *How has* Roe v. Wade *been modified? Do you think that the Constitution legitimizes a "right to privacy"? Why or why not?*

Women's Equality Day, Washington D.C., 1977, Bettmann Archive

Students Should Be Able to:

4D Demonstrate understanding of the contributions of the Warren Court in advancing civil liberties and equal rights by:

▸ **9–12** Analyzing the expansion of due process rights in such cases as *Gideon* v. *Wainwright* and *Miranda* v. *Arizona*. [**Interrogate historical data**]

▸ **7–12** Evaluating criticism of the extension of due process rights for the accused. [**Evaluate alternative courses of action**]

▸ **9–12** Explaining the court's reasoning in establishing the "one man, one vote" principle. [**Interrogate historical data**]

▸ **5–12** Evaluating the court's interpretation of freedom of religion. [**Formulate a position or course of action on an issue**]

| Grades 5-6 | Examples of student achievement of Standard 4D include: |

▸ Construct a role-playing activity, skit, or classroom newspaper explaining the importance of the separation of church and state and freedom of religion in contemporary American society.

▸ Interview local people to investigate issues regarding religious freedom which are important to the community or region.

| Grades 7-8 | Examples of student achievement of Standard 4D include: |

▸ Define "due process of law" and examine the Warren Court's stand on the extension of due process rights for the accused. *What landmark Supreme Court cases extended due process rights? What were the controversies raised by these cases?*

▸ Examine the Warren court's decisions in *Engle* v. *Vitale*. *Why did the decision provoke widespread opposition?*

| Grades 9-12 | Examples of student achievement of Standard 4D include: |

▸ Use selections from court cases — live recordings and transcripts of several major trials since 1957 — edited by Peter Irons and Stephanie Guitton in *May It Please the Court* (1993) cartoons, and speeches to analyze the extension of due process rights during the era of the Warren court. *What is the reasoning used to justify the decision in* Gideon *v.* Wainwright? Miranda *v.* Arizona? *Does the Sixth Amendment's "right to an attorney" mean that a citizen should be provided with one if he/she can't afford it? Is there such a thing as tainted evidence? Is the following statement a justifiable criticism of the Warren court's decisions: "The prisoner goes free because the constable has blundered"? Do you agree or disagree with the statement: "It is better that nine guilty men go free if one innocent man is saved"?* Investigate the reasons why individuals and groups sought the impeachment of Earl Warren.

▶ Examine the Warren court's reasoning in the *Reynolds* v. *Sims* and *Baker* v. *Carr* cases, and explain their effect on representation. What is the "one man, one vote" principle?

▶ Examine the Warren court's interpretation of the First Amendment guarantee of freedom of religion. *What were the landmark Supreme Court cases regarding freedom of religion? Why did the court rule that nondenominational prayers were a violation of the First Amendment? When, if ever, do you think that prayers should be allowed in public schools? Is a moment of silence a violation of the First Amendment? Why or why not? Were the decisions of the Warren court consistent with the concept of separation of church and state?*

Clarence Gideon's handwritten response on prison stationery to Florida's attorney general, National Archives

ERA 10

Contemporary United States (1968 to the present)

The study of the last few decades of American history needs to be approached with a healthy dose of caution since it is too early to judge whether events and trends that seem epic at the time will later seem as important.

There can be little doubt, however, that in global politics the role of the United States has led to seismic changes that every student, as a person approaching voting age, should understand. The detente with the People's Republic of China under Nixon's presidency represents a beginning of a new era whose outcome is still far from determined. Nor can the collapse of the Soviet Union and the overthrow of communist governments in Eastern Europe be translated into any certain appearance of the "new world order" where the United States would have the leading role. But students can understand little about what is happening today without comprehending these momentous events.

Students should study carefully the ability of the political and constitutional system to check and balance itself against potential abuses as exemplified in the Watergate and Iran-Contra affairs. They can hone their ability to think carefully about the American political system, about government's role in the economy, and about how Americans have come to claim entitlements that would have been condemned as socialism half a century ago by studying the "new conservatism" of the Reagan-Bush era. This will alert them to the recurrent shifts in public mood and policy following major wars and domestic dislocation.

No course in American history can reach a conclusion without considering some of the major social and cultural changes of the most recent decades. Among them, a few may claim precedence: first, the reopening of the nation's gates to immigrants that for the first time come from Asia and Central America; second, renewed reform movements that struggle to carry out environmental, feminist, and civil rights agendas that lost steam in the 1970s; third, the resurgence of religious evangelicalism; and last, the massive alteration in the character of work through technological innovation and corporate reorganization.

Overview

Standard 1: Major developments in foreign and domestic policies during the Cold War era

Standard 2: Major social and economic developments in contemporary America

S T A N D A R D   1

Students Should Understand: *Recent developments in foreign and domestic policies.*

Students Should Be Able to:

1A Demonstrate understanding of Nixon's domestic agenda and the Watergate Affair by:

`9-12` Explaining the administration's "southern strategy" and evaluating its political significance. [**Analyze cause-and-effect relationships**]

`7-12` Analyzing the ways in which Nixon initiated and changed social and environmental programs. [**Assess the importance of the individual in history**]

`9-12` Assessing government policy for dealing with the twin problems of recession and inflation. [**Interrogate historical data**]

`5-12` Explaining the Nixon administration's involvement in Watergate and examining the role of the media in exposing the scandal. [**Formulate historical questions**]

`9-12` Analyzing the constitutional issues raised by the Watergate affair and evaluating the effects of Watergate on public opinion. [**Examine the influence of ideas**]

| **Grades 5-6** | **Examples of student Achievement of Standard 1A include:** |

◗ Define terms such as: "law and order," "silent majority," and "New Federalism," and explain how they were used by the Nixon administration.

◗ Define key terms associated with the Watergate Affair such as "plumbers," "enemies list," and "CREEP." Identify and explain the role of prominent people affiliated with the Watergate scandal.

| **Grades 7-8** | **Examples of student achievement of Standard 1A include:** |

◗ Define what was meant by the term "silent majority" and explain the factors that caused so many Americans to support Nixon and his "law and order" stance.

◗ Chart the legislative measures debated in the years 1968-74 that dealt with family assistance and employment opportunities. *What was unique about Nixon's advocacy of these social programs? Why was the administration unsuccessful in attaining congressional approval?*

◗ Draw evidence from public records, special interest groups, newspapers, and magazines to evaluate the Nixon administration record on the environment. *What new programs were established? How did special interest groups react to environmental legislation? To what extent did the Nixon administration sponsor environmental programs?*

♦ Draw upon evidence from a variety of primary and secondary sources including documentary films, books, diaries, audio tapes, news magazines, and newspapers to reconstruct the events of Watergate. *What did President Nixon know about the break-in, and when did he come to know it? How did the attempt to cover up the crime take shape, and what was the role of the press in exposing it? On what grounds did Nixon base his refusal to release certain evidence? How did Congress and the Supreme Court react to his stand?*

♦ Draw upon evidence from differing perspectives to consider the effects of Watergate on public opinion at the time with regard to the presidency, the federal government, and the constitutional system of checks and balances.

♦ Conduct a mock Judiciary Committee hearing examining impeachment charges.

Grades 9-12

Examples of student achievement of Standard 1A include:

♦ Explain how Nixon and Attorney General John Mitchell sought to strengthen respect for law and reestablish order in the aftermath of the riots and violence that had occurred during the Johnson years. *Did the Nixon-Mitchell emphasis on public law and order conflict with their abuse of illegal wiretaps and surveillance, the "enemies list," and the "dirty tricks" campaign?*

♦ After investigating the formation of a new political coalition of southern whites, residents of the rapidly growing western Sunbelt, white working-class ethnics in the North, and conservative white suburbanites, construct a sound argument, debate, or historical narrative on such questions as: *Did the perceived excesses of the civil rights and antiwar movements splinter the old "Roosevelt coalition"? Did the racial and gender characteristics of voters lead them to support one or the other of the major parties? Why or why not? To what extent did Nixon as president create a new political coalition?*

♦ Define the "New Federalism" and explain why Nixon supported it. *What welfare, health, safety, and environmental programs were instituted under Nixon? Why did he support such measures?*

♦ Explain the reasons for congressional imposition of wage and price controls and the devaluation of the dollar. Evaluate their success in dealing with the inflationary spiral. *How did the Nixon administration's sale of wheat to the Soviet Union in 1972 affect the subsequent inflationary spiral? What other factors contributed to inflation? Was Nixon to blame for the inflation affecting the nation during his years in office?*

♦ Drawing on the evidence of the Watergate break-in and involvement of the Nixon administration in the subsequent cover-up, analyze the evidence accumulated by the special prosecutor, the Ervin Committee, and the House Judiciary Committee. Consider questions such as: *What were some of the illegal actions of officials of the Nixon White House? What role did the media play in exposing the illegal actions engaged in by Nixon administration officials? On what grounds did Nixon refuse to turn over subpoenaed tapes of private conversations in the Oval Office to the special prosecutor and congressional investigating committees? What were the grounds for impeachment of the president advanced by the House Judiciary Committee in July 1974? Why did Nixon decide to resign? What major figures in the Nixon administration were convicted of illegal actions in the Watergate affair?*

Students Should Be Able to:

1B **Demonstrate understanding of domestic policy issues in contemporary American society by:**

7-12 Analyzing the Ford and Carter responses to "the imperial presidency." [**Examine the influence of ideas**]

5-12 Evaluating the Republican and Democratic administrations' attempts to deal with the economic "stagflation." [**Formulate a position or course of action on an issue**]

5-12 Explaining the conservative reaction to liberalism and evaluating supply-side economic strategies of the Reagan and Bush administrations. [**Compare and contrast differing sets of ideas**]

7-12 Examining the impact of the "Reagan Revolution" on federalism and public perceptions of the role of government. [**Examine the influence of ideas**]

9-12 Analyzing the constitutional issues in the Iran-Contra affair. [**Identify issues and problems in the past**]

9-12 Analyzing why labor unionism declined in the Reagan-Bush era. [**Interrogate historical data**]

9-12 Evaluating the impact of the recession and the growing national debt on the Bush and Clinton administrations' domestic agendas. [**Interrogate historical data**]

Grades 5-6

Examples of student achievement of Standard 1B include:

▶ Analyze charts, documentary photographs, and films that illustrated how inflation, high unemployment, and escalating energy prices affected Americans during the Ford and Carter administrations. Interview family members to find out how they felt about changes during these years. Use interview data and graphs to show how much it cost to buy essentials such as bread, milk, gasoline, and clothes then and now. *How have prices of basic foods and services changed from the 1970s to our time? What did inflation mean to families in the 1970s?*

▶ Locate the OPEC countries and describe how they controlled oil prices in the 1970s. *What led to the rise in gasoline prices in the 1970s? Why did people have to wait in long lines to buy gasoline for their cars? How did Americans try to limit reliance on foreign oil supplies?*

▶ Draw evidence from documentary films, newspaper and magazine accounts, and interviews with family members to examine the reasons for President Reagan's popularity.

▶ Construct a balance sheet listing in one column the major domestic problems facing Presidents Reagan and Bush and in the second column how their administrations sought to deal with these issues.

Grades 7-8

Examples of student achievement of Standard 1B include:

▶ Construct a sound historical argument, debate, or narrative presenting both sides on the issue of President Ford's decision to pardon Richard Nixon.

▶ Construct a balance sheet listing the successes and failures of domestic policies during the Carter administration.

231

▶ Draw evidence from Reagan's inaugural address to determine the goals of his administration and compare these to his accomplishments. *What were the central issues presented in the address? What did the new administration propose regarding the role of government? What is meant by the "Reagan Revolution"?*

▶ Construct a historical narrative, debate, or project, such as a classroom newspaper, mock congressional hearing, or speeches in support of or opposition to Reagan's environmental program. *To whom did the administration's program appeal? What was the basis of Sierra Club opposition to the program?*

▶ Explain the Iran-Contra affair and examine the role of individuals involved in the affair. *What led to the affair? What was Oliver North's role in Iran-Contra? What was the public perception of Oliver North?*

▶ Construct a balance sheet listing the domestic problems facing President Bush and the programs his administration presented to deal with these issues. *How effective was the administration in dealing with the economic recession? How effective was the Republican administration in dealing with the Democratic congress?*

▶ Construct a time line listing legislation that has promoted or retarded the growth of organized labor in the post-World War II era. Define terms such as "open shop," "closed shop," "featherbedding," and "right to work" laws. *How has the general public perceived labor unions? To what extent have economic conditions affected membership in labor unions? How supportive were the Reagan-Bush administrations of organized labor?*

Grades 9-12

Examples of student achievement of Standard 1B include:

▶ Draw evidence from unemployment statistics and economic appraisals of the Ford and Carter administrations to address such questions as: *What factors contributed to the high inflation rates in the 1970s? What factors contributed to the high unemployment of the period? How did Presidents Ford and Carter attempt to deal with the problem of "stagflation"? What political factors underlined their approaches? Were their programs successful? Why or why not?*

▶ Examine how Presidents Ford and Carter, in the aftermath of Watergate, attempted to address the problems associated with the "Imperial Presidency". *To what extent did Ford and Carter restore credibility to the presidency?*

▶ Explain Carter's program for dealing with the energy crisis and evaluate the effectiveness of his leadership. *To what extent did Carter's "outsider" status affect his dealings with Congress and Washington bureaucrats? Why did critics derisively use the acronym "MEOW" to characterize Carter's conservation plan that he claimed was the "moral equivalent of war"? Why did Carter's support for deregulation of the airline, railroad, and trucking industries and cuts in various social programs alienate liberal Democrats?*

▶ Analyze Reagan's assessment of the Soviet Union as the "evil empire" and explain how it shaped U.S. defense policy. *Where did the phrase "evil empire" originate, and to what extent was it a valid characterization of the Soviet Union?*

▶ Use selections from memoirs, monographs, newspaper articles, and the testimony of Oliver North to analyze the Iran-Contra affair. *How did the relations with the civil war in Nicaragua contribute to the affair? To what extent did the Boland amendment restrict executive foreign policy initiatives? Was the amendment constitutional? Was the president's staff acting above the law? How does the Iran-Contra affair compare to the Watergate crisis?*

▶ Explain the impact of Reagan's tax policies on the national economy. *What were the elements of "supply-side" economics? How was the supply-side tax cut intended to work? How did the increased spending on defense affect the outcome of Reagan's economic program? How did deregulation fit in the overall economic plan? How was the federal deficit affected by the economic program?* Democratic Speaker Thomas "Tip" O'Neill characterized Reagan as "Herbert Hoover with a smile" and "a cheerleader for selfishness". *Is this a fair characterization? Why or why not?*

▶ Draw evidence from statistical data, unemployment figures, union contracts, current periodicals, and public opinion polls to examine the status and perception of labor in the postindustrial economy. *What factors contributed to the rapid decline in manufacturing jobs? How has the public attitude toward labor unions changed in the latter half of the 20th century? What accounts for this change?*

▶ Explain how economic recession and the deficit influenced the 1992 election. *What did the slogan, "It's the economy, stupid!" in the Clinton campaign headquarters mean? What was the impact of the deficit on the Clinton administration's priorities and programs?*

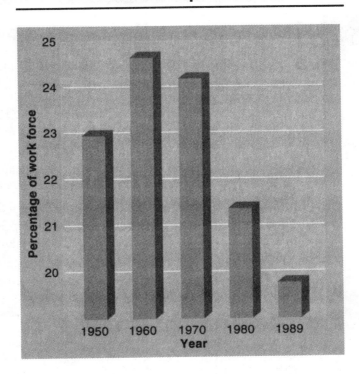

Union Membership, 1950–1989

U.S. Bureau of Labor Statistics

Students Should Be Able to :

1C Demonstrate understanding of major foreign policy initiatives by:

7–12 Assessing U.S. policies toward arms limitation and improved relations with the Soviet Union. **[Examine the influence of ideas]**

7–12 Explaining Nixon's detente with the People's Republic of China and how it reshaped U.S. foreign policy. **[Analyze multiple causation]**

9–12 Examining the interconnections between the United States' role as a superpower with the evolving political struggles in the Middle East, Africa, Asia, and Latin America. **[Analyze cause-and-effect relationships]**

5–12 Explaining Reagan's efforts to reassert U.S. military power and rebuild American prestige. **[Hypothesize the influence of the past]**

7–12 Evaluating the reasons for the collapse of communist governments in Eastern Europe and the USSR. **[Analyze multiple causation]**

7–12 Evaluating the reformulation of U.S. foreign policy in the post-Cold War era. **[Analyze cause-and-effect relationships]**

Grades 5-6

Examples of student achievement of Standard 1C include:

▶ Identify crisis areas around the world and list some of the major peace initiatives made during the Carter administration. Locate places where President Carter tried to influence world events: places where he tried to promote human rights, and places involved in the Panama Treaty, the Camp David Accords, and the Iranian hostage crisis. *What was Carter's human rights policy? Which of Carter's police efforts were successful and which were failures?*

▶ Compare maps of Europe in 1985 with current maps to show changes after the fall of the Soviet Union and communist states in Eastern Europe.

▶ Locate on a world map places in the Middle East, Central America, the Caribbean, Africa, and Asia where U.S. advisers and military forces were involved during the Reagan and Bush administrations. Post current news stories describing the role of the United States in these places today.

Grades 7-8

Examples of student achievement of Standard 1C include:

▶ Interrogate historical data from a variety of sources including contemporary newspaper accounts, weekly news magazines, television journalism, and biographies to evaluate the Nixon administration's policies toward the Soviet Union. *What were Nixon's objectives? To what extent was he successful in achieving his goals in arms control?*

▶ Construct a historical narrative comparing the view of the American public and government toward China in today's world to that at the beginning of the Nixon presidency. *Why was Nixon's trip to China a historic occasion? What effect did the venture have on U.S. relations with the People's Republic of China? How did the public respond to the China initiative?*

▶ Explain the factors that prompted Nixon to send his secretary of state on numerous trips to the Middle East. *Why did Secretary of State Henry Kissinger devote considerable time and effort traveling throughout the Middle East? What challenges did he undertake on behalf of the United States? How successful was he in resolving the Arab-Israeli conflict?*

▶ Chart the measures that led President Carter to assume a leadership role in the Camp David accords, and construct a historical narrative evaluating the importance of that peace initiative for the Middle East. *How successful was Carter's personal diplomacy in negotiating the Camp David Accords? How might Camp David be viewed as the highlight of Carter's foreign policy initiatives?*

▶ Explain the factors that led to the Iranian hostage crisis and evaluate the effects of public opinion about the crisis on Carter's reelection efforts.

▶ Construct a project (e.g., speeches, editorials, poster boards, or collages) analyzing one aspect of Reagan's foreign policy, and illustrate different domestic and foreign reactions to the initiative. *What impact did the Strategic Defense Initiative (S.D.I. or "Star Wars") have on the Soviets? What was the basis of domestic opposition to the S.D.I.? To what extent did the Grenada affair signal a new era in American foreign policy? Did the attack on Libya represent a change from previous U.S. policy or was it a continuation of prior policy? Explain.*

▶ Construct an argument, debate, or historical narrative on the proposition: *Ronald Reagan's defense and military initiatives led to the collapse of communism.*

▶ Explain the foreign policy goals of the Bush and Clinton administrations and evaluate their effectiveness. *Was the administration's Latin American policy a continuation of the Reagan administration's policy? How did the public respond to the Bush initiatives in Panama? How effective was the Bush administration's response the end of the Cold War? How effective was the administration's policy in the Persian Gulf War? How did the end of the Cold War influence Clinton's foreign policy actions? How did human rights issues impact U.S. policy toward the People's Republic of China during the Bush and Clinton administrations?*

| Grades 9-12 | Examples of student achievement of Standard 1C include |

▶ Compare Nixon's foreign policy with that of his Democratic predecessors in the Cold War era. *Why did Nixon, who began his career as an anticommunist crusader, devote his energies as president to negotiate an easing of tensions and conflict with communist states?* Explain Nixon's policy of "linkage" and provide examples of its implementation. *How did Nixon use the "China card" and detente with the Soviet Union to further his foreign policy objectives? How did the Nixon Doctrine redefine the role of the United States in the world? What factors influenced Nixon to issue the doctrine? In what respect were the SALT I and SALT II treaties advantageous to the United States? What was the significance of the Reagan Doctrine?*

▶ Drawing evidence from congressional debates, speeches, newspaper, and magazine articles, and maps of the Middle East, analyze U.S. goals and objectives in the Middle East. Evaluate the success of Henry Kissinger's "shuttle diplomacy" in stabilizing tensions in the Middle East following the Yom Kippur War in 1973 and resolving the oil crisis in the aftermath of the OPEC boycott. Evaluate the significance of the Camp David Accords.

▶ Drawing on a variety of historical sources, analyze the pros and cons of U.S. intervention in the Persian Gulf under Reagan and Bush. *Was Desert Storm justifiable?* Analyze the U.S. role in the creation of a Palestinian homeland on the West Bank.

▶ Evaluate the Reagan administration's policy toward South Africa and debate such questions as: *Was corporate divestment in South Africa a proper response to apartheid? What were the economic and social ramifications of economic sanctions on the black majority in South Africa?*

▶ Analyze the reasons for the collapse of communism in Eastern Europe and the Soviet Union. *To what extent did American foreign policy influence the collapse of communism?*

▶ Analyze the meaning of human rights and explain how it has been used in American foreign policy. *Is an emphasis on human rights an unwarranted interference in the internal affairs of other countries? Is the American concern with human rights a subterfuge for realpolitik?*

Berlin Airlift, 1948, German Information Center

STANDARD 2

Students Should Understand: *Major social and economic developments in contemporary America.*

Students Should Be Able to:

2A Demonstrate understanding of continuing reform agendas by:

9-12 Explaining the arguments for and against affirmative action and evaluating its effects on the social and economic position of women and minorities. [**Consider multiple perspectives**]

5-12 Examining the changing goals of the women's movement and analyzing the issues currently dividing women. [**Explain historical continuity and change**]

9-12 Explaining the evolution of government support for the rights of the physically and emotionally challenged. [**Reconstruct patterns of historical succession and duration**]

7-12 Evaluating the grievances of African Americans, Asian Americans, Hispanic Americans, and Native Americans and the steps they have taken to rectify past injustices. [**Explain historical continuity and change**]

9-12 Examining the emergence of the Gay Liberation Movement and analyzing the arguments concerning the civil rights of gay Americans. [**Marshal evidence of antecedent circumstances**]

5-12 Evaluating how diverse peoples and their cultures have shaped American life. [**Consider multiple perspectives**]

| Grades 5-6 | Examples of student achievement of Standard 2A include: |

▶ Create a collage using the preamble to the U.S. Constitution to show issues involving justice and the common welfare. *Which groups continue to seek rights and opportunities to solve their problems? How successful have they been?*

▶ Draw evidence from biographies, newspapers and magazine articles, and diaries of women in the arts, science, sports, and professional worlds to compare opportunities for women now and in the past. *What accounts for changes since World War II? To what extent have women's roles remained unchanged?*

▶ Use letters, speeches, documentary photographs, stories, and diaries to show how interest groups have tried to achieve their goals of equality and justice. *How have Americans worked to change laws about such things as child labor, unsafe working conditions, and limited suffrage?*

▶ Draw evidence from biographies to create a booklet using illustrations and short quotations to reflect how African American, Asian Americans, Hispanic Americans, and Native Americans have retained their cultural heritage.

Grades 7-8

Examples of student achievement of Standard 2A include:

◗ Draw upon evidence from differing perspectives to assess reasons for the failure to ratify the Equal Rights Amendment.

◗ List the issues that are important to the women's movement and examine different methods in achieving their goals. Draw upon evidence from personal interviews, speeches, newspapers and magazines to appraise the successes of the women's movement in modern America. *What are the most important gains of the women's movement since the late 1960s? To what extent is the women's movement responsible for an increase of women in local, state, and federal offices? What are the unresolved issues? What are the issues dividing the women's movement?*

◗ Survey local community efforts to adapt facilities for the physically challenged. *When did the local community begin addressing the needs of the physically challenged? Were local efforts begun before federal government requirements were established? What additional steps need to be taken?*

◗ Analyze how racial and ethnic stereotyping have affected the perception of African Americans, Asian Americans, Hispanic Americans, and Native Americans. *How have ethnic and racial minorities challenged these perceptions?*

Grades 9-12

Examples of student achievement of Standard 2A include:

◗ Review the major arguments for and against ratification of the Equal Rights Amendment and explain the reasons it failed. *What was the impact of the civil rights movement of the 1950s and 1960s on the modern feminist movement?*

◗ Explain the *Roe* v. *Wade* case (1973) and evaluate its impact on the women's rights movement. *Why did critics such as Anita Bryant and Phyllis Schlafly link the struggle for equal rights, the gay rights movement, and abortion on demand as part of a concerted campaign to destroy the American family and traditional values? How do race and class affect the women's rights movement?*

◗ Assemble the evidence and explain how the modern feminist movement has been both a success and a failure.

◗ Define the term "affirmative action" and construct a historical narrative explaining the ideals associated with that notion. *How successful have such programs been in securing equal opportunity for women, minorities, and other traditionally underrepresented groups?*

◗ Research the issues raised by African Americans, Asian Americans, Hispanic Americans, and Native Americans in contemporary American society, and explain how organizations have gathered support to address grievances. *Are there recurring ethnic and racial problems in American society? What methods are used to redress grievances?*

◗ Draw upon methods of historical research including the use of oral histories, films, local museum exhibits, literature, and the fine arts to evaluate the contributions of diverse peoples and cultures to American society.

▶ Draw evidence from live arguments and excerpts from *Regents of the University of California* v. *Bakke* (1978) from *May It Please the Court* (edited by Peter Irons and Stephanie Guitton) to analyze issues and explain the arguments for and against affirmative action. *What was the court's decision regarding affirmative action? Are critics correct in arguing that the economic and social costs of affirmative action outweigh its benefits? Has affirmative action led to economic and social gains by women and minorities? Does the perception of affirmative action as promoting "reverse discrimination" square with the evidence? Does the perception that women and minorities benefit unfairly from affirmative action handicap them in the work place because they are perceived as lacking in merit?*

▶ Draw evidence from a variety of primary sources reflecting contradictory studies to analyze the arguments over issues brought to the public arena by the Gay Liberation Movement. Interrogate the data with probing questions to discern its credibility, and to detect and evaluate bias and distortion. *What are the constitutional arguments the movement has invoked? What is the basis for opposition to the movement? What evidence is presented by both sides in the issue?*

▶ Draw on a variety of historical and statistical data to analyze the demographic, educational, occupational, and residential characteristics of African Americans, Asian Americans, Hispanic Americans, and Native Americans. *How have changing economic conditions, especially the decline in entry-level manufacturing jobs, affected such groups? Why have many Americans cities today become "reservations for poor people"? What major grievances have been advanced by spokespersons for African Americans, Asian Americans, Hispanic Americans, and Native Americans? How have such organizations as the American Indian Movement, Pan Asian Congress, La Raza Unida, and the United Farm Workers sought to improve the lives of their constituents?*

Murals, Chicano Park, San Diego, CA

Students Should Be Able to:

2B Demonstrate understanding of the new immigration and internal migration by:

`7-12` Exploring the reasons for the internal migrations from the "Rustbelt" to the "Sunbelt" and analyzing its impact on politics. [**Utilize visual and mathematical data**]

`5-12` Explaining the factors that prompted the new immigration. [**Analyze cause-and-effect relationships**]

`9-12` Examining how the new immigration has raised issues concerning intergroup relations and governmental responsibilities. [**Analyze cause-and-effect relationships**]

| **Grades 5-6** | **Examples of student achievement of Standard 2B include:** |

▶ Compare current immigration and migration patterns to earlier times by preparing a class chart showing where ancestors lived before moving to their present residence.

▶ On a classroom map locate areas of the U.S. where immigrants have settled in large numbers. Explain the reasons that sparked increased immigration to the U.S. in recent times. *From which areas of the world have most immigrants come in recent times?*

| **Grades 7-8** | **Examples of student achievement of Standard 2B include:** |

▶ Draw upon evidence from demographic maps, census reports, and periodicals to chart the internal migration from the Northeast to the South and Southwest. *What prompted the migration? Why did industries relocate in the "Sunbelt"? What have been the effects of the reduction in military spending and the recession of the 1990s on growth in the "Sunbelt"?*

▶ Investigate life stories of recent immigrants to explain the reasons for their decisions to emigrate and the challenges they faced in moving to a new land. *What problems do immigrants face in their new home? What organizations help immigrants? How have immigrants relied on their families, friends, or religious communities to help make life easier in their new homeland?*

▶ Construct a historical narrative comparing past immigration history with the reality of present immigration. *What are the push/pull factors that have caused people to move to the United States in the past? How do they compare to the reasons that impel immigrants today? To what extent is the reception afforded immigrants today similar to that of the past? To what extent is it different?*

▶ Explain how the immigration acts of 1965, 1986, and 1991 changed immigration patterns. *Do the new immigration policies live up to the ideas expressed in Emma Lazarus's poem The New Colossus?*

Grades 9-12

Examples of student achievement of Standard 2B include:

▶ Draw on data depicting demographic and residential mobility since 1970 and analyze the factors contributing to the population shift from the "Rustbelt" to the "Sunbelt." Explain how this has affected representation in Congress. *How have the major political parties adjusted to such demographic changes?*

▶ Explain the demographic changes resulting from the Immigration Act of 1965 and consider the following questions: *What areas of the world have provided the most immigrants to the United States since passage of the act? What major factors have promoted immigration to the U.S. from these areas of the world? What effects have the new immigration had on economic opportunity, education, and government services?*

▶ Construct a historical investigation of the factors that led to the Immigration Reform and Control Act of 1986 and examine arguments for and against the legislation and its application. Draw evidence from INS studies, congressional reports, and public opinion polls. *How does the increase in immigration in the 1980s compare to that of the early 1900s in terms of the country of origin and size? How did immigration change after the passage of the 1965 and 1991 immigration acts? How did the 1986 act seek to control undocumented immigrants? Does the act offer fair and balanced treatment? To what extent has the act impacted social services and health care? What is the general perception of the new immigrants? How has it affected their relationship with other groups in society? To what extent is the "melting pot" analogy applicable today? Is the "salad bowl" metaphor more appropriate? Why?*

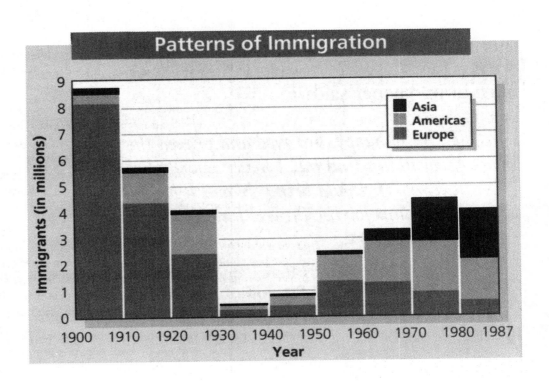

Students Should Be Able to:

2C **Demonstrate understanding of changing religious diversity and its impact on American institutions and values by:**

`5-12` Analyzing how changing immigration patterns have affected religious diversity. [**Explain historical continuity and change**]

`7-12` Analyzing the position of major religious groups on political and social issues. [**Analyze cause-and-effect relationships**]

`7-12` Explaining the growth of religious fundamentalism and the appeal of television evangelists. [**Consider multiple perspectives**]

Grades 5-6

Examples of student achievement of Standard 2C include:

▶ Use the local community to prepare a survey of the different religious groups represented. *What role has immigration played in the growth of religious diversity?*

▶ Identify and describe important issues relating to religious beliefs in contemporary American society. *What solutions have religious groups proposed to solve these important issues?*

▶ Interview family members and friends to investigate the importance of religious beliefs on choices made in the family such as the selection of television programs, movies, and the purchasing of goods and services.

Grades 7-8

Examples of student achievement of Standard 2C include:

▶ Develop a time line indicating the prominent issues regarding the guarantee of no establishment of religion and the free exercise clauses of the First Amendment. Construct a sound historical argument or debate on questions such as: *Is school prayer a violation of the First Amendment? Is a "moment of silence" constitutional? Should local governments promote public signs of religion in seasonal displays? Is public support for religious schools a violation of the Constitution? Has the Supreme Court taken appropriate action in cases dealing with free exercise of religion?*

▶ Research the growth of religious evangelism in the post-World War II era. *To what extent has the growth of evangelism been a reaction to secularism in American society? What has been the appeal of media evangelists? What social issues are at the forefront of evangelical crusades? To what extent have the major political parties responded to issues raised by Christian fundamentalists?*

▶ Conduct a local survey on the significance of religious groups in the local community. *What are the concerns of local religious groups? What differences are evident in their approaches to social issues?*

Examples of student achievement of Standard 2C include:

- Draw on statistical sources such as census data to analyze the changing immigration patterns from the 1970s to the present. Compare how religion and family have eased the transition of past and present immigrants to the U.S.

- Analyze the position of major religious groups on such issues as abortion, gay rights, women in the clergy, and educational issues.

- Analyze the causes and significance of religious evangelism and its effect on American political and religious culture in the 1980s. *What is religious fundamentalism? How has it been a part of American history? How is the 1980s style different? The same? How was President Reagan personally connected to religious evangelism? How does television contribute to the growth of religious evangelism? How has the continuing controversy over* Roe v. Wade *been affected by religious fundamentalism?* Draw evidence from Pat Buchanan's speech at the Republican convention of 1992 to analyze issues relating to fundamental values and religious convictions of conservatives within the Republican party.

- Analyze how Supreme Court decisions since 1968 have affected the meaning and practice of religious freedom. Contrast the position of the Democratic and Republican parties on issues arising from the religious clauses of the First Amendment. *How did Jimmy Carter's "born again" Christianity differ from Ronald Reagan's support for Christian principles?*

Students Should Be Able to:

2D Demonstrate understanding of the modern American economy by:

`5-12` Evaluating the importance of scientific and technological change on the workplace and productivity. **[Explain historical continuity and change]**

`7-12` Analyzing the changing composition of the American work force. **[Analyze cause-and-effect relationships]**

`5-12` Assessing the impact of trade and overseas competition on the economy. **[Interrogate historical data]**

Grades 5-6

Examples of student achievement of Standard 2D include:

‣ Create a scrapbook of the new technologies. Identify and explain the impact of computers, satellites, robotics, telecommunications, and microchips on how people do their jobs.

‣ Drawing on graphical data and newspaper employment advertisements, examine the kinds of jobs available and the education and skills required.

‣ Prepare a list of consumer goods available in your home and the countries they came from. Using a large map of the world in the classroom, create a display of the worldwide pattern of international trade and explain how international trade affects your local community.

Grades 7-8

Examples of student achievement of Standard 2D include:

‣ Drawing on examples from everyday life, analyze the ways in which computers and accessories, such as modems and CD-ROM drives, increase worker productivity and efficiency.

‣ Using areas such as Silicon Valley, the "Sunbelt," or the "Rustbelt," explain how the new technologies and increased global competition affect the contemporary U.S. economy. *What is the impact of the new technologies on educational requirements, job training and job creation, the nature of work, and standards of living?*

Grades 9-12

Examples of student achievement of Standard 2D include:

‣ Define "post-industrial economy" and explain its impact on the changing nature of work and job creation. *What are the social benefits and costs of the new technologies? What impact do the new technologies have on wealth distribution and on gender, race, and class relationships? What effect do the new technologies have on regional, urban, rural, and suburban developments?*

‣ Examine the influence of the new technologies on education and learning? *What is the relationship between earning and learning?*

‣ Analyze the advantages and disadvantages of increased global trade and competition on the U.S. economy. *What economic groups and regions benefit from the NAFTA Treaty? What economic groups and regions are hurt by the treaty? Should the government impose quotas on Japanese imports? Is free trade beneficial or harmful to American workers, businessmen, farmers, and consumers?*

Students Should Be Able to:

2E Demonstrate understanding of contemporary American culture by:

`9-12` Analyzing how social change has affected artistic expression. [**Analyze cause-and-effect relationships**]

`7-12` Explaining the influence of media on contemporary American culture. [**Explain historical continuity and change**]

`5-12` Examining the effects of ethnic diversity on popular culture. [**Interrogate historical data**]

`9-12` Examining the increased commercialization of professional sports and popular culture. [**Analyze cause-and-effect relationships**]

| Grades 5-6 | Examples of student achievement of Standard 2E include: |

▶ Survey your classmates to discover who their heroes/heroines are and examine why they chose such individuals. *How did television and movies influence their selections?*

▶ Organize a cultural jamboree in which the food, music, and art of various ethnic groups are demonstrated.

▶ Create a list of sports and entertainment figures used to advertise specific products. *Do you think this is a good use of sports and entertainment figures? Why or why not?*

| Grades 7-8 | Examples of student achievement of Standard 2E include: |

▶ Examine the influence of MTV (Music Television) on popular culture. *What is the role of image in the success of popular music figures? How does Madonna symbolize the popular culture created by MTV?*

▶ Using examples from the local community, examine how ethnic art, music, food, and clothing have been incorporated into the mainstream culture and society.

| Grades 9-12 | Examples of student achievement of Standard 2E include: |

▶ Drawing on the works of artists such as Willem DeKooning, explain how abstract expressionism is an art form illustrating changing societal concerns.

▶ Analyze the reflection of values in such popular TV shows as *Murphy Brown, Roseanne, Married With Children*, and *The Simpsons*. Compare the depiction of values to those expressed in shows like *Ozzie and Harriet, The Honeymooners, Father Knows Best, My Three Sons, All in the Family,* and *The Bill Cosby Show*.

▶ Evaluate the effect of women's participation in sports on gender roles and career choices. *How are images of women changing because of their involvement in sports?*

Students at West Milford High School, West Milford, NJ. Photograph taken by John Jordan.

CHAPTER 4

Teaching Resources for United States History

Introduction to Resources

While traditional printed sources are still invaluable, the revolution in information-processing technologies provide a new wealth of possibilities for studying the past. Today's teachers and students have a wide array of sophisticated resources and materials available for the improved study of history. The rapid advances in telecommunications and satellite technologies enable learners to engage in a variety of "distance learning experiences," including interactive field trips to historical sites and the use of modems and communications software to tap into distant data banks and sources.

The evolution of CD-ROM and laserdisc technologies provide access to an abundance of diverse printed, audio, and visual data. In addition, publishers increasingly incorporate such multimedia resources into their textbook packages. Finally, an extensive variety of public history resources and materials are available to enhance the study of history. Museums, historical sites, presidential libraries, local and state preservation societies and institutions provide a multitude of resources to teachers and students. The 356 National Park Service Sites , Smithsonian Institution, the countless National and State Historic Preservation sites, and the American Association for State and Local History are just a few of the institutions which provide information and resources for studying the past. The following list is meant to be suggestive rather than inclusive and needs to be updated periodically.

Resources

Media
> Laserdiscs and video
> CD-ROM
> Computer software
> Audio cassettes

Printed Sources
> Primary documents
> Reference materials
> Journals and periodicals
> Visual resources

Teaching Materials
> Curricular units
> Primary source kits

MEDIA

Laserdiscs and Video

▶ **ABC Interactive Programs**
ABC, 1989-1991, interactive laserdisc (CAV) or Macintosh

These interactive laserdisc programs are part of the ABC Instant Replay of History series. The programs includes interviews, speeches, and news footage. With Macintosh HyperCard programs students may print documents and use video clips to compile individual or group reports. The series includes programs such as "Martin Luther King, Jr.," "Communism and the Cold War," and "In the Holy Land." Recommended for grades 7-12.

▶ **America**
BBC/Time-Life, 1973, VHS video cassettes

An award-winning series narrated by Alistair Cooke. The video programs incorporate live action footage, still photographs, period music, and art. Recommended for grades 9-12.

▶ **American Art from the National Gallery of Art**
Voyager, 1993, interactive laserdisc

Students may access over 3600 works of the National Gallery's American art collections. Recommended for grades 7-12.

▶ **The American Document Series**
VHS video cassettes

Newsreel and motion picture footage, still photographs, and radio recordings document the culture and social history of the 1920s, immigration, woman suffrage, the Great Depression, and presidential inaugurals. Recommended for grades 9-12.

▶ **The American Experience**
PBS Video, VHS video cassettes

A series of programs based on a variety of primary sources including archival photographs, diary excerpts, eyewitness accounts, film footage, and music. The classroom series comes with a curriculum package and a comprehensive cross-referenced index. The series includes such programs as "The Donner Party," "In the White Man's Image," "Los Mineros," "America and the Holocaust," "Eisenhower," and "Rachel Carson's 'Silent Spring.'" Recommended for grades 7-12; excerpts from some programs may also be used at grades 5-6.

▶ **Baseball**
PBS Video, VHS video cassettes

An examination of social history from the mid-19th century to the present through a revealing look at America's pastime. The Ken Burns series, narrated by John Chancellor, uses photographs, archival films, interviews, and vintage radio broadcasts. The classroom series of 18 videotapes includes a curriculum package with a teacher's guide, suggested lesson plans, reproducible student handouts, and a comprehensive, cross-referenced index.

▶ **The Civil War**
PBS, 1990, laserdiscs (CLV) or VHS video cassettes

The award-winning series directed by Ken Burns uses archival photographs, music, diary entries, and commentaries by leading historians. Recommended for grades 7-12.

▶ **The Divided Union: The Story of the American Civil War, 1861-1865**
Laserdiscs (CLV) or VHS video cassettes

Reenactments of key Civil War battles, archival photographs, paintings, excerpts from diaries and letters, and analyses by historians. The index and guide provides quick access by bar codes or chapter stops. Recommended for grades 7-12.

▶ **Equal Justice Under Law Series**
Metropolitan Pittsburgh Public Broadcasting, VHS, 3 video cassettes

A dramatization of three landmark Supreme Court cases, *Marbury* v. *Madison*, *McCulloch* v. *Maryland*, and *Gibbons* v. *Ogden*. Each video program examines the historical and legal significance of the court case. Recommended for grades 7-12.

▶ **Estevanico and the Seven Cities of Gold**
All Media Production, 1993, VHS, video cassette

The story of Estevan, a Moroccan, who accompanied Cabeza de Vaca in the journey across the Southwest following the failed Narvaez expedition and Coronado in the search for the "Seven Cities of Gold." Recommended for grades 5-8.

▶ **Eyes: Images from the Art Institute of Chicago**
Voyager Co., interactive laserdisc, Macintosh

Over 200 works from the Chicago Institute with music, poetry, sound effects, and narration about each work. The program provides an introduction to the world of art for younger students. Recommended for grades K-6.

▶ **Eyes on the Prize, Parts I and II**
PBS Video, 1987, laserdiscs (CLV) or VHS video cassettes

A highly acclaimed chronicle of the civil rights struggle between 1954 and 1985. The programs as based on eyewitness accounts and dramatic news footage. Recommended for grades 7-12.

▶ **The Fabulous 60s**
VHS video cassettes

A kaleidoscopic view of the political, social, and cultural climate of the 1960s. Peter Jennings narrates the documentary which includes the Bay of Pigs, civil rights marches, Watts and Detroit riots, and Woodstock. Recommended for grades 7-12.

▶ **Gordon Hirabayashi v. The United States**
Produced by John de Graaf with the Constitution Project, 1992, VHS, video cassette

The story of Gordon Hirabayashi who refused to be interned in 1942, defying Executive Order 9066. The video chronicles Hirabayashi's 42 year struggle to overturn his conviction. Recommended for grades 9-12.

▶ **GTV: A Geographic Perspective on American History**
National Geographic Society, interactive laserdisc, Apple and IBM

Approximately 40 short programs which define the broad concepts of US history from the pre-Columbian era to the present. Recommended for grades 5-8.

▶ **History of the 1980s**
ABC News, VHS video cassettes

Documentary films of the major political, social, and cultural events in the 1980s. Recommended for grades 7-12.

▶ **Lincoln**
PBS Video, VHS video cassettes

A four-part series on Abraham Lincoln and the Civil War drawn largely from Lincoln's writings and letters and diaries of his contemporaries. An educational resource package including a teacher's guide, a class set of a student magazine, and a cross-referenced index accompany the series. Recommended for grades 7-12.

▶ **Motion Picture and Made-for-Television films**

Numerous films are available for classroom use such as *Grapes of Wrath, Tora, Tora, Tora, Roots, 1776, Sarah, Plain and Tall, Salt of the Earth, The Autobiography of Miss Jane Pittman, Glory,* and *Matewan* represent only a few of available videos. The length of major motion pictures may preclude using the entire work; however, selections are appropriate. Movies on laserdisc are especially useful as pre-selected sections are easily accessible. Each of the videos must be reviewed prior to showing to determine the appropriateness for grade levels and student maturity. Various motion picture guides are available and should be consulted for additional titles.

▶ **Talking History**
Produced by Spencer Nakasako, 1984, VHS, video cassette

Oral histories of Japanese, Chinese, Korean, Filipino, and Laotian women immigrants. Recommended for grades 7-12.

CD-ROM

▶ **The American Indian: A Multimedia Encyclopedia**
Facts On File, 1993, CD-ROM for IBM

The program uses documents, photographs, drawings, images, maps, and sounds to explore the history of American Indians. Students may access biographies of over 700 leading figures along with a collection of legends and folktales. Recommended for grades 5-12.

▶ **The Archives of American History: A Moving-Image Retrospective of the 20th Century**
Multimedia, 1993, CD-ROM for Macintosh

Film and video archives from 1896 to the present. Materials include the Spanish-American War, the Nuremberg trials, Nixon's visit to China, and the Challenger disaster. Recommended for grades 7-12.

▶ **Atlas of U.S. Presidents**
Applied Optical Media, 1992, CD-ROM for MPC compatibles

The program includes biographies of the presidents, speeches, political appraisals, and traditions and symbols of the executive office. Recommended for grades 7-12.

▶ **CD Sourcebook of American History**
Infobases, 1992, CD-ROM for IBM

A collection of primary sources, selections from the works of eminent historians, and visuals. The program consists of thousands of entries including Madison's notes on the Philadelphia Constitutional Convention, *The Federalist Papers*, Alexis de Tocqueville's *Democracy in America*, presidential inaugural addresses, the journal of Meriwether Lewis, and the Emancipation Proclamation. Recommended for grades 7-12.

▶ **Jazz: A Multimedia History**
Compton's NewMedia, 1993, CD-ROM for IBM compatibles and Macintosh

This history of jazz from its origins to the 1990s includes swing, bebop, fusion, and the avant-garde. The program incorporates audio clips, historic photographs, and profiles of leading musicians including Louis Armstrong to Miles Davis. Recommended for grades 7-12.

▶ **The 1993 *Time* Magazine Compact Almanac**
Compact Publishing, 1993, CD-ROM for IBM, MPC compatibles, and Macintosh

A full text reference of every issue of *Time* for 1989 through the January 4, 1993 issue with CNN videos of major stories. The disk also includes a "*Time* Capsules" section with some articles dating to the first issue of the magazine in 1923, a "Compact Almanac," maps, and the CIA World Factbook with State Department notes. Recommended for grades 9-12.

▶ **The Oregon Trail**
MECC, 1993, CD-ROM for Macintosh

A simulation of mid-19th century westward expansion. Animated color graphic, music, and digitized speech. Recommended for grades 4-8.

▶ **The Presidents: It All Started With George**
National Geographic/IBM, 1991, CD-ROM for IBM

Students use timelines, texts and audios of famous speeches, personal views of the presidents, and photo essays to investigate the presidency at their own pace. The program includes color photographs and video clips of major events surrounding the presidents. Recommended for grades 4-8.

▶ **Who Built America? From the Centennial Celebration of 1876 to the Great War of 1914**
Voyager, 1993, CD-ROM for Macintosh

Archival films, audio, still images, and documents extends two chapters of the two-volume textbook written by the American Social History Project. Recommended for grades 9-12.

Computer Software

▶ **Escalation: Decision Making in the Vietnam War, 1964-1968**
Kevin O'Reilly, 1990, Apple 5.25" disks, IBM 5.25" or 3.5" disks

A computer simulation on Johnson and the Vietnam War. Students work in small groups with different disks at separate terminals. The program includes reproducible handouts, maps, and other student information. Recommended for grades 9-12.

▶ **Hometown: A Local Area Study**
Active Learning Systems, Apple, IBM

A computer program which guides students in collecting, storing, and analyzing demographic data about their local community. Recommended for grades 4-8.

▶ **Lincoln's Decisions: Simulation**
Educational Activities, not dated, Apple 5.25" disk, IBM 5.25" disk, IBM 3.5" disk

A computer simulation which focuses on important events and turning points in Lincoln's life. Recommended for grades 7-8.

▶ **Mac TimeLiner**
Tom Snyder Productions, Inc., 1990

This timeline maker sorts the entered events into chronological order and arranges them proportionally. Recommended for grades 4-8.

Audio Cassettes

▶ **American History Through Narration and Song**
WEM, not dated, audio cassettes, notes

Audio cassettes boxed in five sets: "Colonial and Revolutionary Songs," "Moving West," "Civil War Songs," "Cowboy Songs," and "Working and Union Songs." Each set includes historical narration and notes on the songs. The cassettes vary in length from 1.5 to 3 hours. Recommended for grades 4-12.

▶ **Band Music in American Life: A Social History: 1850-1990**
Golden Owl Publishing Company

A Jackdaws portfolio of historical documents and audio documents on cassette. The portfolio explores the great band movement from the end of the Civil War to the 1920s. The audio cassette presents 15 representative selections from Gospel to Sousa marches. The program was developed in conjunction with the Smithsonian Institution. Recommended for grades 7-12.

▶ **Blues in America: A Social History**
Golden Owl Publishing Company

A Jackdaws portfolio of essays, historical documents, and 13 audio documents on cassette. The portfolio traces the Blues from the Mississippi Delta to the industrial cities of the North and West. The program was developed in conjunction with the Smithsonian Institution. Recommended for grades 7-12.

▶ **Legacies: An Audio Cassette on the History of Women and The Family in America**
Annenberg, CPB Project

Diary excerpts, songs, and stories about women in different periods of U.S. history. The program includes "New England Farm Families" and "Black Families in Freedom." Recommended for grades 7-12.

▶ **Lincoln Live**
Griessman & Associates, Inc., 1993

An audio cassette in which Gene Griessman portrays Abraham Lincoln. The cassette includes the Gettysburg Address, period songs, and humor. Recommended for grades 5-8.

▶ **May It Please the Court: The Most Significant Oral Arguments Made Before the Supreme Court Since 1955**
New Press, 1992, audio cassettes with text

The audio tapes present edited oral arguments before the Supreme Court for 12 landmark cases including *Miranda* v. *Arizona*, *Gideon* v. *Wainwright*, and *Roe* v. *Wade*. The tapes are accompanied by a hard cover book with transcripts of the tapes. Recommended for grades 9-12.

PRINTED SOURCES

Primary Documents

▶ *The Annals of America*. Chicago: Encyclopedia Britannica, Inc., 1976.

A 21-volume collection of primary source material from the European discovery to last decade of the 20th century. An invaluable library resource for secondary schools. Recommended for grades 9-12; however, selected readings may be used with grades 7-8.

▶ *Documents of American History*, **10th edition, edited by Henry Steele Commager and Milton Cantor. Englewood Cliffs: Prentice Hall, 1988.**

A two-volume collection of primary sources arranged in chronological order from privileges granted to Columbus by Ferdinand and Isabella to the Report of the Congressional Committees investigating Iran-Contra. An invaluable source book. Recommended for grades 9-12.

▶ *The Library of America*

An on-going series supported by the National Endowment for the Humanities and the Ford Foundation. The series includes speeches, debates, letters, and memoirs of important historical figures and the selected writings of American literary luminaries. The series includes *The Debate on the Constitution, Autobiographies of Frederick Douglass, Abraham Lincoln: Speeches and Writings*, and *Writings of W. E. B. Du Bois*.

▶ **Primary Source Collections**

A number of publishers have produced source books as supplements to basic texts. Still others take thematic approaches such as readings on the American Revolution, women in history, labor history, and the post-World War II era. Primary source readings are appropriate at all grade levels; read-a-rounds and paraphrased documents offer two of many different approaches for younger students. Anthologies such as *The American Reader: Words That Moved a Nation* is but one of many currently available source books which have readings which may be effectively used at grades 5-12.

▶ *The World's Great Speeches*, **edited by Lewis Copeland and Lawrence Lamm. New York: Dover Publications, 1973.**

A collection of 278 speeches from United States and world history. Speeches include Jonathan Edwards's "Sinners in the Hands of an Angry God," Tecumseh's speech to Governor Harrison in 1810, Susan B. Anthony on woman's suffrage, Fiorello LaGuardia on American labor, Bernard Baruch on the control of atomic weapons, and Eleanor Roosevelt on the United Nations. Recommended for grades 9-12.

Reference Materials

▶ **Almanacs and Encyclopedias of American Ethnic Groups and Women**

There are a number of single and multi-volume reference books on ethnic groups and women. Such sources include *Harvard Encyclopedia of American Ethnic Groups*, *Dictionary of African American Biography*, *Hispanic American Almanac*, *Handbook of Native American Indians*, *Dictionary of Asian American History*, and *Notable Black Women*. Recommended for teachers and students at various grade levels depending on individual titles.

▶ *The American Indians*
Time-Life Books

A comprehensive series of illustrated books chronicling the history and culture of Native Americans. Books in the series include: Keepers of the Totem, The Buffalo Hunters, The Way of the Warrior, Tribes of the Southern Woodlands, and War for the Plains. Recommended for grades 7-12.

▶ *Civitas: A Framework for Civic Education* **edited by Charles F. Bahmueller. Calabasas, CA: Center for Civic Education, 1991.**

Civitas is a comprehensive framework for civic education. The work provides objectives, key understandings, and historical background information for curriculum developers and classroom teachers. Recommended as a teacher resource.

▶ **Cordier, Mary Hurlbut, and Maria A. Perez-Stable.** *Peoples of the American West.* **Scarecrow Press, 1989.**

An annotated bibliography of over 100 children's literature books that deal with the settlement of the American West. A good resource for elementary and middle school libraries. Recommended for teachers.

▶ *Dictionary of American History* edited by James Truslow Adams (Revised Edition). New York: Charles Scribner's Sons, 1976.

A multi-volumed dictionary of American history recommended for teachers and students, grades 9-12. A companion work, *Album of American History* (1961) is an illustrated six-volume dictionary edited by Adams. *Album of American History*, recommended for grades 5-8, focuses on all aspects of American life including arts and crafts, housing, costume, and weaponry.

▶ *Encyclopedia of American Biography* edited by John A. Garraty. New York: Harper and Row, 1974.

A one-volume encyclopedia of notable Americans. Recommended for grades 9-12.

▶ *Encyclopedia of American History* edited by Richard Morris. 6th edition. New York: Harper and Row, 1982.

A one-volume reference encyclopedia. Recommended for teachers and students, grades 9-12.

▶ *Encyclopaedia of the American Left* edited by Mari Jo Buhle, Paul Buhle, and Dan Georgakas. Urbana: University of Illinois Press, 1992.

A one-volume reference encyclopedia on radicals and radicalism in American society. Recommended as a reference for teachers and students, grades 9-12.

▶ *The Federalist Papers* edited by Jacob E. Cooke. Middletown, CT: Wesleyan University Press, 1961.

This is considered by historians to be the most complete and accurate edition of *The Federalist Papers*. Recommended for grades 9-12.

▶ *Federalists and Antifederalists: The Debate Over Ratification of the Constitution* edited by John P. Kaminski and Richard Leffler. Madison, WI: Madison House, 1989.

A collection of the writings of leading Federalists and Anti-Federalists. The documents presented in the work are organized around key ideas in the ratification debate. Recommended for grades 9-12.

▶ *Harvard Guide to American History* edited by Frank Freidel. Cambridge, MA: Harvard University Press, 1974.

A two-volume reference guide to monographs and journal articles on all aspects of U.S. history. Recommended for teachers and as a student reference for grades 9-12.

▶ Kammen, Carol. *On Doing Local History: Reflections on What Local Historians Do, Why, and What it Means*. Nashville: American Association for State and Local History, 1986.

A guide for exploring local history. The text examines the special factors which confront historians in local history projects. The book also investigates how local history is practiced around the world. Recommended for teachers.

▶ Kyvig, David and Myron A. Marty. *Nearby History: Exploring the Past Around You*. Nashville: American Association for State and Local History, 1983.

This reference book explains how to find and use visual sources, artifactual records, interviews, and published and unpublished records in exploring family and community history. Kyvig and Myron are editors of the "Nearby History Series," a set of books or the study of local history. Recommended for teachers.

▶ *Native American: An Illustrated History* edited by David Thomas, et al. Atlanta: Turner Publishing, Inc., 1993.

A one-volume, richly illustrated history of Native Americans. Recommended for grades 9-12; however, the illustrations may be used effectively with grades 5-8.

▶ *Readers Companion to American History* edited by Eric Foner and John Garraty. Boston: Houghton Mifflin, 1991.

An encyclopedic reference book recommended for grades 7-12 and as a teacher resource.

▶ Silverblank, Fran. *An Annotated Bibliography of Historical Fiction for the Social Studies, Grades 5 through 12*. Dubuque, Iowa: Kendall/Hunt Publishing Co., 1992.

A bibliography of historical fiction with grade level recommendations. Brief annotations of hundred of children's trade books in United States and world history. Recommended for teachers.

▶ *Telling America's Story: Teaching American History Through Children's Literature*. Produced by Tom McGowan and Meredith McGowan

A resource book which incorporating popular children's literature into the study of U.S. history from the colonial era to the 20th century. Selections include a story summary, lesson plans, and critical thinking activities. Recommended for grades 5-8.

Journals and Periodicals

▶ *American Heritage*

A well-established magazine of United States history with high-interest articles on various political, diplomatic, economic, military, and social topics. Recommended for grades 9-12.

▶ *Cobblestone, The History Magazine for Young People*

A magazine for students, grades 5-8, which focuses on a different in-depth theme or topic in U. S. history each month. Events and individual characters are brought alive through articles, illustrations, and student activities. Recommended for grades 4-8.

◗ *Concord Review*

A quarterly journal devoted to student written articles on topics in United States and world history. An exceptional teaching tool modeling outstanding essays research and written by high school students. Class sets are available. Recommended for grades 9-12.

◗ *Magazine of History*

A quarterly publication of the Organization of American Historians. The magazine, with thematic issues such as "Rethinking the Cold War," "Geography and History," and "Peacemaking in American History," includes articles by prominent historians and practical lessons using historical documents. Materials appearing in the OAH *Magazine of History* may be copied for classroom use. The Spring issue each year focuses on the current National History Day theme and provides suggestions on topics and bibliographical sources. Recommended for teachers.

◗ *Social Education*

Published periodically by the National Council for the Social Studies with articles of interest to educators. The magazine regularly features annotations of children's trade books, reviews of newly developed computer programs, and lessons using primary source documents. Recommended for teachers.

◗ *Social Studies and the Young Learner*

A quarterly magazine of the National Council for the Social Studies which includes articles of interest for K-6 teachers. Issues provide critiques of children's trade books. Recommended for teachers.

Visual Resources

◗ Art Resources

Art museums often feature special exhibits focusing on individual artists or themes in United States history. Although educational field trips may be impractical in some cases, special exhibit catalogues such as the Corcoran Gallery's "Facing History: The Black Image in American Art 1710-1940" and the Smithsonian's National Museum of American Art "Homecoming: The Art and Life of William H. Johnson" are exceptional classroom resources. In addition illustrated theme books such as *Propaganda, The Art of Persuasion: World War II* demonstrate the power of visual images through art, architecture, motion pictures, poster art, cartoons, and caricatures. Museum catalogues and art books may be used at different grade levels depending on student maturity.

◗ Caricatures and Cartoons

There are a wide variety of books and portfolios of political cartoons which enrich the study of history. Among those available are portfolios such as "History Through Political Cartoons," and numerous books including *Rebellion and Reconciliation: Satirical Prints on the Revolution at Williamsburg, Draw! Political Cartoons From Left to Right, A Cartoon History of American Foreign Policy, 1776-1976, The Image of America in Caricature and Cartoon,* and the series *Best Editorial Cartoons of the Year.* Recommended for grades 7-12.

◆ **Documentary Photographs**

A number of companies produce documentary photographs and posters which may be used as an integral part of instruction. Among the many documentary visuals are: "Child Labor," "America Revisited," and "The Living Constitution Poster Series." Recommended for various grade levels depending on the scope of each publication.

TEACHING MATERIALS

Curricular Units

◆ **American Literature**
Center for Learning, 1990

A two-volume resource of activities which examine U.S. history and culture through literature. Volume 1, "Beginnings through the Civil War," covers 15 authors from Bradstreet through Whitman. Volume 2, "Civil War to the Present," includes 13 authors from Twain to Updike.

◆ **Classroom Plays and Simulations**

Numerous short classroom plays and simulation activities enhance the study of history. A number of companies have produced excellent interactive activities in U.S. history. Grade level recommendations vary. Among the many plays and activities which should be reviewed for classroom use include "American History through Plays," "Southwest: A Simulation of the Spanish/Mexican Influence Upon American History," and "Great American Confrontations."

◆ Haynes, Charles. *Religion in American History, What to Teach and How.*
Alexandria, VA: Association for Supervision and Curriculum Development, 1990.

A series of lessons based on religious issues in United States history. The lessons are based on primary source materials and provide reproducible facsimiles of documents. Recommended for grades 9-12 but may be adapted for grades 7-8.

◆ *Living With Our Deepest Differences: Religious Liberty in a Pluralistic Society*
First Liberty Institute

Curricular notebooks for upper elementary, junior and senior high school which focus on the place of religious liberty in society. Lessons are designed to provide teachers with maximum flexibility so that they may be used either together as a unit or infused into the study of United States history.

◆ **National Center for History in the Schools**
University of California, Los Angeles

A series of curriculum units based on primary source materials. The teaching units are recommended for various grade levels; however, they may be adapted for use in most classes, grades 5-12. The units cover the scope of U.S. history from the colonial era to the present. Titles include: "William Penn's Peaceable Kingdom," "Women in the American Revolution," "The Southwest," "Women in the Progressive Era," "The Harlem Renaissance," and "The Cold War."

♦ **National Women's History Project**
Windsor, California

The National Women's History Project produces curriculum units and kits which explore the scope of U.S. history. The units and teaching kits are appropriate for different grade levels. The units include "Women in Colonial and Revolutionary America, 1607-1790," "Women and the Constitution," "Woman Suffrage Movement, 1848-1920," and "Multicultural Women's History."

♦ Patrick, John J. *James Madison and the Federalist Papers. Bloomington, IN*: **ERIC Clearing House, 1990.**

An in-depth study of the Federalist and Anti-Federalist positions during the ratification debate over the Constitution. The lessons are based on primary source documents. Recommended for grades 9-12.

♦ Patrick, John J. *Lessons on the Northwest Ordinance of 1787: Learning Materials for Secondary School Courses in American History, Government and Civics.* **Bloomington, IN: ERIC Clearing House, 1987.**

Lessons on the Northwest Ordinance is a set of nine lessons using primary source documents to discuss issues such as civil liberties and governance of new states. Recommended for grades 9-12.

♦ Patrick, John J. and Richard Remy. *Lessons on the Constitution: Supplements to High School Courses in American History, Government, and Civics.* **Boulder: Social Science Education Consortium, 1986.**

A series of short lessons on the Constitution, principles of government, and landmark Supreme Court cases using primary source materials. Recommended for grades 9-12; however, some lessons may be used at grades 7-8.

♦ Schug, Mark, *et al. United States History: Eyes on the Economy.* **New York: National Council on Economic Education, 1993.**

A two volume guide using economic concepts to supplement the study of U.S. history. Units such as "The Road to Revolution," "Boom and Bust in the Early 1800s," "The Emergence of Big Business," and "Economic Growth after World War II" include various lessons exploring economic issues in American history. Recommended for grades 7-12.

♦ *Teaching With Documents: Using Primary Sources From the National Archives.* **Washington, D.C.: National Archives, 1989.**

A collection of over 50 short lessons using facsimiles of a variety of documents, maps, photographs, drawings, and cartoons. This is a compilation of lessons published since 1977 in Social Education along with practical suggestions for using documents in classroom settings. The documents are appropriate for upper elementary through high school. Worksheets in analyzing written documents, data retrieval, and cartoon analysis are extremely helpful in introducing students to work with documents. Recommended for grades 5-12.

♦ *We the People.* **Calabasas, CA: Center for Civic Education, 1993.**

A series of teaching units divided into books for elementary, middle, and senior high school students. The units are intended to give students an understanding of the background, creation, and subsequent history of the Constitution and Bill of Rights.

▶ *With Liberty and Justice for All: The Story of the Bill of Rights.* Calabasas, CA: Center for Civic Education, 1991

A unit of study designed to give students a better understanding of the background, creation, and application of the Bill of Rights. A teacher's guide states objectives and offers practical lesson strategies. Recommended for grades 9-12.

Primary Source Kits

▶ **The Cuban Missile Crisis: A Resource Unit**
John F. Kennedy Library and Museum

A collection of declassified primary source documents on the Cuban missile crisis which students use to reconstruct the negotiations from the U.S. and Soviet perspectives. Recommended for grades 7-12.

▶ **Jackdaws Portfolios of Historical Documents**
Golden Owl Publishing

Over 50 teaching portfolios to supplement the study of U.S. history. The Jackdaws kits provide primary source documents and essays by historians on the featured topic. Documentary photographs and political cartoons accompany the documents. Some of the case studies are: "Women in the American Revolution," "Indian Resistance: The Patriot Chiefs," "Immigration: 1870-1929: Immigrants in the Industrial Revolution," "Coxey's Army," "The CIO and the Labor Movement," and "Japanese-American Internment: The Bill of Rights in Crisis." Recommended for grades 7-12.

▶ **National Archives Teaching Kits**
Published by SIRS, Inc.

A collection of boxed teaching units designed to supplement the teaching of U.S. history by incorporating reproductions of documents for the National Archives. Each unit includes a list of objectives, introductory exercise, lessons, worksheets, glossary, and an annotated bibliography. The publications include, "The Bill of Rights: Evolution of Personal Liberties," "The Civil War: Soldiers and Civilians," and "World War I: The Home Front." Recommended for grades 7-12.

Contributors and
Participating Organizations

Organizational Structure of the National History Standards Project

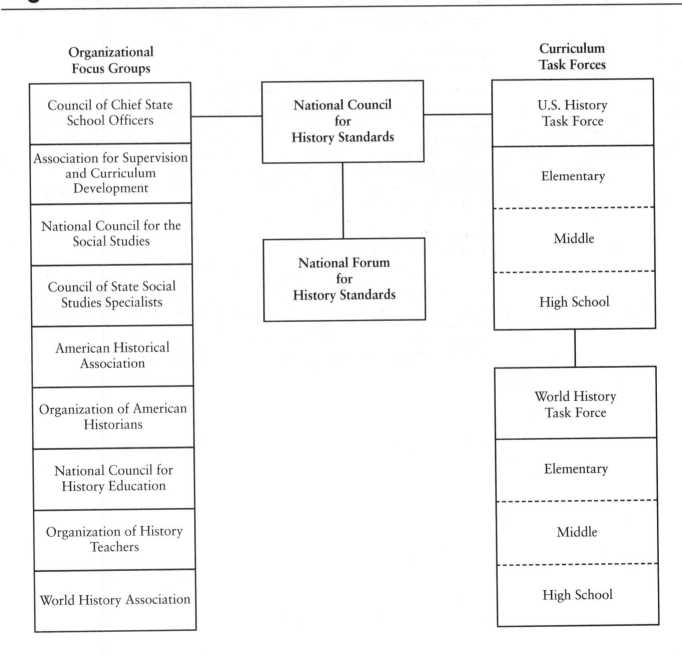

Organizational
Focus Groups

Curriculum
Task Forces

Council of Chief State
School Officers

National Council
for
History Standards

U.S. History
Task Force

Association for Supervision
and Curriculum
Development

Elementary

National Council for the
Social Studies

Middle

Council of State Social
Studies Specialists

National Forum
for
History Standards

High School

American Historical
Association

Organization of American
Historians

World History
Task Force

National Council for
History Education

Elementary

Organization of History
Teachers

Middle

World History Association

High School

Participating Organizations

American Association of School Librarians

American Association for State and Local History

American Federation of Teachers

American Historical Association

Association for the Study of Afro-American Life and History

Association for Supervision and Curriculum Development

The Atlantic Council of the United States

Center for Civic Education

Council for American Private Education

Council for Basic Education

Council of Chief State School Officers

Council of the Great City Schools

Council of State Social Studies Specialists

League of United Latin American Citizens

Lutheran Schools, The Lutheran Church-Missouri Synod

National Alliance of Black School Educators

National Association for Asian and Pacific American Education

National Association of Elementary School Principals

National Association of Secondary School Principals

National Association of State Boards of Education

National Catholic Educational Association

National Congress of Parents and Teachers

National Council for Geographic Education

National Council for History Education

National Council on Economic Education

The National Council for the Social Studies

National Education Association

Native American Heritage Commission

Organization of American Historians

Organization of History Teachers

Quality Education for Minorities Network

Social Studies Educational Consortium

World History Association

Organizational Rosters

National Council for History Standards

Officers

Charlotte Crabtree, Co-chair
Professor of Education Emeritus
University of California, Los Angeles

Gary B. Nash, Co-chair
Professor of History
University of California, Los Angeles

Linda Symcox, Coordinator
Associate Director, National Center for History in the
Schools
University of California, Los Angeles

Members

Charlotte Anderson, President
National Council for Social Studies, 1992-93

Joyce Appleby, President
Organization of American Historians, 1992-1993
Professor of History
University of California, Los Angeles

Samuel Banks, Executive Director
Division of Compensatory and Funded Programs
Baltimore Schools

David Battini, Teacher
Durham High School
Cairo, New York

David Baumbach, Teacher
Woolsair Elementary Gifted Center
Pittsburgh, Pennsylvania

Earl Bell, President
Organization of History Teachers
Teacher, Laboratory Schools
University of Chicago

Mary Bicouvaris, Teacher
Hampton Roads Academy
Newport News, Virginia

Diane Brooks, President,
Council of State Social Studies Specialists, 1993
Manager, California Department of Education

Pedro Castillo, Professor of History
University of California, Santa Cruz

Ainslie T. Embree, Professor of History Emeritus
Columbia University

Elizabeth Fox-Genovese, Professor of History
Emory University

Carol Gluck, Professor of History
Columbia University

Darlene Clark Hine, Professor of History
Michigan State University

Bill Honig, President,
Council of Chief State School Officers, 1992
Distinguished Visiting Professor of Education
San Francisco State University

Akira Iriye, Professor of History
Harvard University

Barbara Talbert Jackson, President
Association for Supervision and
Curriculum Development, 1993-94

Kenneth Jackson, Professor of History
Columbia University

Morton Keller, Professor of History
Brandeis University

Bernard Lewis, Professor of History
Princeton University

William McNeill, Professor of History Emeritus
University of Chicago

Alan D. Morgan, President,
Council of Chief State Officers, 1993
State Superintendent of
Public Instruction, New Mexico

Stephanie Pace-Marshall, President
Association for Supervision and Curriculum
Development, 1992-93

John J. Patrick, Director, Social Studies Development
Center and Professor of Education
Indiana University

Theodore K. Rabb, Chairman,
National Council for History Education
Professor of History
Princeton University

Members (Continued)

C. Frederick Risinger, Associate Director, Social Studies
Development Center and Professor of Education
Indiana University

Denny Schillings, President
National Council for the Social Studies, 1993-94
Teacher, Homewood Flossmoor High School
Flossmoor, Illinois

Gilbert T. Sewall, Director
American Textbook Council

Warren Solomon, Curriculum Consultant for
Social Studies
Missouri Department of Elementary and
Secondary Education

Michael R. Winston, Vice President Emeritus
Howard University and President,
Alfred Harcourt Foundation

Organizational titles of all members were current at the
time of their first participation in the project.

U.S. Curriculum Task Force

Kirk S. Ankeney, Teacher
Scripps Ranch High School
San Diego, California

Earl Bell, Teacher
The Laboratory Schools
University of Chicago

Charlotte Crabtree, Professor of Education Emeritus
University of California, Los Angeles

Mark W. Gale, Teacher
Coupeville Junior/Senior High School
Coupeville, Washington

Melvin Garrison, Teacher
Kearny High School
Philadelphia, Pennsylvania

Stan Miesner, Teacher
Reed Junior High School
Springfield, Missouri

Lawrence A. Miller, Head
Social Studies Department
Baltimore City College High School
Baltimore, Maryland

Lori Lee Morton, Teacher
Riverside Elementary School
Alexandria, Virginia

Gary B. Nash, Professor of History
University of California, Los Angeles

Minna Novick, Curriculum Consultant
Chicago, Illinois

John J. Patrick, Professor of Education
Indiana University

Daniel A. Preston, Teacher
Umatilla High School
Umatilla, Florida

John M. Pyne, Humanities Supervisor
West Milford High School
West Milford, New Jersey

Angeline Rinaldo, Teacher
Eaglecrest High School
Aurora, Colorado

William C. Schultheis, Teacher
Lake Clifton/Eastern High School
Baltimore, Maryland

Gloria Sesso, Teacher
Half Hollow Hills East High School
Pix Hills, New York

Linda Symcox, Associate Director
National Center for History in the Schools
University of California, Los Angeles

Helen Treacy, Teacher
Kettering High School
Detroit, Michigan

David Vigilante, Teacher Emeritus
Gompers Secondary School
San Diego, California

National Forum for History Standards

Ronald Areglado
National Association of Elementary School Principals

Kathy Belter
National Congress of Parents and Teachers

Nguyen Minh Chau
National Association for Asian and
Pacific American Education

Cesar Collantes
League of United Latin American Citizens

Mark Curtis
The Atlantic Council of the United States

Glen Cutlip
National Education Association

Graham Down
Council For Basic Education

Mary Futrell
Quality Education for Minorities Network

Keith Geiger
National Education Association

Ivan Gluckman
National Association of Secondary School Principals

Ruth Granados
Council of the Great City Schools

Joyce McCray
Council for American Private Education

Sr. Catherine T. McNamee
National Catholic Educational Association

Patricia Gordon Michael
American Association for State and Local History

Mabel Lake Murray
National Alliance of Black School Educators

Cynthia Neverdon-Morton
Association for the Study of Afro-American
Life and History

George Nielsen
Lutheran Schools,
The Lutheran Church-Missouri Synod

Charles N. Quigley
Center for Civic Education

Christopher Salter
National Council for Geographic Education

Adelaide Sanford
National Association of State Boards of Education

Ruth Toor
American Association of School Librarians

Clifford Trafzer
Native American Heritage Commission

Hai T. Tran
National Association for Asian and
Pacific American Education

Ruth Wattenberg
American Federation of Teachers

Council of Chief State School Officers
Focus Group

Sue Bennet
California Department of Education

Pasquale DeVito
Rhode Island Department of Education

Patricia Dye, History/Social Studies Consultant
Plymouth, Massachusetts

Mary Fortney
Indiana Department of Education

Connie Manter
Maine Department of Education

Alan D. Morgan
New Mexico State Superintendent of Public Instruction

Wayne Neuburger
Oregon Department of Education

Charles Peters
Oakland Schools, Waterford, Michigan

Thomas Sobol
New York Commissioner of Education

Robert H. Summerville
Alabama Department of Education

Staff
Fred Czarra, Consultant in International Education,
Social Studies and Interdisciplinary Learning

Ed Roeber, Director of the State Collaborative on
Assessment and Student Standards

Ramsay Selden, Director, State Education
Assessment Center

Association for Supervision and Curriculum Development
Focus Group

Glen Blankenship, Social Studies Coordinator
Georgia State Department of Education
Atlanta, Georgia

Joyce Coffey, Teacher
Dunbar Senior High School
District Heights, Maryland

Sherrill Curtiss, Teacher
Chairman, Dept. of History/Social Studies
Providence Senior High School
Charlotte, North Carolina

Geno Flores, Teacher
Arroyo Grande High School
Arroyo Grande, California

Alan Hall, Teacher
Chairman, Social Studies Department
Yarmouth High School
Yarmouth, Massachussetts

Erich Martel, Teacher
Wilson Senior High School
Washington, D.C.

Marilyn McKnight, Teacher
Milwaukee Public Schools
Milwaukee, Wisconsin

Mike Radow, Teacher
Tops Middle School
Seattle, Washington

Karen Steinbrink, Assistant Executive Director
Bucks County Intermediate Unit
Doylestown, Pennsylvania

Staff

Diane Berreth, Deputy Executive Director
Brian Curry, Policy Analyst

National Council for the Social Studies
Focus Group

Linda Levstick, Professor of Education
University of Kentucky

Janna Bremer, Teacher
King Philip Regional High School
Foxborough, Massachusetts

Jean Craven, District Coordinator/Curriculum Devel.
Albuquerque Public School District
Albuquerque, New Mexico

Mathew Downey, Professor of Education
University of California, Berkeley

Rachel Hicks, Teacher
Jefferson Jr. High School
Washington, D.C.

Jack Larner, Coordinator of Secondary
Social Studies, Department of History
Indiana University of Pennsylvania

Tarry Lindquist, Teacher
Lakeridge Elementary
Mercer Island, Washington

Denny Schillings, Teacher
Homewood-Flossmoor High School
Flossmoor, Illinois

Judith S. Wooster, Assistant Superintendent
Bethlehem Central Schools
Del Mar, New York

Ruben Zepeda, Teacher
Grant High School
Van Nuys, California

Council of State Social Studies Specialists
Focus Group

Norman Abramowitz, New York
Margaret (Peggy) Altoff, Maryland
Wendy Bonaiuto, South Dakota
Patricia Boyd, Nevada
Diane L. Brooks, California
Harvey R. Carmichael, Virginia
John M. Chapman, Michigan
Nijel Clayton, Kentucky
Pat Concannon, New Mexico
Edward T. Costa, Rhode Island
Thomas Dunthorn, Florida
Patricia J. Dye, Massachusetts
John D. Ellington, North Carolina
Curt Eriksmoen, North Dakota
Mary Fortney, Indiana
Rita Geiger, Oklahoma
Daniel W. Gregg, Connecticut
Carter B. Hart, Jr., New Hampshire
H. Michael Hartoonian, Wisconsin
Lewis E. Huffman, Delaware
Barbara Jones, West Virginia
Sharon Kaohi, Hawaii
Mary Jean Katz, Oregon
Marianne Kenney, Colorado
Judith Kishman, Wyoming

Frank Klajda, Arizona
John LeFeber, Nebraska
Richard Leighty, Kansas
Constance Miller Manter, Maine
Nancy N. Matthew, Utah
Nanette McGee, Georgia
Marjorie Menzi, Alaska
William Miller, Louisiana
Kent J. Minor, Ohio
John A. Nelson, Vermont
Bruice Opie, Tennessee
Linda Vrooman Peterson, Montana
Barbara Patty, Arkansas
Ann Pictor, Illinois
Joan Prewitt, Mississippi
Orville Reddington, Idaho
Michael Ryan, New Jersey
Warren Solomon, Missouri
Larry Strickland, Washington
Robert Summerville, Alabama
Cordell Svegalis, Iowa
Elvin E. Tyrone, Texas
Margaret B. Walden, South Carolina
Roger Wangen, Minnesota
James J. Wetzler, Pennsylvania

Organization of American Historians
Focus Group

Earl Bell, Teacher
The Laboratory Schools
University of Chicago

Alan Brinkley, Professor of History
Columbia University

George Burson, Teacher
Aspen High School
Aspen, Colorado

Albert Camarillo, Professor of History
Stanford University

William Chafe, Professor of History
Duke University

Christine Compston, Director
National History Education Network

Terrie L. Epstein, Professor of Education
University of Michigan

Eric Foner, Professor of History
Columbia University

Mary A. Giunta
National Historical Publications and Records
Commission

Scott L. Greenwell, Principal
North Layton Junior High
Layton, Utah

David C. Hammack, Professor of History
Case Western Reserve University

Louis R. Harlan, Professor of History
University of Maryland

George Henry Jr., Teacher
Highland High School
Salt Lake City, Utah

Marilynn Jo Hitchens, Teacher
Wheat Ridge High School
Denver, Colorado

Michael Kammen, Professor of History
Cornell University

Harvey J. Kaye, Professor of Social Change and
Development
University of Wisconsin, Green Bay

Kathleen Kean, Teacher
Shorewood, Wisconsin

Lawrence W. Levine, Professor of History
University of California, Berkeley

William McCracken, Teacher
Pine View School
Sarasota, Florida

Lynette K. Oshima, Professor of Education
University of New Mexico

Pamela Petty, Teacher
Apollo High School
Glendale, Arizona

John Pyne, Humanities Supervisor
West Milford High School
West Milford, New Jersey

Eric Rothschild, Teacher
Scarsdale High School
Scarsdale, New York

Peter Seixas, Professor of Social and
Educational Studies
University of British Columbia

Gloria Sesso, Teacher
Half Hollow Hills High School
Dix Hills, New York

George Stevens, Professor of History
Dutchess Community College
Poughkeepsie, New York

Steven Teel, Teacher
Berkeley High School
Hercules, California

Sandra VanBurkleo, Professor of History
Wayne State University

David Vigilante, Teacher Emeritus
Gompers Secondary School
San Diego, California

Bertram Wyatt-Brown, Professor of History
University of Florida

Deborah White, Professor of History
Rutgers University

Mitch Yamasaki, Professor of History
Chaminade University of Honolulu
Kaneohe, Hawaii

Charles Zappia, Professor of History
San Diego Mesa College

Staff

Arnita Jones, Executive Director

American Historical Association
U.S. History Focus Group

Albert Camarillo, Professor of History
Stanford University

Terrie L. Epstein, Professor of Education
University of Michigan

Ned Farman, Teacher
Westtown School
Westtown, Pennsylvania

Elizabeth Faue, Professor of History
Wayne State University

Donald L. Fixico, Professor of History
Western Michigan University

James R. Grossman, Director
Family and Community History Center
Newberry Library, Chicago, Illinois

Louis Harlan, Professor of History
University of Maryland

James O. Horton, Professor of History
George Washington University

Thomas C. Holt, Professor of History
University of Chicago

David Katzman, Professor of History
University of Kansas

Lori Lee Morton, Teacher
Riverside Elementary School
Alexandria, Virginia

Howard Shorr, Teacher
Columbia River High School
Vancouver, Washington

Kathleen Anderson Steeves, Professor of
Teacher Preparation
George Washington University

Staff

James B. Gardner, Acting Executive Director

Noralee Frankel, Assistant Director on Women and Minorities

Robert B. Townsend, Managing Editor

National Council for History Education
U.S. History Focus Group

Douglas Greenberg, Chair, 1994
Director, Chicago Historical Society

James Bruggeman, Principal
Irving Elementary School
Bozeman, Montana

Miriam U. Chrisman, Professor of History Emeritus
University of Massachusetts

Robert D. Cross, Professor of History
University of Virginia

Carl N. Degler, Professor of History
Stanford University

Paul H. Fagette, Jr., Professor of History
Arkansas State University

Betty B. Franks, Social Studies Chairperson
Maple Heights High School
Maple Heights, Ohio

David Alyn Gordon, Teacher
Tempe School District
Tempe, Arizona

Ann N. Greene, Teacher
National Cathedral School for Girls
Washington, D.C.

Larry A. Greene, Chairman
Department of History
Seton Hall University

Michael S. Henry, Teacher
Bowie High School
Bowie, Maryland

Byron Hollinshead, Chair, 1993
Publisher/Chairman
American Historical Publications
New York, New York

Diane N. Johnson, Teacher
Anne Arundel County Schools
Arnold, Maryland

Melissa Kirkpatrick, Information and
Research Consultant
Cassandra Associates
Reston, Virginia

National Council for History Education
U.S. History Focus Group (Continued)

Josef W. Konvitz, Chair, 1992
Professor of History
Michigan State University

Donald Lankiewicz, Education Consultant
Windermere, Florida

Joel Latman, Teacher
Montville High School
Oakdale, Connecticut

Kurt E. Leichtle, Professor of History
University of Wisconsin, River Falls

Arthur S. Link, Professor of History Emeritus
Princeton University

Arna M. Margolis, Head, History Department
The Bryn Mawr School
Bryn Mawr, Pennsylvania

Susan Mertz, Education Consultant
IMPACT!
Summerville, South Carolina

Edmund S. Morgan, Professor of History Emeritus
Yale University

Mary Beth Norton, Professor of History
Cornell University

Paul H. Pangrace, Teacher
Garrett Morgan School of Science
Cleveland, Ohio

Theodore C. Parker, Teacher
Writer/Education Specialist
Camarillo, California

Kathryn Kish Sklar, Professor of History
University of Binghamton

Peg Killam Smith, Teacher
Seton Keough High School
Arnold, Maryland

Sheldon Stern, Historian
John F. Kennedy Library
Boston, Massachusetts

Jo Sullivan, Principal
Federal Street School
Salem, Massachusetts

Robert H. Summerville, Social Studies Specialist
Alabama Department of Education

Susan Taylor, Teacher,
Withrow School
Cincinnati, Ohio

William L. Taylor, Professor of Social Science
Plymouth State College

Stephan Thernstrom, Professor of History
Harvard University

Carl Ubbelohde, Professor Emeritus
Case Western Reserve University

W. Jeffrey Welsh, Professor of History
Bowling Green State University, Firelands

James Wilkinson, Director
Derek Bok Center
Harvard University

Peter H. Wood, Professor of History
Duke University

Staff
Elaine Reed, Executive Secretary

Organization of History Teachers
U.S. History Focus Group

John Tyler, Chair
Groton School
Groton, Massachusetts

Earl P. Bell, Teacher
The Laboratory Schools
University of Chicago

Ron Briley, Teacher
Sandia Preparatory School
Albuquerque, New Mexico

Ron Buchheim, Teacher
Dana Hills High School
Dana Point, California

Tom English, Teacher
The George School
Newtown, Pennsylvania

Marianne Gieger, Teacher
Sousa Elementary School
Port Washington, New York

Joe Gotchy, Teacher
Thomas Jefferson High School
West Milford, New Jersey

Paul Horton, Teacher
The Laboratory Schools
University of Chicago

Doris Meadows, Teacher
Wilson Magnet School
Rochester, New York

John M. Pyne, Humanities Supervisor
West Milford High School
West Milford, New Jersey

Robert Rodey, Teacher
Marion Catholic High School
Chicago Heights, Illinois

Gloria Sesso, Teacher
Half Hollow Hills High School
Pix Hills, New York

Peggy Smith, Teacher
St. Mary's High School
Annapolis, Maryland

Richard Swanson, Teacher
The McCallie School
Chattanooga, Tennessee